Information Warfare

How to Survive Cyber Attacks

Michael Erbschloe

Osborne/**McGraw-Hill**

New York ▶ Chicago ▶ San Francisco ▶ Lisbon ▶ London ▶ Madrid ▶ Mexico City
Milan ▶ New Delhi ▶ San Juan ▶ Seoul ▶ Singapore ▶ Sydney ▶ Toronto

Osborne/**McGraw-Hill**
2600 Tenth Street
Berkeley, California 94710
U.S.A.

To arrange bulk purchase discounts for sales promotions, premiums, or fund-
raisers, please contact Osborne/**McGraw-Hill** at the above address. For information
on translations or book distributors outside the U.S.A., please see the International
Contact Information page immediately following the text of this book.

Information Warfare: How to Survive Cyber Attacks

1234567890 DOC DOC 01987654321

ISBN 0-07-213260-4

Publisher
Brandon A. Nordin

Vice President & Associate Publisher
Scott Rogers

Editorial Director
Roger Stewart

Acquisitions Editor
Jane Brownlow

Project Manager
Deidre Dolce

Project Editor
Laurie Stewart

Acquisitions Coordinator
Alissa Larson

Technical Editor
Jim Helm

Copy Editor
Lunaea Weatherstone

Proofreaders
Sachi Guzman
Tory McLearn

Computer Designer
Maureen Forys,
Happenstance Type-O-Rama

Series Design
Maureen Forys,
Happenstance Type-O-Rama

Cover Design
Fallentree Designs

This book was composed with QuarkXPress 4.11 on a Macintosh G4.

To my mother
To Bruno

—Michael Erbschloe

Contents

Preface

This book provides a new look at information warfare strategies and how they could impact the operations and economic viability of private companies. The historical focus on information warfare has been from a military perspective. Although the military perspective toward information warfare has merit, it is based on a traditional perception of warfare as strategies and tactics that are designed to achieve military goals or protect military capabilities and the infrastructure of a military-industrial complex.

I have gone beyond the traditional military view and presents a multidisciplinary analysis of information warfare that encompasses economics, politics, social behavior, and international relations and how these forces will influence the initiation and response to information warfare attacks. This book presents a new approach to analyzing information warfare strategies and provides an in-depth look at the potential impact of ten different types of information warfare.

This book also examines tactics that will be employed during information warfare attacks and how private companies and government agencies can prepare to respond to attacks. In addition, the emergence of the information warrior is examined and how these warriors may impact national security and international political relationships. Finally, this book presents an analysis of how governments can better prepare for the potential of information warfare and evaluates the skill sets and personalities that will be required to police cyberspace in the future.

Acknowledgments

The Osborne/McGraw-Hill team that worked on this book includes Jane Brownlow, acquisitions editor, Jim Helm, technical editor, and Deidre Dolce, project manager. There was also the team of Laurie Stewart, project editor, Maureen Forys, computer designer, Lunaea Weatherstone, copy editor, Sachi Guzman and Tory McLearn, proofreaders, and Jack Lewis, indexer. They did a great job.

I also acknowledge Kelly Erbschloe and Joe Erbschloe, my brothers. Kelly has an inherent understanding of systems and conflict and a unique view of the future, which, when it unfolds, will further the art and science of information warfare. Our discussions helped me formulate my perspectives on information warfare. Joe grasped the potential impact of information warfare immediately, and his comments and input make me wish that all policy makers had his straightforward understanding and insights.

I also acknowledge three former coworkers: Catie Huneke, Adam Harriss, and Samir Bhavnani who helped collect and analyze a mountain of data on the economic impact of computer virus attacks while they were at Computer Economics, Inc. During and after the Love Bug attacks, Catie, Adam, and Sam worked long hours and made a significant contribution to developing a new perspective on the economic impact of these attacks. They also spent countless hours presenting the analysis to the media and to private companies who were assessing the impact, and coordinating the flow of information to government organizations and investigators. They have all gone on to pursue new professional endeavors, in which I wish them the greatest success. I also acknowledge the support of Anne Zalatan, Kathryn Hall, and Ginger Rittenhouse, who diligently prepared and published the results of the research. I want to express my thanks to Bruno Bassi, former president of Computer Economics, for his support of those research efforts. It is because of all of their efforts that, as a team, we were able to break new ground and advance the understanding of the darker aspects of life in a wired world.

Introduction

This book presents a new and independent viewpoint on information warfare. One of the many things that are different about this analysis, compared to other perspectives of information warfare, is that this analysis is not military-centric. There are many reasons for the departure from the traditional military perspectives. The Internet has helped change the world of communications and commerce a great deal since information warfare strategies were first developed by the military. A global communications infrastructure has now made it possible for a wider assortment of groups to wage information warfare. This makes the threat of information warfare far greater than it was in 1990 and has produced a wider variety of targets to be attacked.

Putting Information Warfare into Context

Information warfare must be considered within the context of war in general. Traditionally, many types of groups have been able to wage a variety of types of wars. Huge groups of military forces have used sophisticated tactics and weapons, as was done in the Gulf War. In Vietnam, a dedicated but fairly scraggly horde of soldiers took on a well-equipped, centrally controlled military organization. In Mexico, small bands of freedom fighters have been willing to fight the entire national army and police force. In Afghanistan, indigenous forces defeated the might of the Soviet military machine that had previously invoked fear on the part of many more sophisticated armies. In other words, war comes in all shapes and sizes.

Before the Internet, information warfare was a war that would be fought among giants. The widespread use of the Internet and readily available access to the global communications systems and an arsenal of software tools has brought information warfare down to levels that all types of warfare eventually fall back to—once again, almost anyone can launch an information warfare attack.

The warfare tactics are very similar across the ten information warfare strategies. What differentiates the strategies are the purpose of the fight and the philosophies and motivations of the fighters. In ruinous information warfare strategies, for example, a sophisticated military operation can be launched to totally destroy the information technology and communications infrastructure of a nation or a region. In sustained terrorist information warfare strategies, a well-funded but small group of terrorists can attack a country, a city, an industrial sector, or a company and halt its operations or severely stifle economic activity. In many ways, the Internet has made some information warfare strategies cheap and relatively easy to implement, thus making the strategies usable to almost anyone in the world.

In this analysis, information warfare is comprised of ten different deliberate strategies to totally destroy or partially disable the military war fighting capability, industrial and manufacturing information infrastructure, or information technology-based civilian and government economic activities of a target nation, region, or population. Military organizations, terrorist groups, or rogue criminals can use these strategies to attack military systems, government operations, industrial infrastructures and communications systems, as well as civilian economic services such as electronic commerce. The ten strategies are examined in Chapter 1.

Is It a Question of If or When?

At the end of World War II, the threat of nuclear war loomed high in everyday life. Perhaps nuclear war is still possible, but it does not loom quite as high in the minds of citizens. The nuclear holocaust did not happen, but it could have, and the mighty nations of the world were prepared for mass destruction of the planet. We have now entered the information age and face the possibility of virtual destruction instead of physical destruction. Will it happen? When will it happen? Who will do it? These are questions that twenty-first century information warfare planners and strategists are grappling with as they prepare for the next war of wars.

The focus of military preparation has long been on devising plans to protect the national infrastructure from attacks from afar and take down the infrastructures of the enemy. This has certainly been a prudent and worthwhile pursuit. But what good would it do for one massive army of information warriors to attack one of their economic-interdependent allies? None! Especially when considering the dynamics of the global economy. Any nation that is capable of waging such an all-out information warfare attack is so tightly woven into the global economy that the attacker would suffer equal if not greater economic damage in the event of successful information warfare attacks on a super economic power.

Terrorists and rogue criminals, on the other hand, have less to protect and often little to hold onto and could perhaps even benefit from a successful attack. The military mind in the United States is still geared for big wars and is equipped to fight big armies. The focus of the military is on protecting the infrastructure while the budding digital economy is being built on ground outside the fort and is easy prey for attackers. Indeed, the infrastructure should be protected, but it is time to start thinking beyond the infrastructure protection strategy. An analysis of the economics of information warfare is included in Chapter 1 within the new framework for analysis, which offers a fresh look at the dynamics and nature of information warfare.

New Targets for Information Warriors

Terrorists strike at weak points, and rogue criminals steal what is the most valuable and the least protected. Both groups have their own cost/benefit equations. Terrorists and rogue criminals are the information warfare threat of the future. They will not attack the infrastructure, partially because it is so well guarded, but also because there is less chance of achieving drama for the terrorist and riches for the rogue. The terrorist and the rogue would rather not fight the military.

The terrorist, of course, loves headlines and drama, and strives to make people fearful while simultaneously embarrassing one or more governments in the process. The rogue loves money and would rather steal than fight. He is motivated by wealth, not fame, and certainly not by the religious salvation promised to so many terrorists who have died in the name of their country and their god.

The terrorist and the rogue will cause tremendous damage to national economies while completely avoiding the military. They will strike at what is easy, and electronic commerce companies, banks, and stock brokerages remain very easy targets compared to the expansive military communications systems, and the relatively well-guarded electric utility grid and telecommunications infrastructure. The economic impact of information warfare is further explored in Chapter 2.

Chapter 3 presents a scenario outlined for massive attacks, not by the military, but by would-be terrorists, that illustrates how ten people could cause severe economic damage. The scenario is called PH2, for Pearl Harbor Two. It is good drama that could readily happen—in fact, almost all of the tricks, hacks, and bugs that the PH2 team use in their attack are already proven tactics and techniques. It is just a matter of how they are put together in combination, sequence, and frequency that makes the difference between mischief and war.

New Weapons and Defense Strategies

How information warfare will be waged will be dependent on the resources of the attackers at the time they attack. New technologies are constantly emerging to help the defender ward off attackers, as are many new weapons for the attacker to use to foil the defenses established by the guardians. Chapter 4 establishes a process to assess defensive and offensive information warfare capabilities. Information warfare strategies and tactics are examined from a military perspective in Chapter 5.

An overview of defensive strategies for private companies that may well become the direct target of information warfare is provided in Chapter 6 through an examination of information warfare strategies and tactics from a corporate perspective. The emergence of the computer-literate terrorist and criminal is examined in Chapter 7, and the reasons why terrorists and rogues have an advantage in information warfare are analyzed. The importance and process of industrial mobilization in information warfare is covered in Chapter 8 as the mobilization requirements for technology companies in information warfare are analyzed.

In most wars, there are civilian casualties, and information warfare attacks will leave many civilians economically wounded and perhaps even destroyed. Chapter 9 examines the impact that information warfare can have on the innocent—and maybe the not-so-innocent—bystanders on the information superhighway. It is important that cybercitizens understand what can happen to them. Perhaps even more important is that military planners come to grips with the fact that the next war could have economic consequences for everyone, especially those who have assets that are computer-based or accounted for in an information system somewhere in the vast caverns of data maintained by the financial complex of the western world.

The New Information Warriors

Not all of the new information warriors are good guys. In fact, on some days the bad guys could easily outnumber the good guys. Chapter 10 examines the emergence of the new terrorists and rogue criminals that are wandering cyberspace. It is important to get to know these people because they are the ones who will be the mostly likely information war aggressors. This analysis delves into the minds and motivations of the new techno terrorists and criminals by reviewing the crimes of the past and speculating on the crimes of the future. Chapter 10 also examines the motivations of information warriors, both those who fight for good and those who serve evil. It explores many reasons why a talented computer professional may find the dark side of the information warrior elite more attractive than the humdrum everyday life of a programmer working in a bank somewhere in New Jersey.

Cyber Law Enforcement Challenges

The defenders on the information warfare front have already found that is tough to find a few good warriors. Recruitment and training of information warriors is critical if the good guys are going to have enough troops. The process and challenges are examined in Chapter 11. The mentalities and motivations of the good guys are also examined along with their training requirements, pay scales, and some of the temptations the guardians may face. The needs of law enforcement agencies are examined, as is the need to develop an information highway patrol and profiling methodology for cyber-terrorists and rogue criminals.

Things to Remember When Reading this Book

The author has interviewed hundreds of people over the last five years who were involved in computer security, information warfare planning, intelligence gathering, and law enforcement. These interviews were conducted for a variety of projects, including market analysis, product evaluations, and articles for journals and magazines. It is important to note that during all of these projects the people who were interviewed did not compromise any sensitive material. Although their input helped the author forage out the perspectives that are the foundation of this analysis, the work in this book is an independent perspective and is by no means to be considered an exposé of insider or confidential information regarding military or law enforcement operations.

Chapter 1

Information Warfare: A New Framework for Analysis

Information warfare strategies and tactics have been of utmost concern to defense planners in industrialized nations since the middle of the 1980s. The growth in popularity of the Internet and the widespread use of the World Wide Web and related technologies have dramatically increased this concern. The U.S. Department of Defense and its counterparts in NATO and other military alliances have been training both offensive and defensive information technology warriors since the late 1980s. This concern and the training that has evolved have been primarily focused on the protection or the destruction of the strategic information infrastructure and military technologies. There is no doubt that the protection of these technology assets should be of concern, as should the ability of the military to attack and disable or destroy the information infrastructure of enemy states as an offensive strategy or counteroffensive measure. This perspective, although sound within itself, is far too narrow for planning defensive or offensive information warfare in the age of electronic commerce. Considerable effort has gone into protecting the infrastructure and securing military capabilities, but the commercial information and electronic commerce technologies on which so many corporations have become dependent remains highly vulnerable.

A simple and straightforward analogy is the vulnerability of civil aviation and how the need for airport and in-flight security has evolved over the last 40 years. Military airbases have always been under fairly tight security because of the need to protect national defense assets and personnel. As civil air transportation became the target of hijackings and bombings in the 1960s and 1970s, it became apparent that there was a need for security at public airports. As a result, the use of metal detectors, security forces, explosive-sniffing dogs, and x-ray equipment for baggage contents has become almost universal. In addition, there are the key questions by airline staff at check-in regarding the control of passenger baggage and the chance that a stranger has asked an innocent passenger to transport a package for him or her. Although not 100 percent foolproof, these simple security precautions make it more difficult for terrorists to abscond with a civilian aircraft or to smuggle weapons or explosives. Other examples of shifts in security attitudes are apparent at courthouses, public schools, and other civilian facilities. The Internet, however, has no such protections. The open access of the Internet is what makes Internet-connected organizations more vulnerable to terrorist attacks and economic espionage.

To begin to address the vulnerabilities that are inherent in the age of the Internet and electronic commerce, a new framework of analysis of information warfare, electronic terrorism, and economic espionage is absolutely necessary. The old school of information warfare that focuses on the protection or the destruction of military and industrial infrastructure is no longer adequate as a basis for planning national defense strategies against cyber attacks. This chapter presents elements of the framework that are necessary to include the protection—or for that matter, the destruction—of civilian activities in cyberspace, as information warfare strategies and tactics evolve.

To help establish a good understanding of the principles, dynamics, and economics of information warfare, this chapter examines, updates, and expands on several aspects of information warfare, including:

▸ The ten categories of information warfare strategies and activities

- ▶ The probability of various information warfare strategies being implemented

- ▶ The establishment of a national information warfare defense structure

- ▶ The military side of information warfare

- ▶ The origin and mentality of technology terrorists

- ▶ How private companies will need to defend themselves during an information warfare attack

- ▶ The dynamics and viability of international treaties

Types of Information Warfare Strategies and Activities

To prepare for information warfare, it is necessary to define what information warfare is and—as with any type of warfare—identify and classify what types of information warfare can be practiced. Information warfare strategies, like physical warfare strategies, are designed to hinder or disable military forces, disable industrial infrastructures and manufacturing capabilities, or disrupt civilian and government economic activities in order to put an aggressor or a target country at a disadvantage. The purposes of establishing an advantage can run along a continuum from improving the negotiating position of the aggressor to the absolute destruction of a nation. Information warfare activities fall into ten major categories:

Offensive ruinous information warfare An organized deliberate military effort to totally destroy the military information capabilities, industrial and manufacturing information infrastructure, and information technology-based civilian and government economic activities of a target nation, region, or population.

Offensive containment information warfare An organized deliberate military effort to cripple or disable military information capabilities, halt industrial and manufacturing information activities, and disrupt information technology-based civilian and government economic activity to leverage a strong negotiating posture for an aggressor over a target nation, region, or population.

Sustained terrorist information warfare The ongoing deliberate efforts of an organized political group against the military, industrial, and civilian and government economic information infrastructures or activities of a nation, region, organization of states, population, or corporate entity.

Random terrorist information warfare The sporadic efforts of an organized political group or individuals against the military, industrial, and civilian and government information infrastructures or activities of a nation, region, organization of states, population, or corporate entity.

Defensive preventive information warfare An organized deliberate military protective effort to prevent an aggressor from destroying military information technology capabilities, industrial and manufacturing information technology infrastructure, and civilian and government information technology-based economic activities of a nation, region, or population.

Defensive ruinous information warfare An organized deliberate military effort to totally destroy the military information technology capabilities, industrial and manufacturing information infrastructure, and information technology-based civilian and government economic activities of an aggressor nation, region, population, or military/terrorist force.

Defensive responsive containment information warfare An organized deliberate military effort to cripple or disable military information technology capabilities, halt industrial and manufacturing information technology activities, and disrupt information technology-based civilian and government economic activity to leverage a strong negotiating posture over an aggressor nation, region, population, or military/terrorist force.

Sustained rogue information warfare The ongoing deliberate efforts of an organized nonpolitical, criminal, or mercenary group against the military, industrial, civilian, and government economic information infrastructures or activities of a nation, region, organization of states, population, or corporate entity.

Random rogue information warfare The sporadic efforts of an organized nonpolitical, criminal, or mercenary group or individuals against the military, industrial, civilian, and government information infrastructures or activities of a nation, region, organization of states, population, or corporate entity.

Amateur rogue information warfare The sporadic efforts of untrained and nonaligned individuals or small groups against the military, industrial, civilian, and government information infrastructures or activities of a nation, region, organization of states, population, or corporate entity.

The Probability of Various Information Warfare Strategies Being Implemented

The Cold War and the existence of nuclear weapons is proof that a strategy or a weapons system can exist and not be used by the nations or groups that have the ability to use it. Of course, this does mean we are operating under an assumption that a nuclear weapon was not used in an act of aggression since the end of World War II. Letting the assumption stand, we can conclude that the wide range of information warfare strategies in this analysis can exist and that nations can be prepared to implement such strategies during political conflicts, but the strategies never need to be used. We can also assume that even though it is not likely that an extreme information warfare strategy will be used, it is still prudent to be capable of defending against a wide variety of strategies. As in any warfare, a key element in predicting what kind of information warfare to be prepared to defend against is to analyze what resources are required to implement an information warfare strategy. Each of the ten categories of information warfare has a price tag, a required organizational structure, and a timeline for preparation and implementation.

Offensive ruinous information warfare requires a well-trained military force that is capable of attacking and destroying an information infrastructure from both afar and on location. The strategy requires a wide range of mental and physical skill sets and an in-depth understanding of information architectures, programming, telecommunications, hardware, software, security, and encryption. It also requires access to a wide variety of telecommunications systems and many types of computers. It may also require a physically capable and equipped task force to physically penetrate a computer or communications facility, retrieve or modify information, and possibly even destroy the equipment. This information warfare strategy is extremely expensive and could only be implemented by a nation that is willing to spend billions of dollars to develop specific methods and train the hundreds, if not thousands, of people necessary to implement the strategy. Very few nations can afford to implement offensive ruinous information warfare strategies.

Offensive containment information warfare strategies are similar to offensive ruinous information warfare in resource requirements. It is not likely that real containment could be achieved without a highly skilled force. It is possible to achieve a harassing effect and be menacing using terrorist tactics—which could be also referred to as guerrilla or resistance tactics—and cause disruption. Depending on the circumstances, containment of an isolated region could be possible—even the least-equipped warriors of the past knew to cut the telegraph lines so the cavalry could not be wired to send help. Sophisticated offensive containment information warfare strategies, however, still require substantial investment and years of development and training of forces. As with offensive ruinous information warfare strategies, very few nations can afford to implement offensive containment information warfare strategies.

Sustained terrorist information warfare is not an expensive process and can be implemented and maintained over long periods of time with an investment of a few million dollars. Certainly good skill sets are needed, but the process of terrorism is far more focused on disruption and harassment than complete destruction or containment. In a complete destruction or containment scenario, it is necessary not to do things to information architectures that will impede or injure one's allies. Since terrorists usually have few allies and generally have the worst of manners in the first place, they can use sloppy techniques that can disrupt and to some extent probably destroy some aspects of information technology-based economies. There are, or at least have been, several terrorist groups that can afford to carry out this type of information warfare strategy.

Random terrorist information warfare is even less expensive than sustained terrorist information warfare. Sporadic terrorism does not require the ongoing recruitment, maintenance, and training of information warriors and thus can be implemented on a really slim budget. In general, random terrorist acts have little lasting impact except on those people who are immediately injured or killed. These random terrorist acts can have great public relations value for political causes, and if such acts are directed toward information technology, the press coverage will be widespread and dramatic. Again, there are, or at least have been, several terrorist groups that can afford to carry out this type of information warfare strategy.

Defensive preventive information warfare has the same basic set of requirements that offensive ruinous information warfare has in terms of personnel, organization structure, and costs. Defensive preventive information warfare is necessary to defend against virtually all forms of offensive information warfare strategies. All information technology-dependent countries must develop defensive strategies, either independently or in a coalition. These strategies take years to develop and cost billions of dollars to implement and sustain.

Defensive ruinous information warfare is a counteroffensive strategy that requires the full set of skills, organization structure, and cost structure associated with offensive ruinous information warfare and offensive containment information warfare strategies. It costs billions of dollars to implement and probably requires a coalition to implement and maintain.

Defensive responsive containment information warfare and offensive containment information warfare strategies are similar except in the circumstances in which they are deployed. The cost is high, and it takes considerable time to develop strategies and tactics and train forces. There are few countries that can independently implement this strategy.

Sustained rogue information warfare has a similar overhead requirement to that of sustained terrorist information warfare. It is not an expensive process and can be carried out over long periods of time with an investment of a few million dollars. Good skill sets are required, but staff may be relatively easy to recruit given the fact that legitimate information technology jobs are not the best-paying positions. The process of embezzlement, fraud, and blackmail pays well for those who get away with it, and those activities are likely to be the focus of rogue information warriors. In addition, pseudo-legitimate mercenaries hired by governments or corporations may also find it profitable to utilize their skills in politically motivated subversive activities.

Random rogue information warfare has a cost structure similar to that of random terrorist information warfare and can be implemented on a relatively slim budget. The major differences are a lack of political motivation when compared to terrorists, and a probable lack of style and grace when compared to professional rogue activities. There are numerous criminal organizations that can readily implement these strategies.

Amateur rogue information warfare is by far the least expensive type of information warfare to wage. A computer, a modem, and an Internet access account are about all it takes to get started. We have had decades of hackers and crackers, virus writers, and malicious computer trespassers, and these activities will continue. Amateur rogues usually operate in isolation and perhaps in small groups, which make them a menace but not a threat to global information infrastructure security. The biggest problem with the amateur rogue is that it costs as much to defend against them as it does to defend against an organized terrorist information warfare force.

Given these cost structures, the types of information warfare that will be most likely waged against large industrial computer-dependent countries are sustained terrorist information warfare, random terrorist information warfare, sustained rogue information warfare, random rogue information warfare, and amateur rogue information warfare. To be able to finance, organize, and mount offensive ruinous information warfare and offensive containment information warfare is so expensive that the publicly political enemies of the large industrial nations cannot afford to use such strategies. But that does not mean that the lesser tactics would not be extremely damaging to infrastructures and economies.

The strategies that would be most effective against smaller, somewhat computer-dependent countries are offensive ruinous information warfare and offensive containment information warfare. In the case of aggressor nations or groups, defensive responsive containment information warfare is the most likely tactic. The strategies that will be the most effective against nations that have done little in terms of developing a computer dependency are those of offensive containment information warfare. The smaller, less-developed nations in no way can afford to mount and sustain defensive ruinous information warfare or defensive responsive containment information warfare strategies. At best, they could mount random terrorist information warfare or random rogue information warfare strategies and most likely would depend on amateur rogue information warfare carried out by a few patriots or geographically dispersed allies.

The private sector in industrial computer-dependent nations does need to be concerned about large-scale offensive ruinous information warfare in widespread conflicts that get out of hand. However, the most likely immediate threats to corporate operations outside of organized conflicts are random terrorist information warfare, sustained rogue information warfare, random rogue information warfare, and amateur rogue information warfare. The most vulnerable corporations are those that are heavily involved in and derive the majority of their revenues from electronic commerce, or what we so lovingly call dot-coms.

It will cost corporations much more to defend themselves against these information warfare strategies than it will cost terrorists or rogues to mount such attacks. In addition, the only organizations in the industrialized nations that can afford to effectively counter or ultimately eliminate the attackers, especially if they are outside the country of the corporation that is being attacked, are maintained and controlled by the military. Because civilian law enforcement is in a weak position to deal with information warfare attacks on private corporations, those companies without strong ties to the military will become easy targets with little recourse. All in all, this may create a role for—as well as employment opportunities for—rogue information warriors who can provide mercenary information warfare services for corporations that are under attack.

The Anatomy of a National Information Warfare Defense Structure

Each of the industrialized computer-dependent nations needs to develop and implement an information warfare defense strategy. This strategy will require the establishment of an integrated defense structure that delineates responsibility across military, civilian government, law enforcement, and private sector organizations. Developing this structure poses organizational, political, and legal challenges. The nature of these challenges will certainly vary in different countries, but there are common challenges that can be addressed by creating a global model with local components. This approach will better enable the international cooperation that is required to counter offensive information warfare in the borderless Internet environment. In addition to the global cooperative process and the local components in computer-dependent nations, there should also be a process to assimilate less computer-dependent nations into the information warfare defense structure. The process of developing the information warfare defense structure involves:

▶ Establishing national information warfare defense organizational structures

▶ Staffing and training information warfare defense organizational units

▶ Developing and implementing steps for international cooperation between national defense organizations

▶ Testing international cooperation abilities through information warfare games

▶ Assimilating less computer-dependent nations into the information warfare defense structure and processes

It is very difficult to properly access existing national information warfare defense structures because of a lack of comprehensive information. In the United States, for example, there are numerous areas of responsibility in each of the military branches and in civilian government agencies. The Love Bug attack in May of 2000 clearly showed that the processes within the U.S. government failed to protect both civilian government and military units from the attack and failed to prevent damage to computer systems. Civilian government agencies were fairly open about the impact of the Love Bug attack, with, for example, the Veterans Administration admitting that it had received more than 7 million Love Bug messages. Military organizations, prudently, tended to run their usual obfuscation and denial exercises about the impact of the attack. There is also a lack of comprehensive information about existing information warfare defense structures and capabilities in NATO member nations. It is clear also that many of these nations suffered damage from the Love Bug attack, but the details of that damage have also been suppressed.

It is noteworthy that there are many successes in information warfare defense processes and structures in the United States. The information infrastructure of the U.S. military is under constant attack and has obviously survived. A truly accurate assessment of damages and successful intrusions will never be made public and rightfully so. It is not prudent to provide potential attackers with any information about success rates and possible weaknesses. It is also prudent for analysts and policy makers to be very skeptical about any and all information released by the military regarding attacks. Anything that is released will certainly have a spin of some direction put to it in order to bolster the desired position of the military.

Defining the Role of the Military in Information Warfare Defense

Given a lack of comprehensive data about the information warfare defense organizational structures of the U.S. military and those of other allied nations (as well as their natural and necessary tendency toward obfuscation of defense), it is impossible to judge the effectiveness of existing structures. There are, however, logical principles that can be applied to the military role in a national information warfare defense structure:

- ▸ The primary role of the military in national information warfare defense structures is to protect military systems and ensure the security readiness of these systems.

- ▸ The secondary role of the military in national information warfare defense structures is to be able to effectively deploy countermeasures against aggressor nations, groups, or individuals in the event of information warfare.

- ▸ The third role of the military is to assist civilian government and law enforcement agencies in the protection of government and commercial information infrastructures.

The primary and secondary roles of the military, at least in the United States, are being pursued and, as noted, have been successful to some degree. However, it is unclear at this time how the military has helped—or even *can* help—to protect the information systems of civilian government and private sector organizations. During civil unrest, disasters, and global conflicts, the military has certainly contributed to the protection of infrastructure assets. This has been accomplished by deploying National Guard units or regular troops to provide various types of support. Deployment under these circumstances can sometimes take a considerable amount of time. In addition, the personnel that are deployed usually provide support in less technical areas such as physical security, transportation and logistical support, evacuation of injured civilians, and establishing emergency shelters. All of these things have been necessary under many circumstances in the past, and military units have shown a high level of capability in accomplishing such missions. In the case of the Love Bug attack, much of the damage had been done before people were out of bed in the morning. In less than 24 hours, the virus had spread worldwide. It is easy to conclude that the type of support the military has successfully provided for the civilian population in the past and the model under which the support was provided is not adequate in the event of information warfare. Thus, if the military is to expand its role in protecting civilian government and private sector information infrastructures, new organizational structures and new deployment methods will need to be implemented.

Establishing New Roles for Civilian Law Enforcement in Information Warfare Defense

Civilian law enforcement agencies will also play a key role in protecting government and private sector information infrastructures in the event of information warfare. At this time, however, civilian law enforcement organizations are in an extremely weak position to provide any assistance. The Love Bug attack was an embarrassment for the U.S. government, the Department of Justice, and the Federal Bureau of Investigation. Attorney General Janet Reno made her usual "we will protect our nation" speech, but the reality is that the Department of Justice was caught by surprise as much as any other government agency and could do little to provide assistance in the form of information warfare defense.

To be an effective player in the national information warfare defense structure, the role of civilian law enforcement agencies will need to go beyond investigating a crime after it occurs. This is where the politics of establishing a national information warfare defense structure get really thick. The traditional role of civilian law enforcement has only partially been focused on preventing crime. The main focus has been investigating crimes, collecting and compiling evidence, and apprehending criminals. The conclusion is simple: civilian law enforcement agencies, although their role in defense is critical, are not adequately trained and do not have much, if any, experience in helping to defend the information infrastructure from attack. In addition, to effectively help defend against information warfare attacks, civilian law enforcement agencies will need to be active in cyberspace at all times. This absolutely reeks of a big-brother totalitarian state, which makes the politics of changing the role of civilian law enforcement in an information warfare defense structure even stickier. The civilian law enforcement defense structure in national information warfare needs to focus on:

- ▶ Patrolling cyberspace to monitor illegal activity and domestic threats to the information technology infrastructure

- ▶ Cooperating with military organizations in the investigation of information technology infrastructure attacks

- ▶ Working with private sector companies to help identify potential sources of threats to the information technology infrastructure

- ▶ Working with private sector companies that produce information technology to help identify potential weaknesses in technology that can be exploited by cyber-terrorists and information warriors of enemy states

Cooperation from the Private Sector in Information Warfare Defense

The role of the private sector in a national information warfare defense structure takes two major forms. First, those companies that are involved in the development, production, and sale of information technology and services have the responsibility of cooperating with civilian law enforcement agencies and military organizations. This cooperation involves reporting suspicious behavior and incidents to the organizations that have responsibility for national defense. In addition, technology producers need to cooperate with the national information warfare defense process by providing a continuous flow of information regarding the known and suspected weaknesses and faults of their products. This is controversial in that most technology producers are not willing to admit their systems have weaknesses and faults. Most will claim that such a process would potentially violate the protection of their trade secrets. Technology producers are also likely to be defensive about how information regarding weaknesses and faults of their technology may impact their marketing strategies and their ability to sell products to government and military organizations. Private sector companies that produce information technology can contribute to the national information warfare defense structure by:

- ▶ Working with civilian law enforcement and the military to help identify potential sources of threats to the information technology infrastructure

- ▶ Working with civilian law enforcement and the military to help identify potential weaknesses in technology that can be exploited by cyber-terrorists and information warriors of enemy states

The second area where private sector companies have responsibility in the national information warfare defense process is to report security incidents and trends in system attacks. By doing this type of reporting, private sector companies could help provide early warnings on increased activity and enable information warfare defenders to anticipate and perhaps even prevent larger-scale attacks. It is not likely, however, that the private sector will provide this information without being required to routinely report. The reason for private sector companies' reluctance is that they need to avoid potentially negative publicity. The primary responsibility of private sector company managers is to protect the value of the company and ensure that dividends are paid to investors. Bad press is bad for stock prices and bad for revenue. Private sector companies that are primarily end-users of information technology can contribute to the national information warfare defense structure by:

- ▶ Reporting suspicious activity and attacks on their information technology infrastructure to civilian law enforcement. Doing so will help effectively monitor growing threats as well as aid in tracking and apprehending cyber-terrorists.

- ▶ Actively participating in the prosecution of apprehended cyber-criminals and potential cyber-terrorists by providing data on attacks on their information technology infrastructure.

International Cooperation in Information Warfare Defense

The development of international cooperation in an information warfare defense structure can be easily grounded in existing international alliances such as NATO. The organization structure is already in place, and there is a well-established mechanism for discussion and establishing cooperative processes. The primary obstacle to establishing an effective approach to international cooperation in information warfare defense is that these existing alliances and structures are inherently slow in responding to a call to action. The ability and willingness of alliance members to cooperate was certainly demonstrated in the Gulf War. However, in the case of the Gulf War there was sufficient lead-time for cooperative efforts to be established and for resources to be mobilized. Defending against information warfare attacks will require an instant response in order for an effective defense to be mobilized.

The nature of information warfare defense is similar to what existed during the Cold War era: "always on defense." It was easy to muster an always-on defense during the Cold War because there was a readily identifiable enemy. The USSR was clearly the bad guy, and the NATO allies were clearly the good guys. The threat was always present, and the good guys were always on alert and ready to respond with defensive actions or counterattacks. In the age of the information warfare threat, there is no clearly defined enemy, and the always-on defense mechanisms have been largely mothballed.

The onset of information warfare can occur in an instant. Early warnings are likely to be short, if they exist at all. Cooperation from allies also needs to be instant. The only way to have an effective international information warfare defense structure is to return to a Cold War always-on defense mentality. This must be accompanied by an organizational structure that can respond with the speed and effectiveness necessary to defend against attacks that will occur without warning. As in the Cold War, there needs to be a common understanding of defensive strategies and what countermeasures will be implemented under specific circumstances. Members of international alliances can contribute to the information warfare defense structure by:

- ▶ Actively participating in international information warfare defense organizations and programs

- ▶ Reporting suspicious activity and attacks on the information technology infrastructure in their countries to other members of the alliance, and to help effectively monitor growing threats as well as track and apprehend cyber-terrorists

- ▶ Training military and civilian law enforcement personnel to defend against attacks on their information technology infrastructure

Assimilation of Non-Computer Dependent Nations into Information Warfare Defense

One of the biggest challenges in establishing a strong national and international information warfare defense structure is to assimilate the non-computer dependent nations into a global alliance to fight against information warfare and cyber-terrorism. Most of these nations have little, if any, stake in the security of information technology infrastructures. Some are very corrupt, and others harbor and support terrorists. The Love Bug case and the impotence or the unwillingness on the part of the Philippine government to act swiftly to apprehend a suspect will long stand as an example of the need to assimilate the non-computer dependent nations into the global defense process. The assimilation process is going to be a long and difficult road. One option is to provide grants and funding to support the passage of appropriate legislation and to train civilian law enforcement personnel in those nations that show a willingness to cooperate.

Global assimilation, however, is likely to fail. Therefore, the alliances of the computer-dependent nations must be prepared to take swift and decisive action to halt attacks on the information technology infrastructure that originate in part or are supported by non-cooperating nations. This may very well mean some form of physical intervention and the apprehension or elimination of attackers or cyber-terrorists. Military invasions, of course, are frowned upon and can be very expensive as well. Covert operations, if they remain covert, may be the only viable and affordable alternative to dealing with attacks or cyber-terrorists that work from or are supported by non-cooperating nations. Non-computer dependent nations can contribute to the information warfare defense structure by:

- ▶ Passing appropriate legislation against cyber-crime and terrorism
- ▶ Training law enforcement to investigate cyber-criminal and terrorist activities
- ▶ Cooperating with international alliances that are defending against information warfare

War Games for Information Warfare Defense

Another big challenge in establishing a national information warfare defense structure is creating a training and practice environment where defenders as well as attackers can practice their skills and where international alliances can conduct exercises. In preparation for conventional warfare, different branches can conduct exercises to gain additional experience in managing the battle process. Alliances can also carry exercises on a larger scale, moving troops and equipment and conducting war games. Military exercises and war games have always been an expensive process, but they are conducted with real equipment that could serve the dual purposes of training and actually conducting war.

In the case of information warfare, it is difficult to utilize the existing information technology infrastructure to conduct training. There have been situations such as Sandia National Laboratories' establishment of the Red Team, which tested the security on actual information technology systems. But the Red Team was not bent on the destruction of systems. Other intrusion and security tests have also been conducted on military, government, and private company information systems, but these tests were really not designed to destroy systems. The best results that can come from this type of testing is improved experience for defenders and a greater knowledge base for eradicating security weaknesses. Overall, these types of exercises do not come close to replicating the actual environment of information warfare compared to the war games that have been used to test conventional warfare methods.

The best alternative to train defenders and attackers is to establish actual data infrastructures that replicate or emulate such environments as banking, Wall Street stock exchanges, electronic commerce companies, and telecommunications centers. These environments would provide an opportunity to train information warriors in implementing or defending against all of the categories of information warfare. This is a very expensive endeavor and comes with a price tag in the billions. Cooperation from information technology producers could help reduce some of the costs, and participation from members of the NATO alliance could also help offset some of the costs.

Putting International Treaties into Perspective

The myriad treaties that exist in the world today are complex and voluminous, and when it comes to directly addressing the international dynamics of cyberspace, they are seriously lacking. Cyber-law is one of the greatest hurdles that needs to be overcome before the Internet and electronic commerce can further evolve. We have witnessed tremendous and rapid growth of Internet applications in commerce, government, and personal individual use. But there are many legal issues that remain. Taxation of Internet-based commerce and cross-border trade are two areas where national and international laws need to be evaluated and probably rewritten before the commercial side of the Internet can grow to its greatest potential. Other cyber-law issues are less business-oriented and more politically volatile. France, for example, wants Yahoo! to prohibit people in that country from having access to purchasing Nazi-related items that are freely traded in the United States both on- and offline. While it would appear that the Chinese government is embracing the Internet on the one hand, the government wants Chinese citizens to only see websites that are approved by the government. Other religious and political groups and governments have a long list of dos and don'ts that they would like to impose on the Internet. These issues will probably be with us for the next several decades.

Cyber-law and regulation at the national level is a complex and passionate problem. Until national issues are resolved, it is going to be extremely difficult to address international issues. When cultures, religions, and politics clash on the borderless Internet, the old methods of localized censorship quickly fail. The old paradigm of local control and structured compromise in the international arena will probably no longer succeed to everyone's satisfaction. Treaties have always been difficult. Governments want local control and feel they are entitled to it. The international governance process through mechanisms like the United Nations has certainly helped, but there is still a great deal of disagreement on international issues. In the past, without the Internet being a change agent, treaty makers—like road builders—could weather out the storms and move ahead at a steady and deliberate pace when and where they could make progress. The Internet, however, accelerates process and decreases the time the treaty makers have to work out new agreements.

These difficult circumstances are compounded further because the Internet can be a vehicle for cross-border terrorism, espionage, and criminal activity. This is not news to seasoned Internet observers. The Love Bug, however, was a global wakeup call in terms of dealing with cyber-crime and terrorism. The Philippine government and law enforcement officials showed little concern that a local student may have set loose a destructive email virus that shut down companies and governments around the world and caused billions of dollars in damages and lost productivity. As a result of the lack of concern and lack of international coordination to conduct a thorough investigation, we may never know the full circumstances of the Love Bug attacks. The Philippines is only one of dozens of countries that are not equipped to deal with cyber issues, and the response of the Philippine government has now become a benchmark for future incidents. It is clear that the industrialized computer-dependent nations will not be able to count on governments that do not have similar cyber interests to be supportive in future incidents—with or without a treaty.

Treaty making is a noble endeavor that has greatly contributed to world stability, and treaty makers certainly do deserve praise. Regardless of all of their efforts and fifty years of ever-increasing success in forging out international treaties, the world remains a rather hostile and not so civilized place. There are massive and continuous human rights violations in many countries. Slavery, torture, and government and police corruption exist in at least 25 percent of the countries in the world. There are international prostitution rings, gunrunners, and drug smugglers operating around the globe. There are governments that make their money on exporting terror and crime. None of these people are ready to embrace a new treaty to control activity on the Internet. They do not care about security on the Internet and, in fact, will use the Internet as another tool and mechanism to continue their existing illicit and ill-mannered behavior patterns.

The process of addressing issues of international cyber-terrorism, crime, and information warfare should indeed be pursued through the treaty-making process. It will help align the computer-dependent nations with the global perspective and possibly prompt them to help out in fighting against information warfare attacks. This, however, may be the only immediate benefit. It will inadvertently also help to accentuate the gap between the industrial and non-industrial, between the rich and the poor, and between the law abiding and those who ignore law. Just as the Internet helps to advance commerce, governance, and individual freedom, the Internet will make these things more vulnerable to terrorist attack and provide inviting targets in global information warfare.

Yes, move forward with the treaties, but as in the nuclear arms race and the Cold War, we must be prepared to defend the infrastructure of information technology and we must be prepared for information warfare. The process of defense goes beyond just watching the gate. We must be prepared to counterattack and to locate—and if necessary, physically eliminate—information warriors, terrorists, or rogue criminals who attack the information infrastructure of computer-dependent nations. The alternative—the disruption and perhaps even the destruction of computer-dependent economies—is not acceptable.

The Military Side of Information Warfare

The military has two major roles in information warfare—defensive and offensive. The defensive role of the military in information warfare, as previously mentioned, is to protect military systems, ensure the security readiness of those systems, and work with civilian government and law enforcement agencies in the protection of government and commercial information infrastructures. In addition, the military must be capable of effectively deploying countermeasures such as defensive responsive containment information warfare against aggressor nations, groups, or individuals. The offensive role of the military is to be capable of implementing offensive ruinous information warfare strategies and offensive containment information warfare strategies against a target nation, region, or population.

Offensive ruinous information warfare strategies and offensive containment information warfare strategies have several tactics in common, but what makes them different is the overall tone of the mission. When implementing an offensive ruinous information warfare strategy, the goal is clear: destroy, to the extent possible, the information infrastructure and computer-based civilian and government economic activities of a nation, region, or population. When implementing an offensive containment information warfare strategy, the military mission is accomplished in degrees. The philosophy or goal is focused on disrupting or disabling the information infrastructure and computer-based civilian and government economic activities of a nation, region, or population. Both strategies are designed to provide an advantage over an enemy.

Defensive Preventive Information Warfare

Defensive preventive information warfare is an organized, deliberate military protective effort to prevent an aggressor from destroying military information technology capabilities. The defensive role is the most difficult role the military faces in information warfare. Over the last decade, military computer systems in the United States have been the target of hundreds of thousands of break-in attempts. Attackers have ranged from teenagers looking for a challenge and a hacking victory to unknown parties in Europe and Asia. U.S. key weapons systems are well protected, and although they have been the targets of numerous attempts it appears that the vast majority of these attempts have been unsuccessful. The business systems of the U.S. military, including websites and email systems, have fallen victim to repeated break-ins and have also been susceptible to virus infections such as the Love Bug.

Defensive tactics used by the military are very similar to those used by any organization that needs to keep intruders out. The U.S. military has deployed the same firewall and other intrusion products that government organizations and private sector companies are now using to protect their systems. This has both positive and negative points. Because military systems are under constant attack, the firewall and intrusion detection and prevention software packages that most organizations rely on are certainly being well tested in a military environment. However, the deployment of these products makes military business and email systems just as vulnerable as any system using off-the-shelf products. The main advantage the military has in defending its information systems is a strong enforcement effort, with hackers (at least those found to be located in the United States) being vigorously pursued and prosecuted.

The vigorous prosecution of domestic hackers who attack military systems can certainly act as a deterrent against amateur rogue information warfare, sustained rogue information warfare, and random rogue information warfare attacks. Another asset of the military in fighting against information system attackers is that, of all the organizations in the world, the U.S. military probably has the most experience in compiling and presenting evidence of intrusions and attacks. This experience provides the military with an advantage when dealing with more serious offenders, including individuals or groups that conduct random or sustained terrorist information warfare attacks against military systems. If a terrorist can be apprehended, the military is well equipped and experienced in pursing prosecution.

Although it is obviously a crime and cannot be condoned, the various amateur rogue information warfare attacks and organized terrorist attacks against information systems have helped the military develop defensive tactics and train systems defenders. An experienced military is a far greater asset than a dedicated but inexperienced military, and in the case of information warfare this very apparent. The experience of the U.S. military in compiling evidence and prosecuting cases is an asset that can certainly be leveraged in protecting civilian systems.

The weapons systems of the military also contain information systems elements and are targets of information warfare tactics. The electronic nature of the weapons systems and the need for accurate information to be fed into the systems in order to obtain optimal performance of the systems is a major concern of military organizations around the world. The protection of monitoring, measurement, and control instrumentation is no longer just a military concern. Many industries, including civil aviation, manufacturing, aerospace, and logistics, are using some of the same types of technology that are central to military weapons systems. This makes the problem of developing solid defenses for monitoring, measurement, and control instrumentation broader than the protection of military systems alone. There are several types of technology that need to be defended from intrusion and interference, as shown in Table 1-1.

Table 1-1: Vulnerable Monitoring, Measurement, and Control Instrumentation

Type of System	Purpose of System
Avionics	Aircraft functioning and control
Navigation	Accurate movement of aircraft, ships, and land transportation devices
Positioning (GPS)	Accurate location and movement of equipment and personnel
Detection (radar, sonar)	Detection and tracking of equipment and personnel
Calibration	System functioning and accuracy
Internal system communications	Proper integration and phasing of system elements
System-to-system communications	Proper coordination and phasing of related systems

The military and private industry need to be able to protect monitoring, measurement, and control instrumentation from both destruction and interference. The need to protect systems from destruction is obvious, because if a system is destroyed it hinders military capability.

Protection from interference, however, is equally important. If systems are not functioning properly and accurately, military capability is certainly hindered. More importantly, malfunctioning systems can cause injury or death to the wrong parties. It is important to provide military personnel with the safest possible war-fighting equipment, and protecting the information elements of weapons systems is critical in this effort. It is also important from a political and diplomatic perspective that equipment function properly. If the information elements of weapon systems are interfered with and accuracy is compromised, the unintentional killing of innocent people or destruction of allied resources can easily occur.

To protect weapons systems from interference, the most effective tactic is to identify potential sources of interference and immediately and decisively disable those sources. This requires the military to develop and maintain sophisticated signal monitoring systems that can identify potentially interfering transmissions and locate the source of those signals. Similar technology needs to be developed to protect private sector technology from the same sort of interference. These detection systems, regardless of their perceived present sophistication, require considerable funding and development to ensure that monitoring, measurement, and control instrumentation is not interfered with in a conflict situation.

In addition, military systems need to operate in an authentication mode and only accept signals that are from a known, trusted, and official source. The military has long used encryption for messaging and communications, and this practice will continue. Encryption, however, is becoming more vulnerable as cheap and easily obtainable high-end computer systems become available around the world. The U.S. military and intelligence community has opposed and often stalled the export of high-end computer systems. By doing so, it hopes to make breaking encryption codes more difficult and hinder the ability of foreign powers to develop information warfare capabilities. The companies that produce and export information technologies have overcome many of the barriers supported by the military, and high-end computer systems are being exported from the United States at a very rapid rate. This may be good for the companies that profit from the sale of these systems. It is not good in that the availability of high-end computer systems will definitely enable cyber-terrorists and the development of information warfare skills and personnel in undesirable locations.

Offensive and Defensive Ruinous Information Warfare

The key difference between offensive and defensive ruinous information warfare is not in tactics, but in purpose. Offensive ruinous information warfare is an organized deliberate military effort to totally destroy the military information capabilities, industrial and manufacturing information infrastructure, and information technology-based civilian and government economic activities of a target nation, region, or population. Defensive ruinous information warfare is an organized deliberate military effort to totally destroy the military information technology capabilities, industrial and manufacturing information infrastructure, and information technology-based civilian and government economic activities of an aggressor nation, region, population, or military/terrorist force. Put more simply, offensive ruinous information warfare is used against a target that is not an aggressor, and defensive ruinous information warfare is used against an aggressor.

The traditional tactics used in ruinous information warfare have been centered in the physical destruction of communications systems, computer systems, and monitoring, measurement, and control instrumentation. This has usually required bombardment with missiles or aircraft, or onsite sabotage and destruction through overt military operations or covert underground operations. The grand theory of information warfare is that such systems can be virtually destroyed by electronically penetrating the systems and disabling them by deliberating modifying software or infecting the systems with viruses or other destructive software modules. The key difference between the physical destruction versus the virtual destruction tactics is that virtual destruction leaves the physical plant intact so it can be reused after the conflict has ended instead of having to be physically replaced and rebuilt.

The success factor in virtual destruction is largely dependent on the age and sophistication of a system, as well as the extent to which the system is connected to communication pathways that can provide access for information warriors. Thus the tactic of virtual destruction will only be effective against the most electronically sophisticated nations, which at this time are mainly allies of the United States. The likelihood then of the United States deploying the virtual destruction tactic is relatively low. At the same time, however, the electronic sophistication of the United States and its allies makes these countries prime targets for virtual destruction tactics.

The capability required to effectively launch a ruinous information warfare effort is very expensive. Therefore, only a few countries can deploy the totally ruinous strategies. But many countries and several terrorist groups can readily use virtual destruction tactics and cause considerable disruption to military operations and government and civilian economic activity. The specific tactics used in ruinous information warfare are explained in Chapters 5, 6, and 7. The most likely systems to be targets for either virtual or physical destruction—and the impact of systems attacks—are shown in Table 1-2.

Table 1-2: Ruinous Information Warfare Targets and Impact of Attacks

Type of System	Impact of Attack on Target Nation
Military defense systems	Makes the country more vulnerable to invasion
Military offensive systems	Hinders the ability of the country to take offensive military actions
Cross-border voice and data telecommunications connections	Hinders the ability to communicate outside the country
National voice and data telecommunications infrastructures	Hinders the ability to communicate throughout the country
Local telecommunications systems	Isolates specific areas of the country
Central banking computers	Slows or disables the flow of cash in the economy
Stock and commodity exchanges	Hinders or disables the investment and trading process
Electronic commerce websites	Disrupts local commerce and contributes to economic failure
Manufacturing businesses, supply chain systems, and monitoring, measurement, and control systems	Hinders or disables the military-industrial complex
Aviation control systems	Hinders or disables the military and civilian air traffic
Power grid control systems	Hinders or disables the distribution of electricity

Offensive and Responsive Containment Information Warfare

Containment information warfare strategies are likely to be used on a widespread basis in the future. The key difference between offensive and defensive containment information warfare is not in tactics, but in purpose. Offensive containment information warfare is an organized deliberate military effort to cripple or disable military information capabilities, halt industrial and manufacturing information activities, and disrupt information technology-based civilian and government economic activity to leverage a strong negotiating posture for an aggressor over a target nation, region, or population. Defensive responsive containment information warfare is an organized deliberate military effort to cripple or disable military information technology capabilities, halt industrial and manufacturing information technology activities, and disrupt information technology-based civilian and government economic activity to leverage a strong negotiating posture over an aggressor nation, region, population, or military/terrorist force. Offensive containment information warfare is used against a target that is not an aggressor, and defensive containment information warfare is used against an aggressor.

In a way, containment information warfare strategies can be viewed as limited information warfare, whereas ruinous information warfare strategies can be equivalent to total nuclear destruction. In ruinous information warfare environments, the aggressor—or responsive defender, as it may be—really does not want any of a nation's information technology infrastructure to be left standing and usable in the future. Containment information warfare strategies are designed to cripple or at least slow down the military ability and computer-based economy of a target nation. Containment information warfare tactics can include physical destruction of parts of an information technology infrastructure as well as virtual destruction. The choice of tactic will depend on a long-term political strategy as well as the military or covert ability to implement a specific tactic. The specific tactics used in containment information warfare are explained in Chapters 5, 6, and 7. The most likely systems to be targets for either virtual or physical destruction—and the impact of systems attacks—are shown in Table 1-3.

A favorite macro-strategy of the United States and allied countries is to create change from within a country, or at least create the appearance that change came from within a country and that the indigenous population supported the changes. Containment information warfare strategies and tactics are excellent tools to support such macro-political and diplomatic strategies. The containment strategies can contribute to dissatisfaction of the citizenry or business interests in a country to the point that they ally themselves with outside forces to help dispose of undesirable leadership. As the global economy becomes more integrated and more communications-dependent, these strategies will prove more useful.

Table 1-3: Containment Information Warfare Targets

Type of System	Impact of Attack on Target Nation
Military systems	Makes the military uncertain of its capability
Cross-border voice and data telecommunications connections	Hinders the ability to communicate with allies or arms suppliers
National and local telecommunications services	Disrupts local commerce and contributes to civil unrest
Banking and financial systems	Jeopardizes control of personal wealth of leadership and citizenry
Aviation control systems	Hinders or disables the military and civilian air traffic
Manufacturing businesses, supply chain systems, and monitoring, measurement, and control systems	Hinders longer-term military actions
Electronic commerce websites	Disrupts local commerce and contributes to economic failure
Public utility systems	Makes life difficult for the citizenry and hinders government, military, and business operations

Civilian Law Enforcement and Information Warfare

The political and legal roles of civilian law enforcement and the military are going to remain a major obstacle in the United States and other industrialized computer-dependent nations during the development of national information warfare defense structures. The separate roles of the military and civilian law enforcement certainly serve a constitutional purpose and help keep the military from taking action within national borders unless expressly authorized by civilian governments. This was all well and good under traditional circumstances. The age of information warfare, however, raises new challenges that will require increased cooperation between the military and civilian law enforcement.

In the circumstance of extreme offensive ruinous information warfare types of attacks that are traced to a specific country or source outside of national borders, the military will obviously have the primary defensive role. But civilian law enforcement agencies may be required to investigate potential collaboration between external attackers and internal compatriots. A similar level of cooperation may be required in the circumstance of sustained terrorist information warfare actions where the question of where terrorism ends and war begins must be dealt with, addressed, and defensive strategies changed. The complementary roles of civilian law enforcement and the military when different types of information warfare are underway are shown in Table 1-4.

Table 1-4: Civilian Law Enforcement and Military Roles in Information Warfare Strategies

Type	Military Role	Civilian Law Enforcement Role
Offensive ruinous	Lead the attacks when initiating the strategy or defend the nation when under attack	Investigate and apprehend individuals and groups that could be collaborating with the enemy
Offensive containment	Lead the attacks when initiating the strategy or defend the nation when under attack	Investigate and apprehend individuals and groups that could be collaborating with the enemy
Sustained terrorist	Protect military systems and provide support in protecting government and civilian systems	Investigate and apprehend individuals or groups responsible for terrorist attacks
Random terrorist	Protect military systems and provide support in protecting government and civilian systems	Investigate and apprehend individuals or groups responsible for terrorist attacks
Defensive preventive	Protect military systems and provide support in protecting government and civilian systems	Investigate and apprehend individuals and groups that pose a threat to the national information infrastructure
Defensive ruinous	Lead the attacks when initiating the strategy or defend the nation when counterattacked	Investigate and apprehend individuals and groups that could be collaborating with the enemy
Defensive responsive containment	Lead the attacks when initiating the strategy or defend the nation when under attack	Investigate and apprehend individuals and groups that could be collaborating with the enemy
Sustained rogue	Protect military systems and provide support in protecting government and civilian systems	Investigate and apprehend individuals or groups responsible for attacks
Random rogue	Protect military systems and provide support in protecting government and civilian systems	Investigate and apprehend individuals or groups responsible for attacks
Amateur rogue	Protect military systems and provide support in protecting government and civilian systems	Investigate and apprehend individuals or groups responsible for attacks

Although the roles of the military and civilian law enforcement agencies are relatively easy to delineate, there must be an information warfare infrastructure in place to effectively initiate or defend against information warfare attacks. If offensive or defensive information warfare strategies are implemented, the ability of the military to attack or defend may be hindered if there are saboteurs and informants loose in the country who are providing information or support to external attackers. Information collected by military intelligence units may also aid civilian law enforcement agencies in identifying and apprehending saboteurs and informants. Without a strong communications structure and an integrated strategy between military units and civilian law enforcement agencies, resources could be wasted because of redundant work. More importantly, however, is that in the event of information warfare attacks the only really effective response will be a rapid response. Without cooperation between military units and civilian law enforcement agencies, a war could be over and the information infrastructure in ruins while the bureaucracy churns away trying to figure out how to manage their roles.

Another major obstacle in the potential involvement of civilian law enforcement agencies to contribute to either the offensive or defensive information warfare efforts of a nation is the low level of training that civilian law enforcement personnel have achieved. Civilian law enforcement is dreadfully behind the technology curve, and few law enforcement officers are trained in computer technology and the investigation of computer crime, cyber-terrorism, and information warfare. This lack of training and an agenda to better the training needs of civilian law enforcement personnel are addressed in Chapter 11.

The Impact of Information Warfare on Private Companies

Private companies can be the direct targets of several information warfare strategies, including sustained and random terrorist information warfare, sustained and random rogue information warfare, and amateur rogue information warfare. Private companies can also be impacted by directly offensive and defensive ruinous information warfare. Indirect impacts on private companies are likely to result from offensive and defensive ruinous information warfare and offensive and responsive containment information warfare. Private companies need their own strategies to deal with each of these information strategies. In addition, they need to be prepared to cooperate with civilian law enforcement agencies in all situations and may find it necessary to deal with military information warfare units during full-scale attacks on information infrastructures.

Targeted attacks from terrorist, rogue, or amateur information warriors are the most likely occurrences of information warfare strategies that will impact private companies. This differs dramatically from (and should not be confused with) the random hack attacks by amateurs or amateur groups that have occurred during the last decade. The primary differences are the sophistication and destructive level of the attack and the political or economic motivation behind it. Terrorists want to terrorize, and rogues want to extort or steal, and they are very serious about their efforts. The amateurs of the past were merely joyriding and collecting hacker merit badges compared to an organized sustained effort by terrorist or rogues.

In the event of full-scale, deliberate military information warfare actions, all companies in the line of fire between an aggressor and a target nation (or a defender and an aggressor nation) will become targets of containment or destruction. If a company is located in an attacked country, it can expect destruction or disruption. However, if a company has branch offices or subsidiaries in an attacked country, it is likely that the company will experience residual impacts. These could include viruses or other destructive codes launched into corporate systems. The potential impact of information warfare strategies on private companies in full-scale wars and less than full-scale wars is shown in Table 1-5. The economic impact of information warfare is examined in Chapter 2, and the information warfare arsenal and tactics of private companies are examined in Chapter 7.

Table 1-5: The Potential Impact of Information Warfare Strategies on Private Companies

Type	Potential Direct Impact in Full-Scale Wars	Potential Indirect Impact in Less than Full-Scale Wars
Offensive ruinous	Destructive attacks on corporate systems by aggressors	Residual viruses or other destructive codes launched during attacks, or loss of communications systems
Offensive containment	Destructive attacks on corporate systems by aggressors	Residual viruses or other destructive code launched during attacks, or loss of communications systems

Table 1-5 Continued: The Potential Impact of Information Warfare Strategies on Private Companies

Type	Potential Direct Impact in Full-Scale Wars	Potential Indirect Impact in Less than Full-Scale Wars
Sustained terrorist	Repeated or sustained destructive targeted attacks on corporate systems by terrorist groups	Hit by viruses and other destructive code launched to attack general populations, or loss of communications systems
Random terrorist	Random destructive targeted attacks on corporate systems by terrorist groups	Hit by viruses and other destructive code launched to attack general populations, or loss of communications systems
Defensive preventive	Accidental disruption of communications during the initiation of preventive measures	Accidental disruption of communications during the initiation of preventive measures
Defensive ruinous	Destructive attacks on corporate systems by attacked nations to destroy an aggressor	Hit by viruses and other destructive code launched during defensive responses, or loss of communications systems
Defensive responsive containment	Destructive attacks on corporate systems from nations attempting to contain an aggressor	Hit by viruses and other destructive code launched during defensive responses, or loss of communications systems
Sustained rogue	Repeated or sustained targeted attacks on corporate systems by criminal groups	Hit by viruses and other destructive code launched to attack general populations, or loss of communications systems
Random rogue	Random targeted attacks on corporate systems by criminal groups	Hit by viruses and other destructive code launched to attack general populations, or loss of communications systems
Amateur rogue	Random targeted attacks on corporate systems by amateur groups	Hit by viruses and other destructive code launched to attack general populations, or loss of communications systems

The likelihood of being targeted by a terrorist or rogue group of information warriors during an all-out attack on a country is very high. It is likely that the information warriors will not concentrate solely on a specific company, but rather, they will repeatedly hit high-profile companies. The worst-case scenario for a private company is to become the direct and sole target of a terrorist or rogue group. If this occurs, it will impact information technology functioning and disrupt business. If the company under attack relies heavily on the World Wide Web for revenue, the disruption could be fatal. Because full-scale information warfare attacks on entire nations are difficult and expensive to launch, terrorists and rogues are likely to target specific government organizations or high-profile private companies in order to bring attention to their cause or, in the case of rogue attacks, attempt to extort the highest amount of money.

One of the major concerns that private companies face if they are singled out by a terrorist or rogue group is getting help from qualified parties to deal with the attack. After isolating and protecting their information systems, private companies then need to turn to civilian law enforcement to report the attack and seek assistance. As previously indicated, civilian law enforcement is not well equipped to deal with information warfare strategies. Civilian law enforcement also has little ability to stop activity that occurs outside the United States unless that activity can be traced to cooperating countries.

Sustained attacks are likely to originate from multiple points, as illustrated in the scenario that we will discuss in Chapter 3. This will make the job of civilian law enforcement investigating incidents even more difficult. At this time, there is also a lack of definition as to when terrorist attacks stop and war begins. War, as defined in the past, happens between political entities. Information wars, on the other hand, can be waged without the political sanction of a specific country. This makes the traditional definition of war rather obsolete.

Add to all of this complexity the fact that the military is most qualified to track attackers, locate the sources of attack, and physically intervene and destroy the ability of the attackers to sustain activity—and if necessary kill the attackers. Since all the governments in the world and all the responsible organizations in the major nations have been unable to develop procedures ahead of time, it is during the first major attacks when the rules will be made and procedures are developed.

Information Warfare Will Result in Civilian Casualties

Civilian casualties during the implementation of information warfare strategies are very likely to occur. Only in extreme circumstances would these casualties actually be physically injurious or result in actual death.

If critical healthcare or emergency service systems were hit during attacks, lives would certainly be at risk. The definition of civilian casualties in this analysis focuses more on the impact on the workforce, personal wealth, and personal technology. During ruinous or sustained information warfare activities where private companies are targets, workers are likely to be displaced, at least temporarily. Depending on the extent of damage, these workers could be unemployed for a lengthy period. Private citizens who have invested directly or purchased stock in publicly traded companies could also experience the loss or decline of investor value and certainly the delay in the payment of dividends. The potential impact of information warfare strategies on private citizens is shown in Table 1-6.

Table 1-6: The Potential Impact of Information Warfare Strategies on Private Civilians

Type	Potential Direct Impact in Full-Scale Wars	Potential Indirect Impact in Less than Full-Scale Wars
Offensive ruinous	Workers displaced and investor value diminished by destructive attacks on corporate systems by aggressors	Personal computers hit by residual viruses or other destructive codes launched during attacks, or investor value diminished in companies that are damaged
Offensive containment	Workers displaced and investor value diminished by destructive attacks on corporate systems by aggressors	Personal computers hit by residual viruses or other destructive code launched during attacks, or investor value diminished in companies that are damaged
Sustained terrorist	Workers displaced and investor value diminished by destructive attacks on corporate systems by aggressors; private data compromised	Personal computers hit by residual viruses or other destructive code launched during attacks, or investor value diminished in companies that are damaged; private data compromised
Random terrorist	Investor value diminished by destructive attacks on corporate systems by aggressors; private data compromised	Personal computers hit by residual viruses or other destructive code launched during attacks, or investor value diminished in companies that are damaged; private data compromised
Defensive preventive	Accidental disruption of communications during the initiation of preventive measures	Accidental disruption of communications during the initiation of preventive measures

Table 1-6 Continued: The Potential Impact of Information Warfare Strategies on Private Civilians

Type	Potential Direct Impact in Full-Scale Wars	Potential Indirect Impact in Less than Full-Scale Wars
Defensive ruinous	Workers displaced and investor value diminished by destructive attacks on corporate systems by aggressors	Personal computers hit by residual viruses or other destructive code launched during attacks, or investor value diminished in companies that are damaged
Defensive responsive containment	Workers displaced and investor value diminished by destructive attacks on corporate systems by aggressors	Personal computers hit by residual viruses or other destructive code launched during attacks, or investor value diminished in companies that are damaged
Sustained rogue	Investor value diminished by destructive attacks on corporate systems by aggressors; private data compromised	Personal computers hit by residual viruses or other destructive code launched during attacks, or investor value diminished in companies that are damaged; private data compromised
Random rogue	Investor value diminished by destructive attacks on corporate systems by aggressors; private data compromised	Personal computers hit by residual viruses or other destructive code launched during attacks, or investor value diminished in companies that are damaged; private data compromised
Amateur rogue	Investor value diminished by destructive attacks on corporate systems by aggressors; private data compromised	Personal computers hit by residual viruses or other destructive code launched during attacks, or investor value diminished in companies that are damaged; private data compromised

Privately owned personal computers and the value of the files and records on these systems can also suffer damage during information warfare. Because so many personal computer users have Internet connections, the likelihood of users getting hit by some type of virus is extremely high. Viruses like the Love Bug can flood email systems, destroy valuable files and electronic documents, and disrupt communications. Self-employed people who are highly dependent on their computers and on Internet communications are very vulnerable during information warfare activities.

Another danger to private individuals during information warfare is that their private data may be compromised. This is most likely to occur because of the attacks of terrorists, rogues, and amateurs who enjoy embarrassing government organizations and private companies. Revealing customers' private data, for example, can cause not only tremendous embarrassment, but also result in long-term damages in the form of individual lawsuits or class action suits. During military offensive actions, it is most likely that records and systems will be destroyed during attacks. However, under certain containment information warfare strategies or when trying to contain an aggressor nation, governments can gain leverage by obtaining information on powerful government leaders, military commanders, and private individuals in target countries. More details on how private citizens can be impacted by information warfare are provided in Chapter 9.

Conclusions and an Agenda for Action

Information warfare strategies and tactics have been of utmost concern to defense planners in industrialized nations since the middle of the 1980s. The growth in popularity of the Internet and the widespread use of the World Wide Web and related technologies have dramatically increased this concern. Now is the time to come to grips with information warfare. Military, civilian government, private industry, and international organizations around the world have a very busy agenda ahead of them in order to catch up to the need to protect the global information infrastructure. This is going to be a long and difficult process, and it's going to cost lots of money. The basic concepts and principles that must be understood—and can help realistically guide the process of moving forward in dealing with information warfare—are detailed in the following pages.

Conclusions Drawn from the New Framework for Analysis

Important conclusions that can be drawn from the material presented in this chapter are as follows:

- ▶ Information warfare strategies, like physical warfare strategies, are designed to hinder or disable military forces, disable industrial infrastructures and manufacturing capabilities, the stock exchanges and brokerage houses, or disrupt civilian and government economic activities in order to put an aggressor or a target country at a disadvantage.

- ▸ Global alliances to fight cyber-crime and terrorism are necessary, and alliance members must be prepared to take decisive action to halt information warfare attacks that originate in part or are supported by non-cooperating nations. Treaties should be pursued, but as in the nuclear arms race and the Cold War, we must be prepared to defend the infrastructure of information technology and be prepared for information warfare.

- ▸ The only way to have an effective information warfare defense structure is to return to a Cold War always-on defense mentality accompanied by an organizational structure that can respond with the speed and effectiveness necessary to defend against attacks that will occur without warning.

- ▸ As the global economy becomes more integrated and more communications-dependent, containment information warfare strategies will prove more useful because these strategies can contribute to the dissatisfaction of the citizenry or business interests in a country to the point that they ally themselves with outside forces to help dispose of undesirable leadership.

- ▸ The United States, the members of the NATO alliance, Japan, Australia, and trade partners in good standing with these nations are the largest stakeholders in the development of the international information infrastructure, the global telecommunications infrastructure, electronic commerce, and the Internet. All have a stake in and a responsibility to deal with information warfare.

- ▸ The capability required to effectively launch a ruinous information warfare effort is very expensive and only a few countries can deploy the totally ruinous strategies. However, many countries and terrorist groups can readily use virtual destruction tactics and cause considerable disruption to military operations and government and civilian economic activity.

- ▸ Because civilian law enforcement is in a weak position to deal with information warfare attacks on private corporations, those companies without strong ties to the military will become easy targets with little recourse.

- ▸ The number of people trained as information warriors will increase over the next five years, enabling better defense against information warfare strategies while simultaneously and dramatically increasing the potential threat of information warfare.

► In order to train information warriors in implementing or defending against all of the categories of information warfare, actual data infrastructures that replicate or emulate environments—such as banking, Wall Street stock exchanges, electronic commerce companies, and telecommunications centers—need to be established.

► Because of a long history of attacks and a vigorous prosecution effort, the U.S. military probably has the most experience in compiling and presenting evidence of intrusions and attacks.

► Systems to protect monitoring, measurement, and control instrumentation in military weapons systems as well as in private industry transportation and manufacturing environments need immediate and critical funding for development, testing, and deployment.

► Terrorists are being bred and trained to be technologically savvy and to attack, disrupt, damage, and perhaps even destroy information technology infrastructures and computer-based economic activities. These people are the biggest future threat to the information infrastructure and the new digital economy.

► Procedures and processes for coordinating the efforts of military units and civilian law enforcement agencies to effectively initiate either offensive or defensive information strategies within the United States (and between the United States and allied countries) are virtually nonexistent.

► If governments in major nations do not establish procedures to deal ahead of time with situations involving random or sustained terrorist information warfare strategies, or random or sustained rogue information warfare strategies, it is during the first major attacks when the rules will be made and procedures developed. Making such rules during chaos can be very messy.

► Civilian casualties during the implementation of information warfare strategies are very likely to occur, including the loss of employment, destruction or damage to personal computers, and compromise of personal data.

An Agenda for Action in Preparing for Information Warfare

The U.S. government needs to set an agenda for action that goes beyond the work already done in preparation for defending against or implementing offensive information warfare strategies. Action steps should include, but not be limited to, the following ten areas:

1. Establish national policy on how to deal with aggressor nations, terrorist groups, rogue criminals, and amateur information warriors who attack the information technology infrastructure or the information technology assets and resources of the U.S. military and government agencies, private companies in the United States, and the general population of Internet and information technology users within the country.

2. Establish national policy on how to deal with aggressor nations, terrorist groups, rogue criminals, and amateur information warriors who attack the information technology infrastructure or the information technology assets and resources of the cooperating and aligned nations' military and government agencies, private companies located in those countries, and the general population of Internet and information technology users within those countries.

3. Develop and implement agreements with cooperating and aligned nations that encompass the implementation of and response to information warfare strategies that are directed toward those nations or implemented by those nations toward an aggressor or a targeted nation, region, or population.

4. Establish an information warfare infrastructure within the United States to manage the response to information warfare attacks or the implementation of an offensive information strategy, and integrate that infrastructure with its counterparts in nations that are cooperating in the fight against information warfare attacks.

5. Within the national and international information warfare infrastructure, define the roles of military units, civilian government agencies, civilian law enforcement agencies, technology-producing companies, and private companies who are dependent on information technology in the response to or initiation of information warfare activities.

6. Establish a national academy of information warfare to help meet the needs of the military, civilian law enforcement, and the military and civilian law enforcement agencies of cooperating and aligned nations to properly train personnel in both defensive and offensive information warfare. Training should be conducted across the spectrum of organizations that can contribute to the protection of the national information infrastructure and the information technology assets and resources of the U.S. military and government agencies, private companies in the United States, and the general population of Internet and information technology users.

7. Fund the development of advanced technology to protect the national information infrastructure and the information technology assets and resources of the U.S. military and government agencies, private companies in the United States, and the general population of Internet and information technology users within relevant countries.

8. Set reporting requirements and procedures for military units, civilian government agencies, civilian law enforcement agencies, companies that produce information technology, private companies that use information technology, and similar organizations in cooperating and aligned nations to report information warfare types of activities.

9. Set reporting requirements and procedures for military units and civilian law enforcement agencies in the United States and for similar organizations in cooperating and aligned nations to report information and data on apprehended individuals who are accused of computer crimes, including hacking, virus attacks, fraud, and extortion.

10. Establish an international SWAT team that can be instantly deployed to seek and destroy terrorist groups or rogue criminals that operate anywhere in the world in their efforts to attack the national information infrastructure and the information technology assets and resources of military and government agencies, private companies, and the general population of Internet and information technology users within relevant countries.

Chapter 2

Measuring the Economic Impact of Information Warfare

The concepts and definitions of economic damage and economic impact have collided in cyberspace. The potential impact that random terrorist information warfare, random rogue information warfare, and amateur rogue information warfare activities have on private corporations and government agencies goes well beyond the traditional civil and criminal definitions of damage. In traditional law, if an individual or group for whatever reason takes actions that close a business down, or if a company sells a faulty product to a business that uses the product, the limits of legal liability are customarily tied to actual damages. In traditional cases, damage has been defined as causing a piece of equipment or other asset to need repair or replacement. Generally speaking damage has been viewed in physical terms.

In the case of the Love Bug virus, the attack hit over 55 million computers. Approximately four percent of the total computers that received the virus required human intervention to reconfigure them or in some way repair them. These computers were actually legally damaged causing hundreds of large companies, government organizations such as NASA, and educational institutions to shut down their email systems. In many cases, shut downs lasted fewer than 48 hours. In other cases shut downs lasted for over a week. The decision to shut these systems down was both prudent and expedient, and if the systems had not been shut down, damages would have been far greater. The debate that followed the release of the Computer Economics' analysis of a total economic impact of $8.7 billion still rages on as corporations, law enforcement, adjudicators, information security professionals, and economists grapple with the new cyber paradigm of economic disruption.

In the age of the digital economy, the definitions of property damage, business disruption, and economic impact need to be rethought. When a dot-com company is hit by attacks, regardless of the reason for or source of the attack, there is a great deal at stake. A dot-com is not a factory or office building which, if attacked, can call in more security guards or the local police. In the physical world, physical force and a greater number of armed guards can deter or even prevent hostile hoards from doing damage. But tear gas does not work in cyberspace. A dot-com company is totally exposed. The police will be able to do very little to prevent damage, and the security guy at the front desk will be able to do nothing at all. But dot-coms are not the only organizations that can fall prey to information warfare tactics. Government agencies are working hard to bring information and services to the populace. They were also damaged during the Love Bug outbreak and remain vulnerable to future attacks of all sorts. This chapter examines several new propositions and formulas for determining the economic impact of information warfare and everyday cyber-terrorism, including:

- ▶ A macro view of the economic impact of information warfare attacks

- ▶ How to measure the strategic and tactical economic impact of information warfare attacks

- ▶ The immediate economic impact of information warfare attacks that can be achieved

▶ The short-term and long-term economic impact of information warfare attacks

▶ An agenda for action in the analysis of the economic impact of information warfare

The Nature of the Economic Impact of Information Warfare Attacks

There are several ways to look at the impact that information warfare attacks can have on an organization. The most basic and traditional model of damage is rather straightforward. If the computer systems of an organization are attacked in an information warfare incident, be it physical attacks or cyber attacks, equipment that needs to be repaired or replaced is classified as damaged. However, the impact of information warfare attacks is likely to go far beyond the traditional and immediate damages to systems. This is especially true in the event of offensive ruinous information warfare strategies directed toward the country in which an organization operates, or sustained terrorist or rogue information warfare strategies where an organization is singled out for destruction or extortion.

There are three types of economic impact on a single organization that will result from information warfare attacks. The immediate economic impact is the cost of repairing or replacing systems and the disruption of business operations and cash flow. A short-term economic impact on single organizations includes the loss of contractual relationships or existing customers because of the inability to deliver products or services, and a negative impact on the reputation of the organization. A long-term economic impact includes the decline in market valuation and stock prices. Types of economic impact of information warfare attacks on single organizations are shown in Table 2-1.

Table 2-1: Types of Economic Impact of Information Warfare Attacks on a Single Organization

Type of Economic Impact on Organizations	Consequences of Impact
Immediate economic impact on a single organization	Damage to systems that require human intervention to repair or replace
	Disruption of business operations
	Delays in transactions and cash flow

Table 2-1 Continued: Types of Economic Impact of Information Warfare Attacks on a Single Organization

Type of Economic Impact on Organizations	Consequences of Impact
Short-term economic impact on a single organization	Loss of contractual relationships with other organizations in supply chains or the loss of retail sales
	Negative impact on the reputation of an organization
	Hindrance of the development of new business
Long-term economic impact on a single organization	Decline in market valuation
	Erosion of investor confidence
	Decline in stock price

Information warfare attacks can also be directed toward a group of companies or an industry sector. There are several ways to look at the impact that information warfare attacks can have on an industry sector. The immediate economic impact on an industry sector includes damages to computer-based supply chain systems and the disruption of sector productivity. The short-term economic impact of information warfare attacks on an industry sector includes the disruption of productivity in organizations that consume sector products and the ability to develop new business. Long-term economic impacts include erosion of investor confidence in the sector and the overall market valuation of the sector. Types of economic impact of information warfare attacks on industry sectors are shown in Table 2-2.

Table 2-2: Types of Economic Impact of Information Warfare Attacks on Industry Sectors

Type of Economic Impact on Industry Sectors	Consequences of Impact
Immediate economic impact on industry sectors	Damage to supply chain systems that require human intervention to repair or replace
	Disruption of sector production
	Delays in transactions and cash flow
Short-term economic impact on industry sectors	Disruption of productivity in organizations that consume sector products or the loss of retail sales
	Negative impact on the reputation of an industry sector

Table 2-2 Continued: Types of Economic Impact of Information Warfare Attacks on Industry Sectors

Type of Economic Impact on Industry Sectors	Consequences of Impact
Short-term economic impact on industry sectors	Hindrance of the development of new business
Long-term economic impact on industry sectors	Erosion of investor confidence
	Decline in stock prices across the sector
	Decline of market valuation of the sector

Offensive ruinous or containment information warfare strategies can be directed toward a specific country or region. There are several ways to look at the impact that information warfare attacks can have on a geographic region or country. In the event of offensive ruinous information warfare attacks, the goal is complete destruction of the information technology infrastructure and computer-based economic activity. Thus the economic impact—or at least the desired economic impact—is extreme and may be very difficult to assess. In the event of partial offensive ruinous or containment information warfare strategies, the destruction would not be absolute, but the level of disruption would be very high.

The immediate economic impact of information warfare attacks on a country or region includes the destruction or disruption of national or regional industrial production and banking and commerce abilities. The short-term economic impact of information warfare attacks on a country or region includes the destruction or disruption of international trade and a negative impact on the commercial and economic reputation. Long-term economic impacts include a decline in stock prices and market valuation of companies in the country or region. Types of economic impact of information warfare attacks on a country or region are shown in Table 2-3.

Table 2-3: Types of Economic Impact of Information Warfare Attacks on Countries or Regions

Type of Economic Impact on Countries or Regions	Consequences of Impact
Immediate economic impact on countries or regions	Destruction or disruption of national or regional banking or commerce
	Destruction or disruption of national or regional industrial production
	Delay of military activity

Table 2-3 Continued: Types of Economic Impact of Information Warfare Attacks on Countries or Regions

Type of Economic Impact on Countries or Regions	Consequences of Impact
Short-term economic impact on countries or regions	Destruction or disruption of international trade
	Negative impact on the commercial and economic reputation of a country or region
	Continued hindrance or halt of military activity
Long-term economic impact on countries or regions	Erosion of investor confidence
	Decline in stock prices of companies in the country or region
	Decline of market valuation of the companies in the country or region

The Immediate Economic Impact of Information Warfare Attacks

Information warfare attacks of all types typically result in some type of immediate economic impact. The two major categories of immediate impact are the destruction or disabling of information systems and the disruption of organization activity. In the event of a physical attack and the real destruction of information systems, the economic impact is higher than the virtual destruction of systems where they are temporarily disabled and cannot provide the services for which they were designed. The disruption of organization activity as a result of information warfare attacks is very significant. It usually results in greater costs than the destruction or disabling of systems that require human intervention to replace or restore.

Calculating the Costs of Repairs or Replacement

The destruction or disabling of information systems is a primary tactic in all information warfare strategies. If systems are physically destroyed, it can take days and in many cases weeks to replace the systems. If the attacked organizations have hot or cold emergency sites from which they can operate systems until their primary systems are replaced or restored, there is the added cost of bringing backup systems live and relocating personnel to the backup sites. If the attacked organizations do not have emergency backup sites already in place, they may need to obtain short-term use of equipment on a rental basis.

Determining the dollar amount of these damages is relatively straightforward. In the case of repair, the damages are the cost of replacement parts and the cost of labor to accomplish the repair. In the event that a piece of equipment must be replaced, the damages are equal to the cost of acquiring replacement equipment, along with the labor costs to remove damaged equipment, install new equipment, load any necessary software, and connect the equipment to the appropriate networks. The cost elements of recovering information systems operations after a physical attack are shown in Table 2-4. The cost elements of recovering from a virtual attack are shown in Table 2-5.

Table 2-4: Cost Elements of Restoring Systems After a Physical Attack

Technology Component	Cost Elements
Implementation of contingency operations plan	Bring backup site live
	Transport personnel to backup site
	Temporary per diem cost for personnel
	Shut down backup site when normal operations are restored
Network equipment, servers, and client hardware	Inspect equipment to determine damage
	Remove equipment that cannot be repaired
	Acquire parts and repair equipment that can be repaired
	Acquire replacement systems for equipment that cannot be repaired
	Install new equipment
	Reload software and files
	Test equipment and operational status
Server and client applications software	Inspect applications to determine damage on machines that are operational
	Reload software if necessary
	Load software on new equipment
	Test functionality
Servers and client data and user files	Inspect files to determine damage
	Restore files from backup if necessary
	Replicate damaged files when no backup is available

Table 2-5: Cost Elements of Restoring Systems After a Virtual Attack

Technology Component	Cost Elements
Network equipment, servers, and client hardware	Inspect equipment to determine damage
	Remove hostile or destructive code
	Reload necessary operating system software
	Restore configurations
	Restore and test operations
Server and client applications software	Inspect applications to determine damage
	Reload software if necessary
	Test functionality
Servers and client data and user files	Inspect files to determine damage
	Restore files from backup if necessary
	Replicate damaged files when no backup is available

Determining the Economic Impact of Disruption

Determining the economic impact of business disruption, especially on a large scale, is challenging for both the attacker and the defender. The fundamental goal of all information warfare is to damage the technology infrastructure of a target organization, region, or country and thus put the targeted entity at a disadvantage. There are several methods that could be applied to measure the economic impact of information warfare attacks. Methods should be selected that are appropriate for the scale of information warfare attacks and the goal of the attacks.

When measuring the economic strategic impact of information warfare attacks on a country or geographical region, the highest level of impact would be to cause a decline in the gross domestic product (GDP). This would demonstrate the effectiveness of the information warfare attacks on the country or region as a whole and could have a long-term impact on economic stability. If the information warfare attacks were extremely successful, it may be difficult to ascertain the GDP and secondary measures may be necessary. Drops in industrial output, per capita income, and financial assets could also be used to measure economic impact.

When evaluating the economic impact of information warfare attacks on an industry sector, the highest-level measure is a drop in sector production. A drop in production could be measured in discrete units produced. In continuous process sectors, a drop in volume of tons, barrels, or gallons would be appropriate. Secondary measures of economic impact of information warfare attacks on an industry sector include declines in sector revenue or stock values. Similar measures are appropriate for measuring the economic impact of information warfare attacks on single companies. The primary and secondary measures of strategic economic impact by type of information warfare target are shown in Table 2-6.

Table 2-6: Strategic Measures of the Economic Impact of Information Warfare Attacks

Target	Primary Measures	Secondary Measures
Country or region	Decline of gross domestic product (GDP)	Drop in industrial output
		Decline of per capita income
		Drop in the value of financial assets
Industry sector	Drop in sector production	Decline in sector revenue
		Drop of stock values
		Drop in market valuation
Single organization	Decline in corporate revenue	Drop in orders processed and shipped
		Drop in company stock values
		Growth of competitor's market share

In many cases, it may not be possible to obtain accurate data to measure the strategic economic impact of information warfare attacks. If this is the case, there are several ways to measure the tactical value of information warfare attacks. In countries or regions, a decline in military activity could be observed or there could be an overall slowdown in business activity, including bank deposits, imports, and exports. If an industry sector is targeted, delays in product shipments or shortages in products in the supply chain could be monitored. When single organizations are targeted, it may be possible to observe business disruptions, problems in processing orders, or a problem in dealing with customer inquires. The primary and secondary measures of tactical economic impact by type of information warfare target are shown in Table 2-7.

Table 2-7: Tactical Measures of the Economic Impact of Information Warfare Attacks

Target	Primary Measures	Secondary Measures
Country or region	Decline in military activity	Drop in business transactions
		Drop in import/export activity
		Decline in international bank transfers
Industry sector	Disruption of product shipments	Shortages in products or commodities
		Plant closings
		Drop in bank deposits
Single organization	Disruption of business operations	Problems in processing orders
		Lack of response to customer inquiries
		Media stories on systems shutdowns and disruptions

The disruption of government, military, and business activities can occur immediately as it did in the case of the Love Bug virus attack when email and other related information systems were shut down for relatively short periods of time. It is certainly possible for such virus outbreaks to recur. Fortunately, information technology managers and network engineers learn from past incidents. The economic impact of disruption caused by such virus attacks has two major components. First, there are the actual labor costs of eradicating the virus from systems and bringing systems back into operation, as previously outlined in Table 2-5. In a simple calculation of economic impact, labor costs and the cost of any equipment that must be replaced are added to the value of lost productivity to determine the total economic disruption. The value of lost productivity can be calculated in two ways:

▶ The hourly wage plus overhead for all employees who were without communication and other services as a result of an attack, multiplied by the number of nonproductive hours that occurred as a result of the service outages

▶ The gross revenue of a for-profit organization divided by the total number of hours of all employees and contract labor hours, multiplied by the total number of nonproductive hours that occurred as a result of service outages

These approaches are adequate for determining the economic impact of attacks that are recovered from relatively quickly. It is certainly possible for companies to suffer a revenue loss, for example, in the amount of time it took to eradicate the Love Bug from their systems. However, revenue loss for dot-coms is not solely dependent on whether their systems are operational. If there are widespread outages, as in the case of the Love Bug, customers (or potential customers) may not have access to the Internet because their systems are not functioning properly, thus causing a potential dip in online purchases. Outages of 24 to 48 hours may not make a huge difference in economic impact. However, an analogy could be made to a major snowstorm hitting the northeastern United States during a peak weekend of Christmas shopping. Obviously, if people cannot get to stores for several days it is likely to impact the seasonal revenue of merchants in the area that is hit by the snowstorm.

The Short-Term Economic Impact of Information Warfare Attacks

Distinguishing the difference between immediate and short-term economic impact may be more a matter of convenience than reality. The immediate impact that occurs when there are virus attacks that rage through systems worldwide is something we have already experienced and can reasonably recover from. Thus immediate impact can be seen as what happens during the first few days of an attack that is contained or repelled. The events that occurred during the Love Bug outbreak are similar to those that would occur in the first hours or days of an organized information warfare attack. However, the difference between virus outbreaks like the Love Bug and organized information warfare attacks is that the latter will likely not be contained or repelled in a few hours or a few days, but will be sustained or repeated on a planned cycle. The short-term economic impact is what occurs over the first few weeks of sustained or random attacks. The long-term economic impact is the result of sustained attacks over weeks or months, or the aftermath of massive attacks that have ceased.

The short-term goals that military, terrorist, or rogue information warriors have in attacking a target will of course depend on the nature of the target. Immediate goals of information warfare when attacking any target (country, region, industry sector, or single organization) are to bring as much activity to a halt as possible, including military action, banking, and commerce, as shown previously in Table 2-3. However, to be an effective warfare strategy, information warfare attacks must accomplish more than just causing temporary discomfort or delaying commerce for a few days or weeks. Alternative systems can be put into practice quickly, and many companies could continue to operate at some level. A country or region could carry on its military actions and commerce, albeit at a hindered pace. The key to a more strategic impact is to destroy the ability to participate in international trade and deliver or take delivery on existing contracts, as well develop new business. The exception is companies that are totally dependent on ecommerce for their revenue, many of which would go out of business if they could not transact business for several weeks or months.

The Impact of Lost Contractual Relationships

As ecommerce continues to expand across the globe, it is anticipated that businesses will be tied together in an Internet-based supply chain system. To remain competitive, countries, regions, and businesses will need to be able to participate and function in the new business-to-business (B2B) infrastructure. This may be good for businesses, but for information warriors—be they good guys or bad guys—it is absolutely great. The more dependent the business community is on electronic communications and the information technology infrastructure, the easier it is for an information warrior to be effective and to be valuable in the future of warfare.

The vision of the future electronic supply chain and marketplace has several components. Certainly any player must be able to participate in the electronic world to remain competitive. But the nature of competition may also change. Assuming that the supply chain does move ahead as envisioned, if a company or even a country were to lose its ability to electronically communicate, it could be readily replaced by other entities that can participate. This means that contractual relationships between suppliers and consumer companies could be easily disrupted.

In the future supply chain model, an information warfare attack could disable a company or region to keep it from participating in the supply chain system. If the disruption lasts long and if there are companies that could almost instantly step in and provide goods or services through the electronic marketplace process, the information warrior has easily achieved the goal of longer-term impact. The loss of such contractual relationships could devastate a company or an economy in relatively short order. The economics of contractual loss will certainly vary across situations. As an example for projecting the success of an information warfare effort, the following case illustrates the potential impact.

A company supplies a commodity product that has $20 million in annual revenue. Eighty percent of that revenue is derived from two major accounts, both of which require electronic supply chain participation. Such a company is an easy target for destruction. The term "commodity product" implies that there are a number of companies around the world that could produce, grow, or somehow supply the product. In a commodity environment, competition is tough and profit margins are slim. When a company derives the majority of its revenue from one or very few sources, it is likely to suffer greatly if one of the largest sources of revenue is lost. Assume that the target company under discussion ships equal amounts of product on a weekly basis over a period of a year and is paid upon receipt of the product at its customers' plants or warehouse. Assume also that the customers have no more than 90 days' supply of the commodity on hand and do not want less than a 45 days' supply on hand.

If the target company's information systems are continuously attacked during the transaction process, and the customers require transactions to be processed electronically, the supplier is at risk. The electronic supply chain processes accentuate the risk because alarms go off in the systems indicating that paperwork is late, or that shipments have fallen behind by a few days or a few weeks. These alarms trigger an automatic posting to an electronic marketplace for bids from alternate suppliers. In a pure electronic supply chain world, there is no human intervention. The original supplier who was a target of information warfare attacks loses a major customer and 40 percent of its revenue. This could happen in less than 30 days because electronic communications were either disrupted or intercepted. The communications never reached their destination, and the supplier was not fully aware of what was happening in the process.

As a second example, a small country that relies heavily on exports as a basis of its economy is in a position similar to that of the target supplier company in the previous example. As the global electronic supply chain is built, international trade and resulting air and seaport traffic of goods and commodities will be managed by large Internet-based systems owned by transportation providers. A seaport that handles twenty ships per month could generate revenue of transported goods estimated at $1 billion. If the information processing abilities of the agents and service providers for this seaport were affected, port traffic could be significantly impacted. This would delay the import and export activities of a country or region for weeks and perhaps months, slowing cash flow and hindering economic growth. As in the previous case, it could also result in the cancellation of contracts, further hindering economic activity.

If annual revenue and resulting annual profits were evenly distributed over weeks and months, a simple calculation of losses for one week of a company or region that is disabled from participating in the supply chain could result in a 1.9 percent loss. The resulting loss of three months of being disabled could result in a 24.9 percent loss in revenue and profits. This assumes that revenue and profits could not be recovered after systems were repaired or participation in the supply chain was restored. The losses could be permanent and even higher if competing companies won contracts to supply commodities or products to the consuming companies in the supply chain. The range of potential impact on company revenue is illustrated in Table 2-8.

Table 2-8: The Potential Impact on Revenue and Profits from Supply Chain Participation Being Disabled

Duration	$100,000,000 Annual Revenue	$10,000,000 Annual Profit	Percent Decline
One week	$1,900,000	$190,000	1.9%
Two weeks	$3,800,000	$380,000	3.8%
One month	$8,300,000	$830,000	8.3%
Two months	$16,600,000	$1,600,000	16.6%
Three months	$24,900,000	$2,490,000	24.9%

The Impact of Disruption Down the Supply Chain

One of the major advantages of electronic supply chain systems is that they give users the ability to more tightly control inventory and create just-in-time inventory environments. The automotive industry, for example, is in the process of creating an industry-wide supply chain system to manage the flow of products through the manufacturing process. As electronic supply chain systems grow and industry sectors become dependent on the systems for ordering parts and supplies, the dependent sectors become more vulnerable to information warfare attacks. In the automotive industry, when there is a labor strike or slowdown in a subsector that produces essential parts, the entire industry experiences a ripple effect and is impacted economically. For example, when workers who produce tires or automotive batteries go on strike, the production of automobiles can be slowed. If the strike lasts long enough, automotive assembly plants are closed and workers are furloughed. This economically impacts the entire industry, from raw material suppliers, parts producers, and component manufacturers, to the companies that sell the finished products.

Sustained information warfare attacks, regardless of their origin, can readily cripple industry sectors that are building the new electronic supply chains. In the case of the automobile industry—which generates more than $1 trillion annually in sales—a 10 percent slowdown in the sector represents an economic impact of $100 billion. This is enough of an impact to cause temporary plant closings, layoffs of workers, decreases in dividends paid to stockholders, and market devaluation of companies throughout the industry sector. The wholesale goods and retail sectors have already become very dependent on automated supply chain systems, as have the consumer electronics and computer industries. The electronic supply chain systems have provided incredible benefits for these sectors, but these systems are also making them more vulnerable to sabotage and weaker in the face of information warfare attacks.

The Extraordinary Vulnerability of Dot-Coms

In the event of any type of information warfare strategy being implemented, the most vulnerable companies are those that are Internet-based and totally dependent on ecommerce for their revenue—the dot-coms. Many dot-coms would go out of business if they could not transact business for several weeks or months. This may not have been true in 1998 or 1999 when dot-coms were in a grace period and revenue investors did not require profits. But by the middle of 2000, investors started taking a different view of dot-coms. The expectation for performance of dot-coms has clearly evolved, and this makes them incredibly vulnerable to business disruption that could occur during information warfare activities.

Dot-coms can suffer during almost any type of information warfare. In the event that offensive ruinous information warfare strategies are implemented, dot-coms become a natural target as an attacker works to disrupt economic activity in the target country. In the case of sustained or random terrorist information warfare attacks, dot-coms are targeted in order to disrupt economic activity in a target country or company for political impact. In the event of sustained or random rogue information warfare attacks, dot-coms are targeted to extort money from a company, industry group, or government. The target status of dot-coms during information warfare attacks are shown in Table 2-9 for each category of information warfare.

Table 2-9: Target Status of Dot-Coms During Information Warfare

Type of Strategies	Target Status	Goal of Attack
Offensive ruinous	Direct if in country or if investment held by companies within target country	Disrupt economic activity in target country
Offensive containment	Direct if in country or if investment held by companies within target country	Disrupt economic activity in target country
Sustained terrorist	Direct or indirect depending on political goals of terrorist groups	Disrupt economic activity in target country or company for political impact
Random terrorist	Direct or indirect depending on political goals of terrorist groups	Disrupt economic activity in target country or company for political impact
Defensive preventive	No target status	Not applicable
Defensive ruinous	Direct if in country or if investment held by companies within target country	Disrupt economic activity in target country
Defensive responsive containment	Direct if in country or if investment held by companies within target country	Disrupt economic activity in target country
Sustained rogue	Direct or indirect depending on goals of criminal groups	Extort money from company, industry group, or government
Random rogue	Direct or indirect depending on goals of criminal groups	Extort money from company, industry group, or government
Amateur rogue	Direct or indirect depending on goals of amateurs	Show skills as information warrior

The Long-Term Economic Impact of Disruption

The long-term economic impact is the result of sustained attacks over weeks or months, or the aftermath of massive attacks that have ceased. Such impact is intended to be devastating. Short-term business disruption, although certainly not desirable, can be recovered from with relative ease compared to the impact of long-term offensive ruinous information warfare or sustained terrorist information warfare attacks. The goal of random rogue or terrorist information warfare attacks is to create more drama than damage. To have severe economic impact, information warfare attacks need to be sustained or ruinous in nature. Such information warfare attacks will result in a substantial loss of business, decline in stock prices, the destruction of market value, and the decline of value of investment funds. These attacks could certainly delay further investment in specific companies or industry sectors.

The Loss of Business

The long-term loss of business that can result from offensive ruinous information warfare or sustained terrorist information warfare attacks is the most serious economic issue that businesses face. Long-term losses include the loss of substantial contracts or position in industry sectors or supply chains. In a competitive global marketplace, disruption of business that occurs because of natural disasters or civil unrest, for example, can take years to recover. These losses can impact a single company, an industry, a region, or a nation. Table 2-8 showed the impact of lost contractual relationships when supply chain participation is disabled for up to three months. If information warfare attacks are substantial enough, the economic impact will go far beyond the disruption of supply chain participation.

The loss of business for a region or nation over substantial periods of time is one of the desired impacts of an offensive ruinous information warfare strategy. If this strategy is successful, disruption of supply chain participation is one of the first desired results of an attack. As ruinous information warfare tactics are implemented, damage becomes progressively worse and more widespread. The first several phases focus on disrupting and disabling business processes. Subsequent phases create embargoes and prevent recovery from early attacks, as shown in Table 2-10. The economic impact of ruinous information warfare attacks on a region or nation, if sustained under the tactical model illustrated in Table 2-10, is far-reaching and results in long-term losses of business, import/export, and banking activities.

Table 2-10: Impact of Business Loss on a Region or Nation in Progressive Phases of Ruinous Information Warfare Attacks

Phase of Ruinous Information Warfare Attacks	Impact Achieved During Phase of Attack
Phase 1: Disruptive attack (days 1 to 3)	Disruption of communications, commerce, and local banking
Phase 2: Disabling attack (days 4 to 6)	Disabling supply chain participation and port activities
Phase 3: Financial infrastructure attack (days 7 to 10)	Destruction of banking systems and financial records
Phase 4: Disabling attack (days 11 to 14)	Disruption of repaired or restored communications systems
Phase 5: Embargo attacks (days 14 to 20)	Embargo on companies or country systems that conduct trade or business with target region or nation
Phase 6: Ongoing disruptive attack (days 21 to 100+)	Continued disruption of new, replaced, or restored information systems

The Potential Decline in Stock Prices

The economic impact of ruinous information warfare attacks can go well beyond just the destruction of business, import/export, and banking activities. Any company located in a targeted country (or foreign businesses with operations in a targeted country) will suffer substantial business loss, including reductions in revenue and profits. This in turn will likely have a relatively immediate impact on the stock price of those companies. If business operations are decreased or halted for several months, the stock price of the companies impacted by the attacks could plummet. This will impact the ability of the companies to raise funds for recovery as well as impact the portfolio value of individuals or investment and mutual funds that are holding corporate stock.

A similar impact on stock prices is also possible for individual companies that suffer from random or sustained rogue information warfare attacks, or random or sustained terrorist information warfare attacks. If a dot-com company, for example, suffers repeated frequent outages or a sustained outage because of rogue or terrorist attacks, stock prices are likely to decline. The decline will result from an overall real decline in company value, caused by dips in revenue or profits. Further declines could be caused indirectly by sell-offs by investment funds that do not want a high-risk stock in their portfolio and by erosion of investor confidence.

If stock price is tied to revenue on a one-to-one ratio, for example, and if revenue declines by 20 percent, stock prices would also decline by 20 percent. However, given probable investor panic, stock prices could decline far more rapidly if it is known that a company has suffered from repeated rogue or terrorist information warfare attacks. If stock prices decline at twice the rate that revenue declines, and a company loses 40 percent of its revenue because of information warfare attacks, stock prices would be only 20 percent of their original value prior to the attacks. The potential impact on stock prices because of declines in revenue caused by information warfare attacks is shown in Table 2-11.

Table 2-11: Potential Impact on Stock Prices from Declines in Revenue Caused by Information Warfare Attacks

Amount of Decline	Revenue Levels	1-to-1 Ratio	2-to-1 Ratio
Level prior to attack	100%	100%	100%
20% decline in revenue	80%	80%	60%
30% decline in revenue	70%	70%	40%
40% decline in revenue	60%	60%	20%
50% decline in revenue	50%	50%	Near zero

The Destruction of Market Valuation

Market valuation of companies in a region or an industry sector and that of an individual company could also be significantly and negatively impacted by information warfare attacks. Although there is considerable debate about the relationship of market valuation and revenue or profits, especially in dot-coms, market valuation is still a vital factor when investors consider a company for inclusion in their portfolio. Regardless of the prospective, bear or bull, toward the estimation of market value, declines in profit and revenue will certainly have an impact on perceived market valuation. If market valuation is determined at a 10-to-1 ratio to profits, a company with $100,000,000 in profits that experienced a 20 percent decline in profits would lose $200,000,000 in market valuation. If market valuation is determined at a 100-to-1 ratio to profits, a company with $100,000,000 in profits that experienced a 40 percent decline in profits because of information warfare attacks would lose $4,000,000,000 in market valuation. A range of examples of profit losses and declines in market valuation is shown in Table 2-12.

Table 2-12: The Potential Impact of Information Warfare Attacks on Market Valuation of a Single Company

Amount of Decline	Profit Levels	10-to-1 Ratio	100-to-1 Ratio
Levels prior to attack	$100,000,000	−$1,000,000,000	−$10,000,000,000
20% decline in profit	$80,000,000	−$800,000,000	−$8,000,000,000
30% decline in profit	$70,000,000	−$700,000,000	−$7,000,000,000
40% decline in profit	$60,000,000	−$600,000,000	−$6,000,000,000
50% decline in profit	$50,000,000	−$500,000,000	−$5,000,000,000

The Impact on Investment Funds and Their Growth

Just as the stock price and market valuation of individual companies and groups of companies in geographic regions or nations can be negatively impacted by information warfare attacks, so can the value and stability of investment funds that hold ownership or stock in these companies. A fund that is largely invested in a geographic region or nation that is hit by information warfare attacks of any type will plummet in value very quickly. Funds that are heavily invested in dot-com stocks or specific industry sectors can suffer from similar types of impacts. In addition to the present value of an investment rapidly declining in value after information warfare attacks, the long-term stability of the fund could also be severely impacted. If an investment fund that was built over a period of ten years suffers a 50 or 60 percent decline in value, in just a few weeks the fund would be set back several years in its ability to grow.

Investment funds attract additional investors because of their reputation for performance as well as their value. If a single fund or group of funds suffers severe losses in value, it will simultaneously suffer a decline in reputation. Investors will be hesitant to buy into the fund if there is a perception that the fund will be troubled over a long period of time and will have difficulty recovering from losses. This would deter further investment as well as cause concern for the companies that did suffer from information warfare attacks but have stock held by the investment fund. Those companies will need to take quick action to protect their stock value from potential sell-offs by the funds that may need to raise cash for operations or reinvestment.

There Is No "Day After" in Cyberwar

Establishing a direct comparison between information warfare and other types of warfare is difficult because information warfare differs from other types of warfare in several ways. The primary difference is that information warfare, as a standalone strategy, is not waged to occupy or control geographic territories as is conventional land-based warfare. It also differs from nuclear warfare because the goal of information warfare is not to physically destroy a country or region. However, it is more similar to nuclear warfare than land-based warfare because the best defensive strategy is to be constantly on the alert for attacks and to be able to stop attacks before they cause a great deal of damage. In nuclear warfare, there was a belief that there would be a "day after"—that is, a time when all of the bombs had gone off and the war ceases. In land-based warfare, there is also a time when fighting ceases and occupying forces move from a destructive mode to maintaining some desired status quo.

The phases of a ruinous information warfare attack described in Table 2-10 are an example of how an information warfare strategy escalates from an initial disruptive attack to an intensified disabling attack which is constantly repeated in order to deter recovery. In addition, phase 5 of the scenario, the embargo attack, is designed to frustrate trade and interaction with allied nations or business partners. To be maximally effective, information attacks will need to continue until a desired political or military change is accomplished. However, even when the goals are accomplished, the effects of ruinous information warfare attacks will be felt for a very long time. The ultimate desired impact of ruinous information strategies is to do executive and long-term economic damage and significantly alter the economic standing, manufacturing processes, and trading ability of the target region or nation.

In the case of offensive or defensive containment information warfare strategies, the goal is to hinder or halt military economic activity until a desired political or military outcome is achieved. The only way for containment strategies to work is for the desired change to occur. The attacker demonstrates its ability to repeat attacks as long as necessary and escalate to a ruinous strategy if desired changes are not achieved. Ruinous and defensive strategies, however, can probably only be achieved by a well-trained and well-equipped military force. Military actions are controllable and can be stopped at any time. Terrorist and rogue attacks, on the other hand, will likely only be stopped if the terrorists or criminals are either apprehended or killed. Regardless if the attacks are random or sustained, the terrorist or rogue would be capable of launching additional attacks at any time as long as the individuals conducting the attacks remain at large.

It will be relatively easy to identify the beginning of an information warfare attack. However, because of the ability to repeat attacks and the long-term economic impact that can be caused by information warfare, it may be years before recovery can be accomplished. Offensive and defensive containment information warfare strategies, and random or sustained terrorist and rogue information warfare strategies, are the equivalent of an electronic siege. Containment efforts must continue, or target groups, regions, or nations must be convinced that containment-oriented attacks can be initiated at any time. Terrorists or rogues will not be feared—and will be unable to accomplish their missions of disruption or extortion—if their target is unconvinced that the terrorist or rogue is capable of continuing the attacks. Thus, the very nature of information warfare makes it likely that there will not be the traditional day after as was once believed to exist in nuclear warfare.

Conclusions and an Agenda for Action

The analysis of information warfare attacks on individual companies, industry sectors, or national economies presented in this chapter shows that potential economic impact of attacks could be very severe. This potential impact means that information warfare is far more important to the private sector than may have been projected in the past, which means information warfare needs to be viewed as something that is more than just a military activity or concern. The business and economic development community needs to understand the potential economic impact of information warfare and prepare accordingly. Important concepts and principles that can help realistically broaden this understanding are as follows.

Conclusions on the Economic Impact of Information Warfare

Several important conclusions about the potential economic impact of information warfare attacks can be drawn from the analysis presented in this chapter:

- ▶ There are three types of economic impact that result from information warfare attacks: immediate, short-term, and long-term. Determining the immediate economic impact of information warfare attacks is far less complicated than determining long-term impacts.

- ▶ The immediate economic impact from information warfare attacks occurs during the first few days of attacks, whether or not the attacks subside or continue. The short-term economic impact is what occurs over the first few weeks of sustained or random attacks. The long-term economic impact is the result of sustained attacks over weeks or months, or the aftermath of massive attacks that have ceased.

- ▶ The wholesale goods, retail, consumer electronics, and computer sectors have already become very dependent on automated supply chain systems, and the automotive industry is working to build an industry-wide supply chain system. The electronic supply chain systems have provided incredible benefits for these sectors, but it is also making them more vulnerable to sabotage and weaker in the face of information warfare attacks.

- ▶ Dot-coms are the most vulnerable commercial enterprise during information warfare attacks because many are solely dependent on their information technology to conduct business.

- ▶ Long-term information warfare attacks will result in a substantial loss of business, decline in stock prices, the destruction of market value, and the decline of value of investment funds. Such attacks could certainly delay further investment in specific companies or industry sectors.

- ▶ The long-term loss of business that can result from offensive ruinous information warfare or sustained terrorist information warfare attacks is the most serious economic issue that businesses face.

- ▶ Stock prices and market valuation of companies in information warfare zones (or those attacked by rogues or terrorists) could be severely and negatively impacted.

► Investment funds that hold ownership or stock in companies or groups of companies in regions that suffer from information warfare attacks will experience a decline in fund value. Such funds could suffer from long-term instability resulting in a decline in reputation and could have difficulties in attracting new investors.

An Agenda for Action in the Analysis of the Economic Impact of Information Warfare

To deal with the potential economic impact of information warfare attacks, governments, private companies, insurers, and investors need to set an agenda for action that enables them to respond and minimize economic damages in the event of attacks. Action steps should include, but not be limited to the following areas:

► Governments need to establish legal definitions of information warfare to guide the financial community in establishing terms and conditions of liability, responsibility for damage, insurance coverage, and tax deductions that could be debated in the event of information warfare attacks.

► Private companies need to develop strategies in advance to protect the value of their assets, the price of their stock, and their market valuation.

► Insurers need to develop policy language that identifies what an information warfare attack is comprised of and the economic loss or damages insurance will cover when an information warfare attack occurs.

► Investors, both individual and institutional, need to develop strategies to minimize the economic impact of information warfare on the value of their holdings.

Chapter 3

The Electronic Doomsday Scenario: How Ten People Could Cause $1 Trillion in Economic Disruption

The true nature of an all-out information warfare attack may never be known. However, the likelihood of terrorist or rogue information warfare attacks is very high. This chapter illustrates how a group of ten people from around the world could launch a sustained terrorist information warfare attack and disrupt businesses and governments for an extended period of time. It also shows how international cooperation in information warfare attacks is absolutely necessary in order to have a reasonable and swift response to attacks. All of the characters in this scenario are fictional and there is absolutely no intent to compare them to any existing people. The names of the attackers and their teams were created by the authors, as was the attack scenario. At the end of the chapter the implications of the attack scenario are analyzed.

The PH2 Team

Pearl Harbor 2 (PH2) is an information warfare scenario. It was created by a group of ten people from different parts of the world. They all had high-level computer skills and knowledge and got to know each other over the Internet and in chat rooms. They all came from different cultural backgrounds and are all educated and intelligent people. One day they decided to conspire to launch a sustained terrorist information warfare attack. They each had their own reasons for participating—some political, some just for fun, some because they were angry at people around them; others were simply alienated or disenfranchised. The individual members of the group of ten are shown in Table 3-1 and their backgrounds are as follows:

Code name: Prince Gilbert Male, born in London, 27 years old, educated in England, degrees in computer science and telecommunications. He spent four years in the military and is employed by the largest telecommunications company in England. He has never been married, his father is deceased, and he provides partial support for his mother.

Code name: Hoffman Male, born in Frankfurt, 30 years old, educated in Germany with degrees in computer science. He spent two years in the German army and is employed by a large bank in Frankfurt. He has never been married, is openly bisexual, and has had difficulty holding a job since he finished military service.

Code name: High-Tech Tonya Female, born in California, 28 years old, educated at Stanford University with degrees in computer science and is a certified Cisco engineer. She is employed by a large software company in Redwood City, California. She has never been married, is openly bisexual, and has a reputation for promiscuity.

Code name: Brandon Male, born in New York, 34 years old, educated at Cornell University with degrees in computer science. He was kicked out of school while working on his doctorate for misuse of university computers, is not employed, and is a social recluse.

Code name: Hiroshima Male, born in Tokyo, 26 years old, educated in the United States and Japan with degrees in computer science. He is employed as a computer programmer by the same conglomerate that his father has worked for all of his life. He is not married and does not date.

Code name: Bit Biter Male, born in Hong Kong, 29 years old, educated in the United States with a degree in compute science. He wanted to continue school in the United States, but his parents relocated to Vancouver in 1997 and could not afford to support his desire for further education. An international computer services firm recruited him out of school, and he works mostly in western Canada and the northwest United States.

Code name: Outback Male, born in Sydney, 33 years old, educated in Australia with degrees in computer science and telecommunications. He worked for IBM for a short period of time and is now employed by the largest telecommunications services firm in Australia. He has never traveled more than 100 miles from home, and he does not date or socialize to any great extent.

Code name: Big Tiger Male, born in New Delhi, 28 years old, educated in the United States and England with degrees in computer science and mathematics. He married according to his family's wishes, has two children, and is a senior programmer in a rapidly growing software firm in India.

Code name: Thomas Jefferson Male, born in Lebanon, 35 years old, educated in the United States and Europe, with degrees in computer science. Israeli soldiers killed his parents when he was 11 years old. He was married for a short time to an American woman, has a son, but has no idea where his former wife and child are living, and was never accepted by her parents or family. He lives part-time in Lebanon, but travels throughout Europe and the Middle East.

Code name: Bad Girl Female, born in the south of Japan, 23 years old, educated in Japan with a degree in computer science. She wanted to continue school, but all of her family resources were going toward educating her brothers. She was ostracized from her family after a quarrel with her father and now lives with her girlfriend in Tokyo where she is employed as a computer programmer.

Table 3-1: Code Names and Geographical Location of PH2 Members

Code Name	Geographical Area of Operation
Prince Gilbert	England
Hoffman	Germany
High-Tech Tonya	California
Brandon	New York
Hiroshima	Japan
Bit Biter	Western Canada and northwestern United States
Outback	Australia
Big Tiger	India
Thomas Jefferson	Lebanon and southern Europe
Bad Girl	Japan

The Conception of PH2

These ten people never met physically as a group. They were familiar with each other's handle, or code name, because they encountered each other in chat rooms. Six of the ten also were members of the same online clubs and mail lists from which they received information about computers and various programming languages. None of them are really full-fledged members of any computer underground or hacking organization. They developed a relationship because most of them came together in the same chat room where there was a discussion of recent virus outbreaks.

It is difficult to determine which of these ten people actually started the conspiracy to attack computer systems around the world. Probably none of them; it probably just grew out of ongoing conversations. Eventually the ten bonded together in a plot to wreak a bit of havoc on the Internet. To some it may have been a game. To Thomas Jefferson, Hoffman, Big Tiger, and Bad Girl it may have just been getting even for things that happened to them in life. The motivation is not really important, but the ten created an information warfare scenario they called Pearl Harbor 2 (PH2).

Day 1: The Launch of PH2

About 9:00 A.M., December 3, 2001, Monday morning in New York City. An email computer virus similar to the Love Bug started sweeping through computer systems on Wall Street and companies up and down the East Coast of the United States. The virus was malicious and had several variants that were circulating at the same time. All of the variants that hit computers using Microsoft Outlook email software would send themselves to the first 50 names found in each computer's email address book. The virus also sent a carbon copy of each email message to preselected email addresses. The carbon copy recipients were different for each variant of the virus.

Variant number one had a subject line of "Emergency Shutdown of Systems in 10 Minutes." This variant sent itself to the first 50 names in each address book, but also sent carbon copies to the customer service email address of several major corporations, such as Amazon, Schwab, and AOL. This variant also corrupted Microsoft Word and Excel files.

Variant number two had a subject line of "We need further information to process your Christmas order." This variant also sent itself to the first 50 names in each address book, but sent carbon copies of the email messages to customer service email addresses at banks and government agencies, including the White House and the U.S. Veterans Administration. This variant also corrupted computer system files.

Variant number three had a subject line of "Free Porn—New Pam Video." This variant, like the other two, sent itself to the first 50 names in each address book, but sent carbon copies to the helpdesk or customer service email addresses at search engines such as Yahoo! and Excite and news websites such as CNN and ABC News. This variant also corrupted Microsoft Windows files.

In Japan, Hong Kong, Australia, Sweden, Finland, Ireland, France, Spain, Italy, India, and dozens of other countries, the same three virus variants were circulating. The subject lines of the email addresses were in local languages, and local companies were targeted with carbon copies of the email messages. Each of the ten members of the PH2 team had orchestrated release of the virus in languages they were familiar with, and they identified the companies to which they sent the carbon copies of the messages.

It took less than four hours for the virus to replicate itself 3 billion times around the world. Within 24 hours, the virus had replicated itself

36 billion times. As with the Love Bug attack, major companies and government organizations that could respond fast enough took their email systems offline to clean up and wait for the fixes to be available from their antivirus software companies. Others were not so lucky or just not fast enough to stop the bug from spreading. The companies that were victims of the carbon copies and their Internet service providers were flooded with massive numbers of email messages that would replenish themselves as fast as they were deleted.

The PH2 team had effectively made their first strike. Email systems were offline, the customer service email addresses of major companies around the world were rendered useless, and it was going to take days for even the fastest organizations to recover. The weakest organizations would face problems for more than a week. Millions of files were corrupted. As in the case of the Love Bug, the PH2 team would get help from people who circulated the viruses in variant forms. For more than two weeks, about 75 variants of the bugs were circulated that the PH2 team had nothing to do with.

Day 2: The Big Bug Bite

About 4:00 A.M., December 4, 2001, Tuesday morning in New York City. Many organizations and individuals that could not use their email systems fell back to their wireless devices such as Palms and smart phones to communicate via email. The PH2 team had anticipated this and had created a deadly virus to attack mobile Internet devices. The virus had three variants, each designed to attack different wireless platforms and operating systems. The PH2 team released the virus, and it successfully and rapidly spread through the world of wireless Internet users. The virus replicated and sent itself to the first 15 email addresses in each email address book of the wireless email devices, then destroyed the operating software of the many wireless devices.

This was the first time that a wireless Internet device virus was so effective. It caught everyone by surprise and left email users without a backup system. The PH2 team released the virus in multiple languages from dozens of points around the world. As with the virus launched on day 1, variant writers took it upon themselves to continue the spread of the virus with different subject lines.

As investigations got underway, the FBI and law enforcement organizations in industrial nations around the world started to attempt to trace where the viruses came from. They had to follow multiple trails, and it quickly became apparent that bugs were launched from multiple points. Most trails led back to university computers, while other trails led to government computers. The PH2 team knew they would be hunted and were taking as many steps as possible to cloak the origin of the messages.

Meanwhile, Internet news sites and the websites that provided antivirus software updates were flooded with traffic. It took several hours for many system administrators to download the much-needed antivirus updates. Ecommerce transactions plummeted, as did online stock trades. Customers who could not use the Internet for purchases or stock trading turned to the telephone to call in orders and trades. The phone systems could not support the volume and there were not enough customer service representatives to handle the incoming calls. Systems and people were being stretched to their limits. By the end of day 2, it was clear that economic activity was gridlocked, and there were long delays in transactions that normally took only seconds to accomplish over the Internet.

Day 3: Is It War Yet?

Wednesday, December 5, 2001. Day 3 was a day of dramatic headlines. Was this a war? Were these people terrorists? The manhunt was on full force. Larger companies and well-staffed government organizations started to recover and bring email systems back online. However, more than 75 percent of the organizations hit by the virus attacks had still not completely recovered by the end of day 3.

The PH2 team launched their third wave of viruses. This time, the virus was designed to strike Apple computer systems that had previously been relatively impervious to many virus attacks. The attack was successful: the virus hit mailboxes on Apples, replicated itself, and then corrupted files, rendering the Apples useless.

The media circus continued, and many experts who were interviewed warned people to not even turn on their computer systems until the viruses were contained and wiped out. Ecommerce companies cringed at this warning and started a campaign to counter such advice. The dot-coms were losing money and losing it fast. Christmas was coming and the ecommerce companies desperately needed the revenue generated by holiday sales. The last thing they wanted was panic and fear.

Day 4: A Russian Connection?

Thursday, December 6, 2001. Several new variants of the original viruses were circulating, but they were not the work of the PH2 team. On day 4, investigators thought they had suspects. An email was traced back to a computer in Venezuela, another in Russia, and yet another in Romania. Other trails led to computers in Hong Kong and the People's Republic of China, which created a touchy diplomatic situation. It was the Love Bug all over again. Local law enforcement officials were ill equipped to investigate. The chaos and the rhetoric continued, but no culprits were apprehended. By the end of day 4, all that was found of the Venezuelan lead was an empty apartment. In Russia, a computer operator in the central administrative office of the government was being interrogated. In Romania, the alleged computer could not be found.

Day 5: Chaos Realized

Friday, December 7, 2001. The PH2 team was in deep silence—they did not communicate, nor would they communicate until day 6, as planned. They had created chaos and had caused more than 100 billion dollars in business disruption and damaged files on more than 30 million computers. Companies and governments in the industrial nations were starting to claim victory over the viruses. All investigative attention was being focused on the computer operator in Russia because many copies of the virus variants with subject lines in several languages had been found on computers in the central government's administrative office. However, several experts warned that he probably was not the person who started the virus attacks, and suspicions of an international terrorist plot started to turn into headlines around the world. One newscaster in San Francisco compared the attack to that of Pearl Harbor on December 7, 1941.

Day 6: It Isn't Over Yet

Saturday, December 8, 2001. It had been a hard and busy week for information technology professionals around the world. Many were stressed and had been pulled and tugged in many directions in their efforts to clean viruses from computers and reload software for millions of computers that had files destroyed. Most would work through this weekend to finish the cleanup task. Many of the technicians had worked 18-hour days. They were exhausted, but they had successfully contained the virus in most organizations, and antivirus software had been updated. There were still variants and many systems that had not come back online. But most major companies had their systems up and operating by the end of day 4, and on day 6, there were only a few systems that had not recovered.

Meanwhile, the investigation focused on the Russian computer operator. Investigators found there had been more than $10,000 deposited in his bank account in the last month and that he had a bank account in Switzerland with more than $200,000 that had been deposited in the last month. The authorities were convinced they had caught their man. As the computer operator was being escorted in handcuffs from one building to another, two black Jeeps with tinted windows sped up to the group of eight policemen guarding the alleged cyber-terrorist. In an instant, men jumped from the Jeeps and shot and killed the computer operator and all of the guards with a shower of machine gun bullets.

At a designated hour, each of the PH2 members logged on to a website they had set up and posted coded messages all starting with the word "Hell" and ending in a three-digit number, starting with the combination "Hell 370." Each of the cyber-gang posted a numbered message. Thirty minutes later, they all logged on again and found ten messages had been posted. This meant they were all in sync and prepared to move ahead with their attacks. The next phase was a free-for-all where each of the ten would act independently to launch more chaos onto the Internet. This was also a game. It was a contest to see which of the ten could be the cleverest in their destructive techniques.

Day 7: Attacks in Germany and Japan

Sunday, December 9, 2001. Investigations of the virus attacks continued, the list of suspects grew larger, and speculation for the reason for the attacks increased. China of course denied that attacks had originated from the PRC, but quietly was rounding up suspects—mostly political dissidents who were always suspected of unacceptable activity by the Chinese government. A tense situation was developing as many Congressional representatives in the United States were making unsubstantiated comments about Chinese or Russian involvement in the attacks. The chaos of the investigation was compounded because it was clear that many people had helped to launch the attack, and it was difficult to facilitate international cooperation in the investigation.

Hoffman, the programmer in the German bank, set his phase two plan into action. He copied files from the bank's computers that contained thousands of credit card and debit card numbers and PINs. He then distributed them to more than a dozen websites in Europe and North America and also sent them to several email addresses in Russia. Within hours, people around the world were using the information to make illegal purchases and withdrawals from accounts. He then launched a program that altered bank deposit and withdrawal amounts for the bank's business and consumer accounts. The alterations were small random numbers ranging from 1 to 100 Deutsche marks. He also planted a time bomb on the computer systems that was designed to shut the systems down just as the bank was opening for business Monday morning, December 10, 2001. Hoffman went home and removed the hard disk from his computer, set a bomb trap that would go off when his apartment door was opened, and then took a train to the Netherlands where he modified his identity. Using a forged passport, he boarded a plane for New York. He dumped the hard disk in the river on his way to the train station.

Bad Girl, the computer programmer in Tokyo, launched her phase two plot. She had worked for several weeks designing a pornographic website that was hosted in California. The site was called "Our Asian Daughters." The site was in two languages, Japanese and English. She set the theme of the site as young Asian girls and had some very compelling photos that porn viewers would love to talk about and share. Bad Girl started posting announcements in newsgroups about free one-week passes to the site as an introductory offer. A credit card number was not required for the free trial, but users had to enter a password that was included in the newsgroup postings. In just a few days, more than 40,000 people visited the site. Upon their visit, two things happened. First, email addresses and IP addresses of visitors were collected and stored in a database. Second, a virus was also installed on the visitors' computers as they interacted with the website, and the virus was set to launch on December 14, 2001.

Brandon, using the computer systems of Cornell and other universities in New York, was preparing to launch a denial-of-service attack on Wall Street computers that would take place on Tuesday, the day after Hoffman's bank hit.

Day 8: A German Bank Goes Down

Monday, December 10, 2001. Hoffman's plot worked just as he had planned. The computer systems of the bank shut down at the start of the business day. By the end of the day, the illegal use of the credit card and debit numbers was discovered, and the bank had to halt transactions on thousands of accounts. The bank and German police started investigating immediately and interrogating employees. All employees who had not shown up for work became immediate suspects, and the police started visiting their homes. When Hoffman did not answer his door, the police entered his apartment and the bomb exploded, killing three German police officers and injuring several residents of the apartment building. It would take several days to determine that Hoffman's body was not among the arms, legs, and torsos at the bombing scene. It would take four more days to find out that account deposits and withdrawals had been altered, and weeks to reconcile the accounts and get the credit and debit card mess cleaned up. Bank operations would be crippled for weeks. By noon in New York City, the news had spread of the incident in Germany.

Day 9: Wall Street Denial-of-Service Attack

Tuesday, December 11, 2001. The German bank hit dominated the news. The investigation of the Russian computer operator took a new twist. He was definitely guilty, but not of originating the virus. It was found that he had been helping to illegally transfer money out of official Russian government accounts into various bank accounts around the world. His gangland-style execution was carried out to keep him from revealing any information about this crime. It was Thomas Jefferson and Hoffman who had learned of the money-theft plot and had planted copies of the viruses on the Russian's computer systems and then sent an anonymous note to Russian authorities about his involvement in the virus attacks.

Brandon's Wall Street denial-of-service (DOS) attack started at 10:00 A.M. He had set up slave programs on hundreds of computers in New York, New Jersey, and Pennsylvania universities. He was not counting on a sustained DOS because slave computers are relatively easy to track, and traffic from the systems could be blocked. He did expect high drama out of the event and expected that users would quickly discover that access time to the trading systems had deteriorated. The DOS focused on the three largest online stock-trading websites. Brandon had developed an attack system that would submit queries to the sites, and the slaves would automatically rotate which sites they were hitting.

DOS attacks were really an old trick. If he was going to impress the PH2 team, Brandon had to add a new twist. He had hacked into the website of a major online stock-trading news site and stole the subscriber list to the site's email newsletter which was sent out several times each day. At 10:30 A.M., Brandon sent a spoofed email newsletter to the list, warning of the DOS attacks. This in turn created more traffic to the sites as legitimate users went to check out if anything was really happening. By 10:45 A.M., the network security teams at the stock-trading websites had determined they were under a DOS attack and they started taking evasive actions.

Brandon also placed calls to CNN, CNBC, and MSNBC about the attacks. The news stations then started calling the stock brokerages to find out the facts. At 11:15 A.M., Brandon sent another spoof email newsletter to the subscriber list he had stolen from the stock-trading news site. This time the subject line read "Service Levels Restored." The email also contained a virus. The virus was similar to those the PH2 team had used the week before. The virus sent emails to every other name in the address book of the recipient computer and to the three stock-trading websites' helpdesks. The emails carried the virus with it. The virus then destroyed system files on the recipient computers.

The DOS was shut down by 1:00 P.M. The universities, the FBI, and the SEC launched more investigations. Reporters went wild. The phones and email systems of the online brokerages were clogged with traffic. Thousands of online stock-trading customers had their computers chewed up by the virus. Brandon destroyed his computers, left the gas stove on in his apartment, and went to meet up with Hoffman. About an hour later, there was an explosion in the apartment and the building burst into flames. The evening news was getting complicated, and there was more of a spectacle than the Monica Lewinsky affair and the 2000 presidential election combined.

Day 10: Middle East Conflict Brews, Wrong Number in Australia

Wednesday, December 12, 2001. Thomas Jefferson, operating from Lebanon and southern Europe, was one of the most politically oriented members of the PH2 team and clearly sought revenge for the death of his parents. He started a campaign of hacks and defacements of Israeli websites, leaving behind various anti-Israeli slogans on the pages. He also launched a variant of one of the early viruses and sent it to tens of thousands of Israeli email addresses, claiming it was from a Palestinian organization. He also started hacking other sites that belonged to companies and government organizations in the Middle East. On each of the websites that were hacked, there were messages left claiming that it was the other side who hacked it, as well as insulting slogans. Using code and techniques Brandon had developed, Thomas Jefferson launched DOS attacks on several Middle Eastern sites. He used university computers in Italy, Spain, and France to launch the attacks.

It does not take much to spark conflict in the Middle East, and Thomas Jefferson was counting on having high impact with little effort. The computer crime or cyber-terrorism investigative skills of the Middle Eastern countries did not match their skills for political rhetoric. The DOS attacks continued for more than 24 hours before all of the slave systems were tracked down and disabled. The email virus circulated for several days before the frequency of messages diminished. Tensions flared again as all of the governments in the Middle East tried to determine who had hacked what site and who was sending email viruses around the region.

The combination of events that had occurred over the last ten days had investigators around the world confused and bewildered. There were numerous law enforcement agencies and division of the U.S. Department of Defense independently investigating attacks and incidents. The FBI and SEC were investigating Wall Street incidents. The Japanese government had not reacted to the Asian Daughters attack because they thought it was probably a prank. The Germans were in a frenzy over the bank attack and had even discussed shutting down Internet service providers in the country. The only thing worse than the cyber-chaos perpetrated by the PH2 team was the chaos being created by an uncoordinated investigative approach. A more coordinated approach was going to be required in the investigative process if anything constructive was going to happen. The White House called for an emergency international summit, and twenty of the top industrial countries sent representatives to the first emergency meeting. But these people were diplomats and they had absolutely no idea what kind of action to take and what to do to better coordinate efforts.

Outback, working for a telecommunications services firm in Australia, like the other members of the PH2 team was watching the drama unfold. He had considered some of the tricks his other team members had already used, and he was very proud of their impact. He wanted to do something different. He did not want Australia to be left out of the excitement, and of course, he did want to impress the PH2 team. His job with the telecommunications services firm gave him access to many of the most sophisticated telecommunications installations in Australia. On the evening of day 10, Australia time, he got the opportunity he had been waiting for—he was sent on a service call to a large telecommunications switching center. He left home to go on the call, leaving his computer dismantled and taking the hard disk with him. He dumped the hard disk on the way to work.

He entered the switching center just as people in Sydney were finishing dinner. Outback was working alone, and he would probably have a few hours to accomplish his task, which would need to be done by early morning. Telecommunications switches had seldom been tampered with over the years because they were not like the open architecture that supported the Internet. Only an insider could accomplish what Outback was going to do. He started modifying programs that would impact how calls were routed through the switches. He also programmed phones for the police department, the phone company's offices, and government organizations to go out of service at 4:30 A.M. Sydney time.

Outback left the switching center about 3:45 A.M. and drove to the edge of town where there was a large satellite-dish farm that supported international telecommunications connections to Australia. There were more than 40 satellite dishes at this location. His intent was to damage most of the dishes in some way so they would need repair. He had used the Internet to research how to make small bombs—such information is readily available—and he created small explosive devices out of material purchased on the open market. Outback entered the dish farm through a hole in the fence well away from the building that housed security and the control center. He planted his homemade explosive devices at different locations on each of the dishes. They were set to detonate at 4:45 A.M. He worked quickly and effortlessly, and drove away from the dish farm at 4:38 A.M.

At 4:45 A.M., the small explosive charges went off, damaging each of the satellite dishes enough to make them inoperable and require repair. The explosions were loud enough to get the attention of the night technician in the control building who, as he was going outside to see what happened, was distracted by alarms on control panels beeping and flashing. The technician picked up the phone to call for help, and for every number he dialed he got the recorded message "The number you have reached is not in service." Sydney woke to a day of malfunctioning telephones. When a telephone number was dialed, callers were connected to a different number than the one they dialed. When people called the phone company's offices, they got "The number you have reached is not in service."

Managers at the telecommunications offices knew it had to be an inside job. By 10:00 A.M., the police were looking for Outback. He had driven his car for about 30 minutes, dumped it, and then picked up a different car, shaved his beard, packed up his new identification and credit cards, dumped his car over a cliff, and drove off to see the world. For the first time in his life, he was going to go more than 100 miles away from home.

At this point in PH2, Hoffman, Thomas Jefferson, Brandon, and Outback were all in transit heading for new locations to regroup and then join the PH2 attack again. Meanwhile in Tokyo, Hiroshima, the computer programmer, launched another virus attack targeting wireless Internet email platforms, this time only in Japanese.

Day 11: The Tiger Prowls

Thursday, December 13, 2001. The work of Thomas Jefferson continued to wreak havoc. Militants from all sides rallied to attack websites and send email viruses to addresses in the countries they were fighting against. The attacks and counterattacks by the fanatics in the Middle East would go on for weeks. His attacks were successful by design. He wanted to ignite existing political and religious conflicts without expending too much effort and without compromising himself in the process. Thomas Jefferson had been operating mostly from Italy, but he knew it would not be long before authorities would be tracking him. He destroyed the computers he was using and took a plane to Canada, supposedly to visit his relatives.

Big Tiger, a senior programmer for a software company in India, had been watching the news of the impact the PH2 team had made. He was in awe, and he was proud. Big Tiger had worked on many projects over the last several years for companies in Europe and the United States that would send their application development work to India in an effort to reduce costs. Every month his company would send new code out to the clients to update their systems. Big Tiger had a surprise in mind for nine of the company's largest clients. He had planted bugs in the new code that would make the programs of the user companies malfunction. He did not want to render the systems inoperable because that would be noticed in an instant. Big Tiger's plan was simple. The software updates were sent out and installed by users, and everything seemed to be working fine. Within 24 hours, databases in the nine large companies were having records slightly altered. Within 48 hours, more than 30 million records were altered, effectively diminishing the data integrity of the customer service databases in the nine companies. It would take days to determine that something was going wrong, and months to correct all of the corrupted database records. Big Tiger was just beginning to prowl, but he only had a little more than a day to work and he wanted to make a dramatic strike while he had the chance.

Prince Gilbert, working for a large telecommunications company in England, was ready to go into action when he heard of the telecommunications system being sabotaged in Australia. He smiled, then he cursed. Outback had beaten him and used some of the same tricks he wanted to use, which meant that he clearly needed to take a different path. He was perplexed and needed to think of some new tricks. Prince Gilbert had done much of the coding work on the first wave of viruses the PH2 team had launched. He had several other variants in mind and, using email servers in France, Brazil, and Hong Kong, launched a new virus. It was fast to replicate itself and started spreading quickly, but not as fast as the multiple-point launch the PH2 team had achieved just eleven days ago. This variant also sent itself to addresses listed in email address books, but sent a carbon copy to only one address—FBI headquarters. Prince Gilbert then started working on a plot to hit the U.K. telecommunications systems. He wanted to make sure that he beat Outback at the game of drama and destruction.

Day 12: Our Asian Daughters

Friday, December 14, 2001. Bad Girl's virus is launched. She sent the list of email addresses collected from the website visitors to several newspapers and television stations in Japan and the United States. Many of the email addresses were anonymous, but not all of them. Then the Asian Daughter virus set itself off and did several things. First, it sent an email message to all of the addresses in each email address book with a photo from the Our Asian Daughters website attached to it that contained a virus. The subject line of the message read "Check Out Your Asian Daughter." The virus then corrupted many of the files on the recipient's computer and placed an Asian Daughter photo on the monitor with phone numbers to call for further information. The phone numbers were for large newspapers in Tokyo and San Francisco.

If the computer the Asian Daughter virus infected was only used by the porn surfer who visited the Our Asian Daughters website, the damage was only to the computer and perhaps to the ego of the porn surfer. On the other hand, if the computer was used in a business and a person in the workplace other than the porn surfer turned on the computer on December 14, 2001, it was a different story. It was indeed a different story if the computer was accessed by family members of the porn surfers, as hundreds of children and wives viewed an Asian Daughter photo in Japan, the United States, and more than twenty other countries. The news spread quickly, leaving many embarrassed closet porn surfers. The story that Bad Girl liked the most took place in a home in the south of Japan: the one she grew up in.

Meanwhile Big Tiger knew that in a day or so he would be caught if he did not run. He was definitely planning on leaving, but wanted one more strike under his belt. One of the companies he did development work for was a major electronic commerce website. He went to his office and used his password to access the site. He stole files with more than 100,000 names and credit cards numbers in them. Using an email address in Italy, he sent the files to several hacker newsgroups around the world and posted them on some bulletin boards. He logged on to his company's servers with an administrative password and erased files that could help trace his activity. Big Tiger had already altered the code that he had sent to the nine client companies to eliminate those lines of instruction that were altering database records. He replaced that code with simple and meaningless lines of instructions to make the patches look the same size. He left on vacation that afternoon, taking his family to the United States to visit relatives.

Bit Biter, working for a computer services firm in Vancouver and the northwestern United States, was ready to go into action. He got a service call to go to Seattle and work on a printing system for an information services company that contracted to print payroll checks for several companies in the area. It was a repair that had to be accomplished quickly. Bit Biter did not normally work on printers, but he was close by and all he was supposed to do was swap out some circuit boards and run some tests.

Bit Biter had not planned this specific action, but knew how to sabotage the printer by making sevens print as ones and ones print as sevens. He had learned this from a friend who was a printer service technician. It was not going to take long to figure out that the 30,000 checks printed that week were incorrect, but the problem would likely be blamed on the aging printer. Thomas Jefferson was on his way to Vancouver, and he and Bit Biter would meet in three or four days to work together on a major PH2 attack.

Day 13: Tonya Strikes

Saturday, December 15, 2001. There was chaos. The international summit was meeting day and night, and they were accomplishing nothing. So much had happened and none of the investigating groups could figure out what was related and what was not. One major newspaper ran the headline "Have Geeks Gone Mad?" This was poetry to the PH2 team.

High-Tech Tonya, a network engineer for a large software company in Redwood City, California, had multiple lives. She was an extremely talented programmer and network engineer by day. But several nights a week she wandered Silicon Valley as a member of an offbeat dating club in which she had several identities. She had hacked the website of the dating club and knew everything about all of its members. She had scheduled three dates, each with network engineers who worked for dot-com companies or Internet service providers (ISPs). The scenario was similar for each date: they would meet and have dinner, then perhaps go to a club or a movie.

Date number one was with a network engineer of an ISP. His name was Simon. For this date Tonya had red hair and brown eyes. They met for dinner, and she ordered wine. Simon did not drink, but she convinced him to have a glass of wine. Tonya was a master of seduction. As planned, they ended up back at Simon's apartment sipping wine as Tonya teased him into delusion and submission. She let Simon kiss her and told him she would have sex with him after they finished their wine. Simon downed his wine and they headed for the bedroom. Simon never had sex that night. He passed out in minutes from the drug that Tonya had added to his drink. He would be out for hours.

Tonya used Simon's computer and the list of passwords on the yellow Post-it stuck to his monitor to log on to the systems at his company. She made quick work of it, modifying IP addressees in routers, changing parameters in email systems, rerouting email from one client to another, and changing administrator passwords on services and applications of the ISP systems. Tonya cleaned up her fingerprints and left without a trace. Early the next morning, Simon woke in a fog to a ringing phone—there was chaos at the ISP. Simon could hardly move, and he remembered almost nothing from the night before. There would never be a trace of the date, as Tonya had deleted all evidence from the dating club's computer.

Hiroshima, meanwhile, had great success with his last virus and decided to repeat the trick. The previous virus had been eradicated for the most part, and he was anxious to strike again. He used a similar virus, but this time he targeted Korea, Taiwan, Hong Kong, and Thailand. The subject lines were a variety of ethnic insults. Hiroshima was just getting warmed up.

Day 14: The Shambles of Electronic Commerce

Sunday, December 16, 2001. The international summit remained confused. There were investigations everywhere. Leads were being followed, and government agencies were all blaming each other for the inability to put a stop to the cyber-chaos. Holiday electronic commerce sales had fallen far below last year's level, and it appeared that there was no chance for recovery.

High-Tech Tonya had another date. This time she had black hair and green eyes. Tonight's victim was a network engineer for a large electronic commerce applications service provider (ASP) that supported the online sales of more than 100 clients. His name was Harold. The outcome was the same for Harold as for Simon. The next morning, more than 20 of the companies the ASP supported would not have any electronic commerce functionality on their websites. It would take weeks for the others to figure out that orders were placed incorrectly and that shipping addresses were incorrect on every other order placed. Tonya also absconded with more than 200,000 credit cards numbers that were circulated around the web just as those from the German bank had been.

Hiroshima hacked into several electronic commerce sites in Japan, ripping off tens of thousands of credit card numbers and circulating them around the web.

Bad Girl had set up another porn site in the United States; this time the theme was child pornography. She was not only after child pornography fans, but also wanted to hit the child porn cyber-cops as well. As porn surfers logged on to the web, they received a virus that sent an email to the top fifty names in each address book with the subject line "I Like Kiddie Porn." The message had an incriminating photo attached. The virus corrupted some system files and reprogrammed the dialer to reconnect the computer to the Internet, but this time to dial 911. This was of course very effective in the United States.

Brandon and Hoffman had met up in Cleveland, Ohio. They were planning their next move. Bit Biter and Thomas Jefferson met up in Vancouver. Big Tiger was visiting family in Boston; he went out for a walk and never returned. It was also time for the PH2 team to touch base again. They logged on to another website they had created and started to leave their messages. This time the messages read "Heaven" followed by a three-digit number. When they logged on again a half hour later, there had only been nine responses. Outback did not report in.

Outback was an easy catch for the authorities in Australia. The police knew who they were looking for and assumed that their suspect was living under a new identity after he launched his attack. Automated searches of new vehicle purchases and new driver's licenses issued during the last few months were easy to run, as were analyses of airline tickets issued for departures from Sydney. Outback was careless on the auto purchase, and extensive footwork on the part of local law enforcement helped identify suspect vehicles. Within three days after the strike, the police were checking out seventeen suspects, which they quickly narrowed to three. On December 16, 2001, police pursued Outback in a high-speed chase less than 200 miles from Sydney. He panicked and attempted to outrun the police. He lost control of his car, it crashed, and he was killed.

The Australian police, in cooperation with the FBI and law enforcement authorities in more than twenty countries immediately attempted to track where Outback had been in cyberspace and with whom he might be associated. Authorities were uncertain if any of the incidents in Australia were related to incidents in other countries, but they had little (if anything) else to investigate. They agreed to attempt to keep all of these incidents quiet until they had further information.

Day 15: Busy Signal in London

Monday, December 17, 2001. News reporters found out about Outback, the high-speed chase, and the death of the most likely suspect in the sabotage of the Australian telecommunications systems. The news broke worldwide. As was previously discussed, if there was a compromise of identity, the PH2 team would have no further contact with each other. Each was now on his or her own to continue the attack or to run and hide. The headlines, of course, were spectacular.

Distraught at the news of the death of Outback, Prince Gilbert was falling apart. He was working the night shift in a large telecommunications switching center. He went to work that night as scheduled. During the lunch break on the graveyard shift, he planted several explosive devices in the switching center. As his coworkers were eating lunch, he set the bombs off and died in the explosion. The blast crippled a good portion of the telephone service in London and surrounding suburbs. Prince Gilbert's strike was certainly effective. The police moved swiftly and started their work to determine if Prince Gilbert and Outback had any relationship. There were now eight members of the PH2 team left.

Brandon and Hoffman decided it was time to strike. They went to visit Harold, a friend of Brandon's who worked at a Shaker Heights, Ohio, branch office of a large stock brokerage. It was getting close to the holidays and there were few people in the office in the middle of the afternoon. Brokerage computer systems have generally been hard to hack into, and Brandon and Hoffman wanted to get into a system fast, gather some technical data, and maybe leave a little something behind as well. Hoffman was somewhat familiar with the brokerage process because of his bank experience in Germany. Harold had also been kicked out of Cornell for improper use of computer systems. He was living with his parents in Shaker Heights and not doing much with his life. He did not hesitate to let Hoffman use the computer system and provided him with considerable information and numerous passwords. While Brandon and Harold caught up on old times, Hoffman took a virtual tour of the computer system. He was not going to be able to access any system-level files from the branch office terminal, but he did learn a lot about the system and was able to devise a hack plan.

Prince Gilbert and Outback were dead. Bit Biter and Thomas Jefferson were now in Seattle. Big Tiger was at large and no one, not even his PH2 team members, had any idea where he was. High-Tech Tonya, Bad Girl, and Hiroshima were still on their home turf. The toll had been tremendous. Dozens of viruses had been released, hundreds of thousands of credit card and debit card numbers had been compromised, bank accounts had been sabotaged, as had the operations of more than 100 electronic commerce companies and hundreds of companies using ISP services in Silicon Valley. The identity of porn surfers and kiddie-porn surfers had been revealed. The Internet and the telecommunications system had been hit harder than ever before.

In India, the crimes of Big Tiger had started to be realized. There were client complaints about functionality and problems in the new code. The electronic commerce from which Big Tiger had stolen credit card numbers was suspecting an Indian connection. Big Tiger's employers were trying to get in touch with him and found that he had disappeared. To the management team in India, Big Tiger's guilt was clear and the hunt was on.

Day 16: Target NASDAQ

Tuesday, December 18, 2001. As Hiroshima was leaving for work in the morning, the Tokyo police were waiting for him outside his apartment. He was arrested without discussion. The police sent a bomb squad into his apartment and after the squad gave clearance the police confiscated Hiroshima's computer and the entire contents of his apartment. The arrest did not stay out of the news for long. By late in the afternoon, television and radio stations were announcing that a cyberterrorist had been arrested. Bad Girl panicked. She dismantled her computer, packed a few things, and left. Her girlfriend was out of town visiting family for a few weeks and would not have any idea that she was gone. Bad Girl dumped her hard drive in the river on her way out of town.

Brandon and Hoffman acquired two computers and went to work to hack the computer systems at Harold's brokerage. They succeeded in short order and brought the system down at 10:30 A.M. Eastern time. The brokerage got their systems up and running in about an hour, but the downtime caused considerable delays in processing transactions, which continued throughout the day. Brandon and Hoffman had also learned more about how the brokerage's computer systems interacted with computers at NASDAQ, which they suspected had been hacked into several times in the past. Hoffman suspected that when NASDAQ reported a systems glitch there may have been hacking activity associated with it. His friends who worked at the exchange in Frankfurt had told him that hackers were always hitting the systems, and although they had never done any real damage, hackers were able to bring the systems down several times. This was Hoffman's goal with the NASDAQ systems.

It was time for High-Tech Tonya's third date. She was nervous. She had not yet heard of the arrest of Hiroshima, but she had a bad feeling that things were going to go wrong. The deaths of Prince Gilbert and Outback had made her ill. She was depressed because she could not get in contact with the PH2 team. She decided not to go on the date with the network engineer she had scheduled for that night. When she went home, Tonya saw the police cars at her apartment complex. She made a quick right turn and got on Highway 101 north, driving toward San Francisco. Parking her car in long-term parking at the San Francisco International Airport, she took a shuttle to the main terminal where she caught a taxi into the city. After shopping for some clothes, Tonya went to the train station and took a train to Seattle, where she planned to spend a day or two and then go on to Vancouver.

About midnight on the Charles River in Cambridge, Massachusetts, a student saw a body floating near a bridge and called the police. It was Big Tiger. High-Tech Tonya and Bad Girl were on the run. Six of the PH2 team were left. None of them were now in their home territory. None of them were totally certain what they were going to do next. Brandon and Hoffman left Cleveland to go to Chicago.

Day 17: PH2 Realized

Wednesday, December 19, 2001. Bad Girl was far from out of the game. She went to visit an old college friend who lived south of Tokyo. He was glad to see her and felt comfortable leaving her at his apartment while he went to work. His full-time roommate was on a business trip to the United States. She was exhausted and slept well. The next morning after her friend left, she used his computer to log on to one of her many websites. She had stored some viruses that Hoffman had written and distributed to the PH2 team. She downloaded several files to a floppy disk and went for a long walk. Bad Girl entered a cybercafé and got a cup of coffee. She sat down at a computer and logged on to a web email service at which she had a few aliases. She started sending the virus to several email lists she had accumulated and stored in her address book. Hoffman was a very good virus writer—his new worm traveled fast, and within 24 hours was being spotted around the world.

Bit Biter and Thomas Jefferson had also unleashed some of their new viruses the night before. The news reports declared another wave of virus attacks, and the antivirus cycle started all over again. None of these new viruses were as destructive as the ones the PH2 team had let loose during their first week of attacks. Bad Girl and Hoffman had learned each other's tricks, and both of the new strains hit address books and sent themselves to the top names in each book, then sent a carbon copy of every message that it produced to corporate email addresses. The new strains spread quickly, but they did little if any real damage other than clogging email boxes. The strains were similar to some of the earlier viruses released by the PH2 team, so the organizations that had updated their antivirus software did not suffer any consequences from the new wave of virus attacks.

Meanwhile, the police in Japan were interrogating Hiroshima, and the FBI in the United States had High-Tech Tonya's computer. They were starting to piece together the PH2 plot. The international investigation team that the White House had helped assemble was learning to work together and share information. High-Tech Tonya had left very little on her computer, but the FBI was beginning to assemble her cyber-trail. Hiroshima cracked and started telling the police about the plot. The FBI sent a team to work with the police in Japan. Hiroshima, however, was falling apart and much of what he said was incomprehensible to his interrogators. In addition, the investigation team for the most part disbelieved what Hiroshima was telling them.

The news about a terrorist plot called Pearl Harbor 2 did get out, and the press went wild. The Chinese and Russian connections were blown out of proportion. There had been chaos in the Middle East as various factions kept hitting each other's computer systems. This was one of Thomas Jefferson's plans, and it worked well because the press and the investigation teams started turning their attention to the Middle East fanatics, which gave Bad Girl, High-Tech Tonya, Bit Biter, Thomas Jefferson, Brandon, and Hoffman more time to work. In India, the authorities were keeping silent about what they had found out, and the company Big Tiger had worked for was attempting to do some damage control. It was in the best interest of the company and of the software industry in India to keep as much distance from the PH2 scandal as they possible could.

Day 18: Stock Brokerage Take-Down

Thursday, December 20, 2001. Chinese dissidents around the world had already started striking back at the Chinese government for the round-up of their comrades. Cyberwar was not new to these rivals who had hit each other's websites in the past with DOS and hack attacks. The dissidents started hacking websites, defacing them with slanderous remarks, and signing their work "PH2." This added to the already massive confusion in the investigation. The press started emphasizing the Chinese connection again.

In Japan, Hiroshima quickly became a folk hero and a wave of hack attacks spread across the country. Some of these attacks originated in the United States as Japanese students attending universities in the United States joined in the cyber-chaos. The attackers defaced websites and also signed their work "PH2."

In Germany, the police had been quietly rounding up known hackers trying to find out more information about Hoffman and attempt to determine if more cyber-crime had been planned within the country. The press knew nothing of these activities, but the hacker underground started spreading the word about their friends being detained by the German police. There were several hack attacks in retaliation, and government and business websites in Germany were defaced. However, few of the German hackers were aligning themselves with the PH2 name.

Brandon and Hoffman arrived in Chicago, and they hit the brokerage company's systems again, bringing it down, but not before they were able to obtain more technical information about the system. The outage lasted for about an hour and caused delays in transactions throughout the day. Brandon and Hoffman had been moving from hotel to hotel and were being cautious not to stay in one place too long. The brokerage company's computer security team had determined the origin of some of the passwords that were being used in the attack and were soon questioning Harold. The FBI was called in and Harold was on the hot seat. He did not care. Harold had been watching the news since early December and after Brandon's visit had pretty much figured out that Brandon was involved. He was not cooperating with the investigation.

The FBI was investigating Harold's background and paid a visit to Cornell University. They found out about Harold's relationship with Brandon and that they had both been kicked out of Cornell for improper use of the university's computer systems. The pieces fell together and the FBI started their search for Brandon.

Brandon and Hoffman made their first attempt to hack the NASDAQ systems. They did not have much luck at first, but by the end of the day they had succeeded in gaining entrance to the systems. They wanted to take the NASDAQ systems down the next day, Friday, December 21, 2001.

Bad Girl met some old amateur hacker friends during one of her visits to a cybercafé. They were talking about Hiroshima and PH2. She did not confess her involvement with PH2, but she started to pull together a small band of cyber-warriors. They were more bored than socially motivated, and they had a desire to do something they thought would be cool. Hiroshima's notoriety appealed to them. Bad Girl departed from her friend's apartment the next day and went to stay in a small apartment with some of her new gang.

Bit Biter and Thomas Jefferson had launched a series of hack attacks. Like Brandon and Hoffman, they stayed on the move. Each day they were hitting an electronic commerce website, stealing credit card numbers, and distributing them over the Internet. It was close to Christmas and the combined PH2 team had stolen and redistributed more than one million credit card numbers. The numbers were being used around the world for fraudulent transactions, and credit card holders were becoming the civilian casualties of PH2 as were the web merchants that were suffering from fraudulent use of the cards. The illegal use of credit card numbers required thousands of cards to be canceled and new ones issued in their place. The audit process to determine the extent of fraud would take months to work through. Bit Biter and Thomas Jefferson were getting ready to hit some large electronic commerce companies. However, their schedule had fallen behind, and the holiday shopping season was all but over—they had little time left for a big take-down.

Day 19: NASDAQ Foiled, Microsoft Hit

Friday, December 21, 2001. The international task force and the investigative teams in various countries were overwhelmed with information they did not know what to do with. The FBI was investigating dozens of hacks on electronic commerce sites, but had no idea what was related to the PH2 team and what was not. They knew they were looking for Brandon, Hoffman, and High-Tech Tonya. Investigators were not yet aware of the involvement of Bad Girl, Thomas Jefferson, and Bit Biter. The FBI also still had no information about the relationship between Big Tiger and the PH2 team. The investigators had no real idea if there was in fact a massive plot or if there were many plots that had originated in the Middle East, or in Russia, or in China. The media loved it, and the speculation about PH2 and the Middle East, Russia, and China raged on.

The police in Japan had pieced together other evidence with the results of their interrogation of Hiroshima and had established the identity of Bad Girl. The search was on. The police detained Bad Girl's girlfriend and started interrogating her. She knew nothing about Bad Girl's activities and in fact knew very little about computers. The newspapers in Japan ran the story and a photo of Bad Girl. The members of Bad Girl's new gang quickly figured out who she was, and they rallied around with intensified dedication. Bad Girl knew they would be caught, and she also knew the police would do everything short of physical torture to extract information from her girlfriend. She intended to go out in a blaze of glory. The news stories resulted in an increase in hacking activity, which led the police to wrongly believe that the plot in Japan was more far-reaching and better organized than it actually was. Bad Girl set about planning her next wave of attacks.

Brandon and Hoffman started their attack early in the morning as the NASDAQ computers started churning. They were moving through the system looking for a way to do damage. What they did not know is that the NASDAQ computer security team was watching every move they made and were attempting to determine from where they were hacking. The security team let Brandon and Hoffman wander a bit, then kicked them out of the system. Brandon and Hoffman immediately started to reenter the system. They were getting very careless and not covering their tracks as much as they should have on a high-profile hack. The security team booted them out again. Brandon and Hoffman went back in, determined to bring the system down. The FBI quietly surrounded the hotel where Brandon and Hoffman were operating from. The FBI entered the hotel room about 11:45 A.M., surprising the hackers. Hoffman jumped up and pulled out a gun. He was shot dead immediately. Brandon sat frozen in front of his computer.

Late that night, Bit Biter and Thomas Jefferson started a hack on Microsoft's website. Both were familiar with Microsoft's products and were highly knowledgeable about the web software and tools Microsoft produced. They had waited for the holiday weekend, hoping there would be a minimum number of people staffing Microsoft's operations. They were right. They managed to enter Microsoft's systems and steal a considerable amount of source code and documentation. They distributed the material across the Internet just as they had done with the credit card numbers they had stolen.

Day 20: Information Warfare, Guns, and Bombs

Saturday, December 22, 2001. Bit Biter and Thomas Jefferson had left for Vancouver. The news of the Microsoft hack had not hit the newspapers—and as Bit Biter and Thomas Jefferson correctly assumed, it never would. They crossed the border without incident and went to an apartment in Vancouver that Bit Biter had rented a month before to serve as a hideout.

The FBI was interrogating Brandon, but not getting much out of him. He was in a state of shock having seen his partner get killed by the FBI. He was also exhausted, and most of what he was saying was incomprehensible. The FBI started tracing the steps of Brandon and Hoffman based on the use of a large number of stolen credit cards they had in their possession when captured. The FBI was gathering a lot more information, but they still had no real idea of the scope of the PH2 plot and how many people were really involved or how deeply they were involved.

Meanwhile the cyberwar between the Chinese government and Chinese dissidents continued to rage on around the world. Later that night, shots were heard in a Los Angeles apartment. When the police arrived, they found four young Chinese men dead and a room full of computers. It took only a few hours for the police to find out that these four men were Chinese dissidents and that they had established an information warfare team that had been hitting Chinese government websites and computer systems. The police would never determine who had shot the four dissidents, but it made for a great newspaper story.

The Middle East cyberwar also remained in full swing as virus attacks and website hacks continued. As is always the case in the Middle East, it was impossible to really tell what was happening and if any of the many sides was actually winning. The Palestinians, however, were finally coming into the information age. They figured out that placing car bombs in market areas and blowing up buses would have far less impact on the state of Israel than hitting the communications infrastructure. That day, a car bomb exploded at a telecommunications substation, knocking out more than 200,000 phones in Jerusalem. Information warfare was going to become a permanent tactic in Middle East conflicts.

High-Tech Tonya was lying low in Seattle and getting ready to cross the border into Canada. She visited a cybercafé and, using one of her many aliases on a web email site, released her Merry Christmas virus.

She also hacked into a Santa Claus website and used the email newsletter of the site to steal more than 100,000 email addresses of children who had registered at the website. Lots of children would have an interesting surprise on Christmas Eve.

Later that night, the Royal Canadian Mounted Police raided Bit Biter's apartment and arrested him and Thomas Jefferson. In cooperation with the FBI, they had figured out that Bit Biter was probably involved in PH2. The two were arrested without incident.

Day 21: Vulnerability and Exposure

Sunday, December 23, 2001. Bad Girl wanted drama. She decided to use another pornographic ploy, this time not to do damage—she wanted to embarrass people, especially the rich and the powerful. She knew the sex underground in Tokyo well because many times when she was a college student people had attempted to recruit her into the business. She set her cyber-gang to work from four locations hacking into websites that offered sex services in Japan and Thailand. She wanted credit card numbers and names of users and clients. They succeeded in obtaining more than 28,000 credit card numbers. She created nine websites and posted all of the numbers on the websites openly stating that they had been stolen from sexually oriented websites or businesses. The evidence was incriminating to government officials, business executives, and public relations firms who were customers of escort and sex services in Japan and Thailand. She also emailed the lists to television stations and newspapers in Japan and the United States. The card numbers were from several countries, including Japan, the United States, Germany, Korea, and Australia. Many were corporate cards from large companies, and others were traceable to high-level executives or their assistants.

The police in Japan were patrolling cyberspace, expecting incidents and trying to track hackers or people they thought might be associated with the PH2 team. Bad Girl was careless and did not cover her cyber-tracks well. She knew it was almost over anyway. The police quickly learned about the websites and attempted to shut them down. However, some of Bad Girl's new websites were in the United States and it would take days for the police to get those sites closed. The police moved quickly, hit two of the gang's locations, and arrested the hackers. It did not take long for the police to determine where Bad Girl was working from because her amateur gang fell apart fast. As the police moved to arrest Bad Girl, she was walking out of a run-down apartment building in Tokyo. She had three guns and started shooting at the approaching police officers. The police returned fire and shot and killed her and two of her cyber-gang. The media quickly jumped on the scandal.

Day 22: Santa Claus Hits

Monday, December 24, 2001. Christmas Eve. High-Tech Tonya's Merry Christmas virus hit was sent out to more than 100,000 email addresses. She had set up several slave programs to send the emails from numerous web-based email services starting about 1:00 A.M. Christmas Eve morning, Tonya's Merry Christmas virus was waiting to spread by the time mom or dad said to the kids, "Let's see if you got an email from Santa Claus." As tens of thousands of kids and parents were checking their Santa Claus email, Tonya smiled with her own version of Christmas joy. The virus did its work as soon as the Santa message was opened: a photo of Santa and a group of naked female and male elves hit monitors across the United States.

The virus program then locked the keyboard so the computer had to be switched off to clear the screen. The virus then changed the phone number that the modem dialed to connect to the Internet. If the computer was not turned off immediately, it was disconnected from the Internet and reconnected, but this time the number that was dialed was 911. If the computer was shut down before it could redial, the next time it was turned on and connected to the Internet the modem dialed 911. At the bottom-right corner of the Santa Claus and naked elves graphic, there was a greeting: "Merry Christmas from the PH2 team." The next time the computer was connected to the Internet and the email program was activated, the virus sent itself to all of the addresses in the email address book. Oh, the horror of it all!

Day 23: Merry Christmas

Tuesday, December 25, 2001. Christmas Day. Except for High-Tech Tonya who remained at large, all of the PH2 team had either been killed or captured. The delays in business operations, stock trading, the theft of credit card and debit card numbers, and the damage and lost productivity caused by a series of virus attacks had resulted in hundreds of billions of dollars in economic impact. One newspaper headline read "The Trillion Dollar Cyberwar."

The Aftermath of Information Warfare Attacks

The PH2 scenario illustrates many potential aspects of information warfare attacks. It is important to understand that any of the information warfare strategies examined in Chapter 1 can utilize tactics similar to those of the terrorists in the PH2 scenario. Military organizations, terrorists, and rogues can all use similar tactics, and the key differences to how they may approach information warfare is far more philosophical than it is tactical. Several conclusions can be drawn from the PH2 scenario, including:

► Because of the international nature of information warfare, existing political structures are not prepared to immediately investigate the source of attacks and to appropriately respond to and counter information warfare scenarios.

► It is not likely that all governments will equally participate or cooperate in the investigation of information warfare attacks or that they will work together to halt attacks.

► Skilled information technology professionals can readily turn to rogue activities or join terrorist groups.

► There are threats from inside organizations if information technology and communications workers are alienated or have criminal orientations. The shortage of skilled information technology professionals around the world adds to the potential for some people having ulterior motives for working in the profession.

► The work of information technology professionals is increasingly being done from remote locations outside organization facilities, which can make entry into systems easier to accomplish.

► Although the impact of some information warfare tactics will be felt immediately, other tactics will leave a longer-lasting impact, including the alteration of records and corruption of databases.

► Information warfare attacks can effectively impact the economies of a nation or region without destroying infrastructures or disabling military capabilities.

▶ In the event that information warfare attacks are widespread and there are many groups operating simultaneously with different motives and different targets, it may be difficult to determine which activities are related.

▶ Information warfare attacks can be virtual—that is, accomplished through remote electronic connections—as well as physical, including the destruction of communications facilities.

▶ As in other types of warfare, information warfare has political, military, social, economic, and psychological aspects.

Chapters 4 though 9 provide a more technical review of information tactics and how organizations can defend their information technology infrastructures and the integrity of their information processing activities.

Chapter 4

Preparing to Fight Against Major Threats

To defend and fight against large-scale threats to the information technology infrastructure, there will need to be a high level of cooperation between national governments around the world, between governments within a country, between agencies within governments, and among industry groups and individual corporations. To ensure that there is the capability to deploy offensive information warfare strategies and to maintain this capability as a deterrent are equally important. To prepare to defend or to attack requires an assessment of the capabilities and experiences of governments, militaryunits, industry, and terrorist and criminal groups.

The process of assessment and evaluation involves:

▶ Assessing the level of preparedness to counter or launch information warfare attacks within the United States.

▶ Assessing the level of preparedness of other countries to counter or launch attacks.

▶ Assessing which countries are most likely to support information warfare activities in the future.

▶ Assessing the information warfare capabilities of terrorist and criminal groups.

▶ Assessing the defensive and offensive information warfare capabilities of industry groups.

▶ Assessing the readiness and preparing the diplomatic corps to respond in attack situations.

▶ Assessing the capabilities and preparedness of military alliances to launch or counter attacks.

▶ Addressing the martial law powers of civilian law enforcement agencies and military units to patrol or halt activity on the Internet and other communications systems in the event of information warfare.

▶ Establishing a super cyberspace patrol to monitor activities on the Internet and intervene when national security is at risk.

It is important to note that the assessment of information warfare capabilities requires the disclosure of confidential as well as top-secret information. The framework set forth in this chapter provides policy makers and industry leaders as well as warfare planners with a method to organize the information necessary to conduct an assessment. It is not possible for the author to actually conduct the assessment without access to this carefully guarded information, but the framework is designed to provide a reasonable starting point for those with access. It is also a means of structuring information that policy makers or industry executives need to have access to in order to conduct a thorough assessment.

It is also important to recognize that no single organization in the world has enough resources and a long enough political reach to fight information warfare attacks in a single-handed manner. The fantasy top-secret organizations that are portrayed in *La Femme Nikita* and other popular media are just that, a fantasy. Counterespionage organizations certainly do exist, but they do not have the vast resources and political support that pulp writers like to ascribe to them. Policing the world against terror is in fact a rather dull and bureaucratic process and although done fairly well, it will always take extraordinary efforts for the good guys to track down the bad guys and either eliminate them or bring them before the justice system.

This chapter addresses the basic principles of assessing global capabilities to defend against information warfare attacks in the most rapid and effective manner. This has many challenges built into it that will make the building of a global infrastructure to defend against information warfare a long and complicated process. These challenges are analyzed and an agenda for action is established.

Assessing the Preparedness for Information Warfare in the United States

The question of preparedness is threefold. First, preparedness and capabilities for defensive information warfare strategy need to be addressed. This includes defensive preventive information warfare, defensive ruinous information warfare, and defensive responsive containment information warfare strategies. Second, preparedness and capabilities for offensive information warfare—including offensive ruinous and offensive containment strategies—need to be assessed from a different perspective. Third, the capabilities and preparedness to conduct covert operations such as those used in terrorist and rogue information warfare strategies, in the event that they could contribute to national security, also need to be evaluated.

The question of the level of preparedness of the U.S. government to deal with information warfare attacks can be answered in several ways. First, the U.S. government, including all military and civilian law enforcement organizations, is more prepared to deal with information warfare attacks than in the past. Second, the abilities of the United States to counter attacks have never been thoroughly tested and thus cannot be definitely judged. Add to this a rapidly expanding technology arena and increasing technological capabilities of countries and organizations that are capable of information warfare or likely to use information warfare strategies, and you have a situation in which the United States faces a constant struggle in developing information warfare defensive capabilities.

Conducting a thorough assessment of the defensive information warfare capabilities of the United States is probably impossible. There are two primary reasons for this. First, the government tends to obfuscate. This is true from the smallest agency to the largest department and from the executive branch to Capitol Hill. This makes it difficult to determine the activities of both civilian government and military organizations and what levels of capability have in fact really been achieved. Second, the fragmented organizational approach that is inherent in the military and in government agencies creates an atmosphere that often results in duplication of effort and a lack of cooperative relationships between government agencies and military units.

This obfuscation and fragmentation both serve a purpose and act as a hindrance. The obfuscation, other than when used for political convenience, aids national security efforts. It is simply foolish to reveal what does not need to be revealed about military capabilities. Although potentially beneficial for national security, obfuscation makes it difficult to conduct a realistic assessment of capabilities. The fragmentation of military and civilian efforts serves to make organizational units more anonymous and focused on their independent mission. It also prevents any one agency or military unit from gaining illegitimate power and control over resources, government operations, and the populace. On the other hand, fragmentation often hinders cooperation among units that have similar capabilities and can result in overlap of activity and perhaps even contradictory behavior on the part of different agencies or military units.

There is some public information available about the information warfare activities of the U.S. military. However, details are very scant. The following list shows known U.S. military units that have direct responsibilities for information warfare activities:

- ► Air Force Information Warfare Center

- ► Air Force Computer Emergency Response Team (AFCERT)

- ► Air Force Research Laboratory Information Directorate

- ► Air Intelligence Agency

- ► Army Research Lab

- C4ISR Cooperative Research Program
- Defense Advanced Research Projects Agency
- Defense Information Agency Center for Automated Systems Security Incident Support Team (ASSIST)
- Defense Information Systems Agency's Center for Information Systems Security
- Defense Security Service (DSS) Academy
- Defense Science Board
- Director of Information Systems for Command, Control, Communications, and Computers
- Directorate of Combat Developments
- Global Command and Control System
- Joint Advanced Distributed Simulation – Joint Task Force
- Marine Corps Warfighting Laboratory
- National Defense University
- National Infrastructure Protection Center
- National Security Agency
- Naval Air Warfare Center Weapons Division—Information Warfare Division
- Naval Surface Warfare Center
- PACAF Regional Information Protection Center
- Simulation, Training, and Instrumentation Command (STRICOM)
- Soldier Systems Center
- Space and Naval Warfare Systems Command
- United States Army Intelligence and Security Command
- USAF Information Warfare Battlelab
- Warfighter Training Research Division
- Warrior Preparation Center

How to Inventory Information Warfare Capabilities

A thorough inventory of the information warfare capabilities of the United States would serve to help guide policy makers on organization and funding issues. In this case "thorough" means the identification of all civilian, military, and intelligence agency capabilities in information warfare. However, just as such an inventory would serve as a guide for policy makers, it would also serve as a guide for any nation or organization that is interested in attacking the information infrastructure of the United States. Thus a thorough inventory would be both a blessing and an extreme curse. It is also important to differentiate between an admitted inventory and a thorough inventory. Many things go on in the U.S. government that few people know about and it is not likely any time soon that a thorough inventory will or could be accomplished.

Even if there has been a comprehensive inventory of the defensive and offensive information warfare capabilities of the United States, it probably needs to be conducted again because of the many shifts in organization structure and continuous changes in technology. In the event that a responsible party could facilitate an inventory, the following principles should be applied to the process:

▸ An inventory needs to be updated frequently enough to keep up with changes in organization structure and technology.

▸ An inventory must cover all organization units in the government, regardless of which agency or military unit they are part of, that have a direct role in either defensive or offensive information warfare strategies. (A direct role means that the agency's or unit's primary or major responsibility is information warfare.)

▸ An inventory must also cover the information warfare capabilities of major military commands, civilian organizations, and intelligence agencies that have indirect roles in either defensive or offensive strategies. (An indirect role means that the agency or unit has some responsibility to conduct or prevent information warfare.)

▸ An inventory must cover personnel, including staffing patterns and training levels of all military, civilian, and intelligence workers who have direct or indirect responsibility for information warfare activities.

▶ An inventory must include the technological capabilities of all organizational units with direct or indirect responsibility for information warfare and should include computers, communications, and software and how these technologies are currently used and may be used in the future.

▶ An inventory must classify organizations, personnel, and technological capabilities in how they will or can work in the face of the ten types of information warfare strategies shown in Table 4-1.

The inventory process is a long and tedious task. Table 4-1 shows how information warfare capabilities could be illustrated in an organized fashion covering the major inventory points. The inventory process involves profiling the agency or the military unit by type of information warfare strategy that they are capable of dealing with, how they are staffed, and their technological capabilities.

Table 4-1: Inventory Sheet for Information Warfare Capabilities of the United States

Type	Agency/Unit Name and Responsibility	Staffing Level	Technological Capability
Offensive ruinous			
Offensive containment			
Sustained terrorist			
Random terrorist			
Defensive preventive			
Defensive ruinous			
Defensive responsive containment			
Sustained rogue			
Random rogue			
Amateur rogue			

How to Assess Information Warfare Capabilities

Once inventoried, the process of assessing information warfare capabilities presents another challenge to both policy makers and war planners. There have been decades of experience, and in some cases centuries of experience, in assessing traditional warfare capabilities. In many warfare situations, assessments have been reasonably accurate and beneficial and have resulted in successful warfare efforts. Assessments made during World War II and the Gulf War provided a high degree of success in mounting military campaigns. However, there have also been cases when assessments have been inaccurate, including, in the opinion of many, the Vietnam War and the fighting in Afghanistan. The value of any assessment is largely dependent on what is known about an enemy's capability and motivation and what it will take, from a military perspective, to achieve military or political goals when facing that enemy. Lack of this information is what makes assessing information warfare capabilities so difficult.

However, an assessment must have a starting point. The key factors to include in an assessment of civilian agencies, military units, or intelligence organizations are the type of information warfare engagements in which they have participated and the outcome of those engagements. Table 4-2 shows how this information could be illustrated. Again, the assessment needs to be completed by the type of information warfare activities that each agency or unit has had experience in and what the outcome of those experiences was.

Table 4-2: Assessment Sheet for Information Warfare Experiences

Type	Agency/Unit	Engagements	Outcomes
Offensive ruinous			
Offensive containment			
Sustained terrorist			
Random terrorist			
Defensive preventive			
Defensive ruinous			
Defensive responsive containment			
Sustained rogue			
Random rogue			
Amateur rogue			

A second approach in assessing capabilities is to evaluate what civilian agencies, military units, or intelligence organizations by the type of information warfare simulations or war games in which they have participated. Table 4-3 shows how this information could be illustrated. Each agency or unit needs to be assessed on their participation in exercises or simulations of information warfare by strategy. How well they did in any of these events should be noted.

Table 4-3: Assessment Sheet for Information Warfare Exercise Outcomes

Type	Agency/Unit	Simulation or War Game Participation	Outcomes
Offensive ruinous			
Offensive containment			
Sustained terrorist			
Random terrorist			
Defensive preventive			
Defensive ruinous			
Defensive responsive containment			
Sustained rogue			
Random rogue			
Amateur rogue			

Assessing the Preparedness for Information Warfare of Other Governments

It is prudent to determine which countries are the most prepared and mostly likely to participate in information warfare activities. The same inventory and assessment approaches that can be applied to the United States can also be applied to other countries. This includes an inventory of information warfare capabilities as shown previously in Table 4-1, an assessment of information warfare experiences as shown in Table 4-2, and an assessment of exercise outcomes as shown in Table 4-3.

The countries that are the most capable of mounting strategies which are military-centric (including defensive preventive, defensive ruinous, defensive responsive containment, offensive ruinous, and offensive containment strategies) are allied to the United States. It is not likely that these countries will launch information warfare attacks against the United States—or each other, for that matter. For those inside the military or intelligence complex, these countries are relatively easy to assess because of ongoing military and political relations.

The countries that may be less capable of launching sustained information warfare attacks, at this time, may be the countries that are the most likely to launch such attacks in the future. Many of the countries that have often been classified as terrorist states probably fit such a description. These countries are also the most likely to launch or support random terrorist or rogue criminal information warfare activities. Thus, it is important to go beyond the inventory and assessment approaches previously discussed and add an assessment of motivations and probability that a country would either launch or support information warfare attacks. Table 4-4 shows how the probability of information warfare participation could be illustrated.

A high motivation ranking means that there are recognizable economic, political, or military reasons why a country would participate in or support information warfare attacks. A high probability ranking means that a country is likely to participate in or support information warfare attacks.

Table 4-4: Assessment of Probability of Participation in Information Warfare

Type	Country	Motivation Ranking	Probability Ranking
Offensive ruinous			
Offensive containment			
Sustained terrorist			
Random terrorist			
Defensive preventive			
Defensive ruinous			
Defensive responsive containment			
Sustained rogue			
Random rogue			
Amateur rogue			

Another important evaluation that should be conducted of nations around the world is their willingness to sell technology and provide information warfare training to terrorist groups or criminal organizations. Those countries that have supplied other materials or training to terrorist groups or criminal organizations in the past will likely be willing to sell computers, software, and communications access just as readily as they are willing to supply guns and explosives. Table 4-5 shows a grid that can illustrate the probability that a country can and will support random or sustained terrorist information warfare, random or sustained rogue information warfare, or amateur rogue information warfare activities.

Table 4-5: Assessment of Probability of Supporting Information Warfare

Country	Previous Terrorist and Criminal Support Activities	Access to Computers, Software, and Communications	Probability Ranking

Assessing the Preparedness for Information Warfare of Terrorists and Criminals

One of the major points made in Chapter 1 and illustrated in other chapters in this book is that information warfare strategies can be used by a wide variety of organizations. This includes terrorist and rogue criminals. It is critical to start coming to grips with this threat and to conduct thorough inventory and assessment of the information warfare capabilities of terrorist and criminal groups. It is again prudent to determine which terrorist groups or organizations and which criminal organizations are the most prepared and mostly likely to participate in information warfare activities.

An inventory and assessment approach similar to that applied to the United States and other countries can be used to evaluate terrorists and criminals. This includes an inventory of information warfare capabilities as shown previously in Table 4-1, except it would be terrorist groups or criminal organizations that are being examined rather than government agencies or military units. The assessment of information warfare experiences shown in Table 4-2 can also be applied to terrorist groups or criminal organizations. The assessment of information warfare exercise outcomes shown in Table 4-3 probably does not apply to terrorist groups or criminal organizations. However, the probability assessment of participation in information warfare shown in Table 4-4 should also be applied to terrorist groups or criminal organizations.

The process of evaluating a nation's willingness to sell computer technology, software, and communications access or to provide information warfare training to terrorist groups or criminal organizations can be reverse-engineered to provide another assessment technique. In this assessment, the relationship of the terrorist groups or criminal organizations with countries that have supplied such groups in the past is very important. This is especially true in countries that have started to import and sell larger quantities of computer technology. Many countries are doing so under the guise of proliferating Internet activity. A method of illustrating an assessment of the probability of supporting information warfare is shown in Table 4-6.

Table 4-6: Assessment of Probability of Supporting Information Warfare

Terrorist or Criminal Group	Country from Which Support Was Provided in the Past	Availability of Computers, Software, and Communications in the Country	Probability Ranking

Assessing the Preparedness for Information Warfare of Industry Groups

An assessment of the preparedness of industry groups to deal with information warfare attacks similar to those conducted for nations is a necessary element in determining vulnerability to attacks. Although there is considerable overlap in the approaches, this assessment differs from the assessment of civilian law enforcement and military units in several ways. In this assessment, the incidents and experiences of various industry groups needs to be cataloged along with the outcomes or results of their efforts in defending against or conducting information warfare activities.

All of this information is highly sensitive and is likely to be held confidential by all of the companies that could provide the information to the assessing organization. There have certainly been news stories in the past about banks being hacked or attempts to extract funds from a bank using a variety of illicit methods. Defense contractors have also been targets of attacks of various types. Table 4-7 shows how to illustrate the industry group experience and outcomes of previous information warfare activities. Incidents should be summarized, and the outcomes or final consequences of each event should be noted for each of the information warfare strategies in the left column.

Table 4-7: Assessment Sheet for Information Warfare Experience of Industry Groups

Type	Industry Group (Such as Banking)	Incidents and Experience (Defensive and Offensive)	Outcomes
Offensive ruinous			
Offensive containment			
Sustained terrorist			
Random terrorist			
Defensive preventive			
Defensive ruinous			
Defensive responsive containment			
Sustained rogue			
Random rogue			
Amateur rogue			

The experience levels of each industry sector are likely to be very different from each other. Banks have been fighting off robbers ever since there have been banks and certainly will have a different set of experience than will the retail distribution sector. Similarly, aerospace firms and other defense contractors have their own unique set of experiences.

From a policy making and planning perspective, it is important to understand how the sectors differ and why one sector may be more vulnerable than another sector in the event of information warfare attacks. This information is also helpful when planning offensive information warfare actions because it can help attack forces understand where there are weaknesses and how to best exploit those weaknesses.

Traditional Diplomacy and Information Warfare

Traditional diplomacy should never be underrated. It is not perfect, but it has been a valuable asset for countries and organizations that know how to use it. Information warfare presents several new challenges for the diplomat. The first challenge is to develop an understanding of strategies, who can use them, and who is likely to use these strategies for political, military, or financial gain. The second challenge is to preplan diplomatic actions and responses to information warfare attacks. The third challenge is speed of response. Information warfare attacks will come quickly, and they may very well be totally unanticipated. This all means that an assessment must be conducted as to the preparedness of diplomacy organizations to deal with information warfare and to take steps to train diplomats to respond before an attack happens.

The process of assessment for diplomatic organizations is more internal than external. The major challenges that diplomats face are outlined in the following paragraphs. It is important to understand that the diplomatic process stands in tradition. It is necessary that the ability to deal with information warfare attacks be addressed, not by adding more processes, but rather by maximizing existing processes and diplomatic relationships to respond during attacks. This maximization is what will provide the most benefit during an information warfare attack.

Meeting the first challenge of educating the diplomatic corps is well underway. The U.S. Department of State is well aware of the information warfare threat, as are the diplomatic departments of the top industrial nations. However, the extent of knowledge of the average diplomat and the staffs of embassies and consulates around the world remains questionable. Information warfare does not change the diplomatic process. The goal is to ensure that the diplomatic process can respond in a well-balanced and well-informed manner attacks or incidents.

Information warfare strategies are tools and weapons just like other tools and weapons, and those who benefit from using the strategies will use them. It is only a matter of time. Thus, education of diplomats needs to move ahead in a uniform structured manner, and it is important that diplomats around the world are educated in information warfare just as they have been in traditional warfare methods.

The second challenge of preplanning diplomatic actions and responses to information warfare attacks most likely lags behind the basic educational process. This is because information warfare has not yet been widely practiced. It is important to move ahead on this front for several reasons. First, those countries that are the most capable of launching information warfare attacks at this time are strong allies and do not really pose a serious threat to each other. Second, those countries that are most likely to participate in information warfare attacks or support terrorist or criminal groups who use information warfare strategies are also likely to resist or not respond to traditional diplomatic efforts. The best way to work through the preparation of diplomatic responses is through scenario development and simulations.

The information warfare attack scenario in Chapter 3 was deliberately presented with unknowns. There were people from numerous countries involved and the source of the attacks and the nature of the attackers was not readily apparent. This realistically depicts the likely character of such attacks. In the event that the PH2 attack scenario is implemented, the diplomatic corps will play a key role in responding and soliciting the assistance of nations around the world. An understanding of information warfare combined with planned actions on the part of diplomats will better enable them to fulfill this very critical role in the event of information warfare.

The challenge of speed of response in dealing with information warfare attacks is one of the biggest obstacles that diplomats face. If they are to fulfill the role of soliciting and gaining cooperation from other countries they must act immediately in order to reduce the potential damage of attacks. This need is tied into the basic education of diplomats and their understanding of what they must do when they must do it. There will be no time to brief and train diplomats when the attacks occur. Their rapid response will help locate the people responsible for the attacks and stop information warfare attacks before they cause excessive damage.

The Role of International Organizations

There are many possible roles for international organizations in mitigating and responding to information warfare attacks. Unfortunately, most international organizations with any real political clout are bogged down in dealing with more immediate issues such as human rights, hunger, and health. Obviously, these issues need to be addressed on a global basis, and it is important that those organizations that are best equipped to deal with such issues continue to do so. It does, however, leave a bit of a void at the international level, and there does not seem to be any relief in sight. In addition, international organizations such as the United Nations tend to deal with events after they happen or get involved in events that are prolonged or long-lasting in nature. Information warfare must be dealt with ahead of time because the potential of economic damage or disruption is so high.

An October 1998 press release from the United Nations indicates that information warfare and other new forms of warfare are issues that the organization should address. The United Nations has been dealing with issues of computer crime since the middle of the 1990s, and to a limited extent, has started addressing the use of computers by terrorists and criminals. The Council of Europe has taken little action except to suggest the Organization for Economic Cooperation and Development (OECD) address the issue, and in turn the OECD has taken little action. Similarly, the European Union (EU), which is also wrapped up in more current issues, has taken little if any action regarding information warfare.

Overall, it is doubtful that these organizations or any other international political body can actually do anything to stop information warfare attacks. What they can do and should do is to set the stage for cooperation during information warfare attacks. This could include requiring member states to cooperate and provide assistance to help track down sources of attacks or individuals responsible for attacks. However, to be effective, this position must be taken well before information warfare attacks occur, not after. The first goal needs to be to stop information warfare attacks, not help apprehend perpetrators after the fact. Apprehension of individuals after attacks certainly will be helpful, but only in serving justice, not stopping attacks in progress.

One of the big issues that any lobbying country will face in such international organizations is how to set parameters for cooperation and intervention. The ideal situation is that allied forces are allowed to deploy information warriors or expeditionary forces within a country to track down information system attackers and halt their activity. This is especially true for countries that have a limited police force or organized military capable of dealing with information warfare attacks. The likelihood of any country surrendering their sovereignty in such a manner is not very high. However, it is best that the international organizations encourage these countries to cooperate so interventions can be smoothly executed and heavy-handed military action can be avoided.

If severe responses are required—for example, if defensive responsive containment information warfare or defensive ruinous information warfare strategy needs to be implemented—it is likely that there would be damage or disruption to a host nation's communications infrastructure. This will occur because it is necessary to stop the actions of information warriors who are attacking systems from afar and to conduct such attacks requires access to communications. Unless there is cooperation from a host country, information warriors have few choices. The first choice is to knock out all communications channels, either virtually or physically. The second choice is to locate and physically eliminate information system attackers either with ground forces or through precision bombing. In either case, there could be damage to physical property, disruption of communications and commerce, or perhaps the death of innocent local residents. Overall, it would be best if international organizations address the issues of cooperation and access prior to the time either is necessary.

The Role of the Global Military Alliances

Cooperation among global military alliances is absolutely essential to defend against information warfare attacks of all types. There are numerous alliances in place that have provided mutual support to alliance members during various conflicts that have taken place since the end of World War II. It is necessary to assess the ability of each alliance to determine the level of preparedness to counter information warfare attacks. The obvious organizations on which to focus assessment efforts include the North Atlantic Treaty Organization (NATO), its operational headquarters, the Supreme Headquarters Allied Powers Europe (SHAPE), and the various subcommands of NATO. Commands include the Supreme Allied Commander Europe (SACEUR) and the Supreme Allied Commander Atlantic (SACLANT), which are responsible for the overall direction and conduct of all alliance military matters within their areas of command. Regional commands also need to be assessed, including Allied Forces North Europe—RHQ AFNORTH and Allied Forces South Europe—RHQ AFSOUTH.

NATO members include Belgium, Canada, the Czech Republic, Denmark, France, Germany, Greece, Hungary, Iceland, Italy, Luxembourg, the Netherlands, Norway, Poland, Portugal, Spain, Turkey, the United Kingdom, and the United States. NATO partner countries include Albania, Armenia, Austria, Azerbaijan, Belarus, Bulgaria, Croatia, Estonia, Finland, Georgia, Ireland, Kazakhstan, the Kyrghyz Republic, Latvia, Lithuania, Moldova, Romania, Russia, Slovakia, Slovenia, Sweden, Switzerland, the former Yugoslav Republic of Macedonia, Tajikistan, Turkmenistan, Ukraine, and Uzbekistan. There are several other less glamorous alliances around the world that should also be assessed. These include pacts between and among the United States, Japan, Australia, Israel, and numerous other countries that have standing military forces.

Much of the information necessary to accomplish this assessment would be gained through the previously proposed assessment of the preparedness for information warfare of other governments. The same inventory and assessment approaches that were recommended for the United States were also recommended for use in assessing other countries. This includes an inventory of information warfare capabilities as shown previously in Table 4-1, an assessment of information warfare experiences as shown in Table 4-2, and an assessment of information warfare exercise outcomes as shown in Table 4-3.

However, it is important to take the country assessments up to the military alliance level and determine how prepared the alliance is as an operational entity. Once the country data has been compiled, it needs to be aggregated in a manner that accurately reflects the level of integration of country capabilities into the command structures of military alliances. Key questions to address at the command level include:

▶ Has the alliance command designated specific officers to be responsible for information warfare?

▶ Has the alliance command integrated information warfare strategies into its long-term war planning efforts?

▶ Does the alliance have tactical information warfare capabilities?

▶ Have alliance officers been trained in information warfare strategies?

▶ Does the alliance have standing liaisons with the military information warfare units of member countries?

▶ Has the alliance participated in information warfare exercises, and if so, what were the outcomes?

The role of military alliances in information warfare will depend on the ability of the alliance command to launch or defend against attacks. Until a thorough assessment is conducted, these capabilities will remain unclear. However, it is obvious that alliances are dependent on their member states to provide military capability. The most important thing that the command of any alliance can do is to understand the resources that member states can provide and be able to facilitate proper and expedient use of their capabilities.

Martial Law and Cyberspace

Comprehensive legislation to provide civilian law enforcement agencies and military units with the ability to declare martial law in cyberspace does not yet exist. It also appears that any effort to regulate activity on the Internet will cause an uproar. For example, there has been considerable controversy over the efforts of the Federal Bureau of Investigation (FBI) to use Carnivore, an electronic spy tool to monitor electronic mail. However, the Internet Fraud Complaint Center (IFCC) formed by the FBI and the National White Collar Crime Center (NW3C) to aid and protect consumers from being ripped off on the Internet has met little resistance.

The National Infrastructure Protection Center (NIPC) and the National Domestic Preparedness Office (NDPO), operated by the Counterterrorism Division of the FBI, have also been fairly well received. The NIPC serves as the U.S. government's focal point for threat assessment, warning, investigation, and response for threats or attacks against critical infrastructures. The NDPO coordinates federal efforts to assist state and local first responders with planning, training, and equipment necessary to respond to a conventional or unconventional weapons of mass destruction incident.

The U.S. Federal Trade Commission's (FTC) Internet lab was established to provide agency lawyers and investigators with tools to investigate high-tech consumer problems. The lab allows investigators to search for fraud and deception on the Internet in a secure environment and also provides FTC staff with the necessary equipment to preserve evidence for presentation in court by capturing information from websites that quickly come and go. The FTC lab has worked on hundreds of cases and has developed a reasonably sound reputation for its work. Fortunately, the FTC lab has not met with any resistance to its work.

At the Securities and Exchange Commission (SEC), the Division of Enforcement and the Office of Investor Education and Assistance support the SEC Complaint Center to help address Internet fraud issues. The investigations of the SEC have benefited the public and the investment community. The Complaint Center has investigated hundreds of complaints about Internet fraud and illegal activity in the securities field. The establishment of this center has also met little resistance.

These examples show that under circumstances acceptable to legislators and the general public, the government can and does monitor and regulate activity on the Internet. Furthermore, the U.S. government and the military have fairly broad power during wartime to preempt the use of transportation systems, including the railroad and civilian aircraft when necessary to support a war effort and protect national security. This takes us to the question as to the nature of the Internet and whether or not the government will indeed be able to exercise broad powers to circumvent the use of the Internet and other communications systems in the event of an information warfare attack.

The logical answer is that in the event of information warfare attacks civilian law enforcement agencies and military units could stop some or all activity on the Internet, at least within the United States, in order to slow or hinder attacks. However, there is a certain passion about the Internet that is only beginning to subside. The work of the FBI, FTC, and SEC shows that law enforcement efforts in cyberspace can benefit the citizenry. But so far those actions have been limited and targeted to relatively obvious offenders.

Ultimately, there will have to be a public policy decision on how civilian law enforcement agencies and military units can work on the Internet in the event of information warfare attacks. Generally speaking, when national security is at risk, freedom is compromised. This has been demonstrated numerous times in the past. In World War II, for example, many people of foreign birth were detained and incarcerated in the name of national security. Right or wrong, it was clearly a decision where national security took precedent over individual freedom. In the case of civil aviation security personal, freedom to move weapons on commercial airlines is curtailed for the security of all people using the civil aviation system.

These precedents are yet to be tested when it comes to freedom on the Internet and other communications systems. However, to be fully prepared to counter information warfare attacks, governments have little choice but to curtail activity on the Internet. It is a reality that cannot be denied, and it is an action that inevitably must be taken to deal with information warfare threats.

The Super Cyber Protection Agency

The prospect of establishing a super cyberspace patrol to monitor activities on the Internet and intervene when national security is at risk is a political hot potato. Many people view the Internet as a sacred ground of freedom and will resist government intervention whenever possible. As much as passion may reign over this prospect, it is important that national and international security win out. The FTC, FBI, and SEC already patrol cyberspace for reasons previously stated. In addition, local and regional law enforcement agencies work in cyberspace in their hunt for child pornographers and other criminals. It is inevitable that a super cyber protection agency emerge.

Once the arguments have been made and the political battles fought about the cyber patrol, the questions that remain are, "What should a super cyber protection agency be like, and what powers will it have?" Most likely there will emerge a joint task force or project comprised of members of various civilian law enforcement agencies from several countries as well as members of military units from major alliances around the world. It is likely that many of these organizations are already on patrol, but have little codified power to take drastic action.

The establishment of the super cyber patrol force will need to address several issues, including the following:

- Which governmental units will be authorized to participate in the patrol of cyberspace?

- How will the agencies work together and share information?

- What kind of information will they be able to share?

- What powers of investigation and arrest will the patrol have?

- Under what conditions will the patrol be able to control access to the Internet?

- What will be the extent of the patrol's power and under what conditions will the patrol be able to exercise those powers?

Preparation from a Global Viewpoint

Preparation for information warfare needs to be put into a global context. There are several principles of modern civilization that can be extended to dealing with information warfare threats. From a military point of view, there is already a structure in place for international cooperation through military alliances and various treaties that govern the action of military alliances. There is also a custom of joint military operations that has been maintained and exercised by NATO and the United Nations. When joint action is required to keep the peace or to deal with international threats, nations cooperate and deploy military forces under a single command to address the crisis at hand.

In the commercial arena, there are also several precedents. Treaties as well as customs govern the international waters of the high seas. When maritime disasters strike, nations cooperate to rescue ships, fight piracy, and maintain safety in international shipping lanes. There are also treaties that address the use of international airspace and how and why that airspace is used. Again, in the event of air disaster, nations cooperate to rescue victims and ensure safety in air travel. In the case of natural disasters, nations cooperate by providing aid and assistance in the form of medical supplies, food, clothing, emergency shelters, and reconstruction funds.

These precedents in international cooperation are applicable to cyberspace. In each of these examples, the events that are beyond the control or jurisdiction of a single nation are responded to in a joint and cooperative manner by nations around the world. This level of cooperation and the customary approach to such cooperation is a necessary part of the foundation of global coexistence.

Cyberspace is beyond the control and jurisdiction of any single country. This means that international cooperation is the only workable solution to the patrol of cyberspace and a uniform and thorough response to information warfare attacks. No nation will be able to stand alone, and all nations are at risk if rogue states, terrorist groups, or criminal gangs are left free to wreak havoc in cyberspace. The global economy is interlocked. The peace of the world is dependent on a mutual view that peace is necessary and that war is detrimental. These principles and the process by which they are implemented, maintained, and exercised must be extended to the new frontier of cyberspace.

Conclusions and an Agenda for Action

Preparing for information warfare will take considerable time and effort and require substantial human and financial resources. The work of policy makers, military planners, and private sector security organizations will need to be highly coordinated in order to be successful in defending against information warfare attacks. In addition, to use information warfare capabilities as a deterrent will require that allied computer-dependent nations also cooperate.

Conclusions on Defensive Strategies for Governments and Industry Groups

It is important to achieve a comprehensive high-level understanding of the major building blocks in and obstacles to building sound and sustainable defensive strategies to counter information warfare attacks. The following conclusions are based on the analysis in this chapter.

- ▶ It is difficult to assess the information warfare capabilities of the United States because facts are obfuscated and there is a lot of fragmentation across civilian law enforcement agencies that deal with warfare strategies.

- ▶ It is easier to assess the information warfare capabilities of allied countries that may share military information with the United States than it is to assess the information warfare capabilities of terrorists states, but it is advisable to conduct an in-depth assessment of information warfare capabilities around the world.

- ▶ In addition to assessing the information warfare capabilities of countries outside the major alliances, countries should be ranked regarding their motivations for participating in information warfare attacks as well as the probability that they will participate.

- ▶ It is important to monitor the information warfare capabilities of terrorists and criminals, as well as which countries may be supplying these groups with computer technology and access to communications.

- ▶ The experience of industry groups and how they defend against various types of attacks can provide insight into information warfare defensive and offensive tactics.

- The diplomat will play a key role in securing the cooperation of national governments around the world to respond to information warfare attacks.

- Cooperation among global military alliances is absolutely essential to defend against information warfare attacks of all types.

- Government policy about the use of the Internet for private and commercial purposes during information warfare attacks must be addressed in order to enable civilian law enforcement agencies and military units to halt attacks.

- A super cyberspace law enforcement agency could play an important role in countering information warfare attacks.

An Agenda for Action to Develop Defensive Strategies for Governments and Industry Groups

The U.S. government and governments around the world need to inventory and assess information warfare capabilities and set an agenda for improvement of capabilities and cooperative relationships among allied nations. Action steps should include, but not be limited to the following areas:

- The U.S. government should establish a process to secretly, thoroughly, and realistically inventory and assess its information warfare capabilities.

- Governments around the world should establish their own internal process to secretly, thoroughly, and realistically inventory and assess their information warfare capabilities.

- The United States, in conjunction with its strongest allies, should inventory and assess the information warfare capabilities of all nations, especially those who have supported terrorist or criminal activities in the past.

- The United States, in conjunction with global law enforcement partners, should monitor the development of information warfare capabilities by terrorist and criminal groups.

- The experience of various industry groups such as banking, finance, aerospace, and information technology should be cataloged to help determine patterns of attack and successful defensive and offensive strategies.

▶ Diplomats must be educated and briefed on information warfare so they can quickly respond and obtain the necessary cooperation of various governments to help stop information warfare attacks.

▶ The information warfare capabilities of military alliances should be assessed and proper training programs initiated to enhance the command's information warfare capabilities.

▶ Martial law powers of civilian law enforcement agencies and military units must be codified to enable these organizations to counter information warfare attacks.

▶ Consider the establishment of a super cyberspace patrol to monitor activities on the Internet and intervene when national security is at risk.

Chapter 5

Information Warfare Strategies and Tactics from a Military Perspective

Military organizations face major challenges in developing both defensive and offensive information warfare capabilities. However, military organizations also have opportunities to utilize new strategies and tactics that will be beneficial in future conflicts. Challenges include developing technologies that are defensible against attacks as well as learning how to attack information systems using a variety of strategies and tactics. In addition, military organizations must recruit and train computer-savvy personnel who are capable of working with information technology to create a combat advantage.

The concept and practice of information warfare is not new to military organizations. But unlike conventional weapons, even the most modern weapons, information technology evolves at a very rapid rate that requires constant retraining of personnel and constant reevaluation of strategies and tactics. This chapter examines military opportunities and tactics in the framework of the ten categories of information warfare strategies previously discussed. Each strategy requires different tactics and is bound by different political and diplomatic restrictions in which the military must operate.

The Context of Military Tactics

The key to developing successful military information warfare tactics is to understand how tactics can be used within various strategies and to ensure that individual tactics do not result in unintended and detrimental consequences. The growth of the Internet provides opportunities for more types of organizations and individuals to use information warfare strategies, but it is also a hindrance to aggressive military action because commercial and civilian use of the Internet sets the stage for widespread civilian casualties. In the case of information warfare, an analogy to precision bombing is appropriate. If the wrong targets are hit during bombardment, the military faces unwanted political and diplomatic consequences for the error. If military organizations use the Internet or other public communications infrastructures to launch attacks and damage is done to an innocent target, the military will face the same sort of response as they would if they had bombed civilians, elementary schools, or even foreign embassies.

The potential for error in information warfare, just as in any other type of warfare, must be addressed. Those military organizations that have the highest potential for severe political and diplomatic repercussions belong to the top industrial countries and the major military alliances. It has long been necessary for these military organizations to fight neat and tidy wars or face the onslaught of negative press and the often-resulting negative popular opinion and legislative backlash. On the other hand, rogue states, insurgents, terrorist, and criminals are seldom concerned about potential backlash or how the headlines of newspapers in industrial nations may read.

This in mind, the ten information strategies are analyzed to determine how and when the strategies may be the most effective. In addition, the difficulties in utilizing the strategies are examined, including costs, complexity, and potential unwanted consequences. The strategies are also examined from the perspective of the attacker and the defender.

It is important to understand that although the ten information warfare strategies are analyzed as independent warfare strategies it is likely that many of the ten strategies would be implemented in conjunction with other military actions. Even if a war effort was centered on an information warfare strategy there is still a requirement for numerous types of military activity outside the attack of information systems. Logistics support to move information warriors is essential, as are intelligence gathering and analysis, reconnaissance to measure results, and physical protection of military installations, warships, and aircraft that are utilized to launch the attack.

Offensive and Defensive Ruinous Information Warfare Strategies and Tactics

Offensive ruinous information warfare is an organized deliberate military effort to totally destroy the military information capabilities, industrial and manufacturing information infrastructure, and information technology-based civilian and government economic activities of a target nation, region, or population. This strategy is an all-out destructive effort without any restrictions or any desire to leave any infrastructure intact. When implementing the strategy, there is also no regard for human life or the interlocking economic, social, or political relationships that the target has with neighboring states.

A related strategy, defensive ruinous information warfare, is an organized deliberate military effort to totally destroy the military information technology capabilities, industrial and manufacturing information infrastructure, and information technology-based civilian and government economic activities of an aggressor nation, region, population, or military/terrorist force. The difference between the two ruinous strategies are that the offensive version would be implemented without provocation and used by an aggressor that feels that any political or economic consequences they faced are worth the outcome of the conflict. The defensive version is implemented as a response to the actions of an aggressor, but it is likely that the nation launching the defensive response will have the support of an alliance and be concerned about the interlocking economic, social, or political relationships that the aggressor has with neighboring states. In addition, there will also likely be some concern for human life and a desire on the part of the responding force to maintain a political and diplomatic decorum in their actions.

Complexity and Expense of Ruinous Information Warfare Strategies

To execute a totally successful ruinous information warfare strategy is a complex and expensive process. The complexity and expense are directly related to the size and the location of the target nation, region, or population. Achieving a successful military impact of a ruinous information warfare strategy is directly related to how dependent the target nation, region, or population is on communications and information systems. Table 5-1 shows the relationship between target characteristics, complexity and expense of the attack, and potential military outcomes.

Table 5-1: Complexity, Expense, and Potential Military Impact of Ruinous Information Warfare Attacks

Target Characteristics	Complexity and Expense	Potential Military Impact
Small nation, region, or population geographically close to attacker	Low	Low
Large nation, region, or population geographically close to attacker	High	High
Small nation, region, or population geographically far from attacker	Moderate	Low
Large nation, region, or population geographically far from attacker	High	High

If the target is a small nation, region, or population geographically close to the home or resource bases of an attacker, the complicity and cost of launching a ruinous information warfare attack is low. Because of the size of the target, the military impact is also likely to be low unless the target has strategic value related to other political, economic, or war efforts of the attacker. A small island nation, for example, is certainly dependent on communications as is any modern state, but is probably somewhat less dependent on computer systems with the exception of air and seaport traffic control and management. Thus it would be fairly easy to destroy the information and communications infrastructure because there is so little to destroy. There will also likely be little, if any, military defense capability in place. However, the military impact would also be low because there is likely to be little in the way of an organized military, and the small island state will likely have very little strategic value.

To launch a ruinous information warfare attack on a large nation, region, or population geographically close to the attacker has a higher level of complexity because of the size of the nation of a higher density of communications and computer systems. This in turn raises the costs because there are more systems that must be ruined in order to achieve success. The potential military impact is of course higher because of the likely dependence of such a nation on communications and computer systems. However, because of the technological and military sophistication of the nation is potential higher, attacks will be more difficult and counterstrikes are likely to be launched.

To launch a ruinous attack on a small nation, region, or population geographically far from the attacker would have moderate costs and complexity because of the distance that must bridged to ensure that an attack is successful. But, as with a small nation, region, or population geographically close to the home or resource bases of an attacker, the value of success will also likely be low. The exception is that the small nation, region, or population has other political, economic, or military value.

To launch a ruinous attack on a large nation, region, or population geographically far from the attacker will, as in all warfare, have high costs and be very complex. With few exceptions, larger nations, regardless of their distance from the attacker, are likely to have more complex and dense communications systems that are better protected than those of a small nation. In addition, the general defensive capabilities of a larger nation will be more sophisticated.

The Perspective of the Attacker in Ruinous Information Warfare

The perspective, resources, actions, and tactics of an attacker in a ruinous information warfare attack will depend on the circumstance of the engagement and the political role of the attackers. There are three primary perspectives or motivations of an attacker in ruinous information warfare strategies:

> ▶ The attacker is acting in an official military capacity and in the role of a provoked *legitimate retaliator* who is fighting against an aggressor nation, region, or population on behalf of their constituency or on behalf of an ally.

▶ The attacker is acting in an official military capacity and in the role of a *legitimate unprovoked aggressor* who targets a nation, region, or population on behalf of their constituency.

▶ The *illegitimate attacker* is not acting on behalf of any legitimate government that is diplomatically recognized, but is using the military capabilities and resources of a nation to launch an unprovoked attack against a nation, region, or population to pursue self-interest, mutiny, or revolution.

The legitimate retaliator who is retaliating against an aggressor on behalf of their constituency or on behalf of an ally has several advantages from a military, political, and economic perspective. These advantages would be equivalent to the same advantages that any military action would have regardless of the type of warfare strategies being utilized. The legitimate defender generally has the political support of a nation and any alliance of which the nation is a member. Resources will be relatively plentiful, and there will be cooperation among nations to halt the actions of an aggressor. All of the protocols and expectations of any type of warrior acting on behalf of the sponsoring nation or alliance will also bind the information warrior in this situation.

The legitimate unprovoked aggressor will have the support and resources of the nation on whose behalf the attack is being carried out. However, aggressors tend to have a limited number of allies and will get the support of only small alliances. Their resources will be more limited and without widespread economic and political support will have difficulty maintaining a ruinous attack. This does not mean that they will not be able to quickly cause considerable damage before there is a defensive responsive action. The aggressor in this scenario will probably ignore international protocol and may well cause damage to other nations or regions through the careless use of information warfare tools.

The illegitimate attacker who is not acting on behalf of any legitimate government, but is using the military capabilities and resources of a nation to launch an unprovoked ruinous information warfare attack is probably the most unpredictable information warrior that would dare utilize this strategy. They will act similar to a terrorist, but may have the political or economic support of one or more nations that would benefit from insurgency within a nation or the ruinous attack of another nation. However, the illegitimate attacker will also have very limited resources and will not be able to garner widespread support for their actions. They will also likely invoke a swift response on the part of alliances with an interest in a region or who have a generalized interest in world order.

The Perspective of the Defender in Ruinous Information Warfare

The perspective, resources, actions, and tactics of a defender in a ruinous information warfare attack are far narrower than that of the attacker. There are two primary information warrior perspectives or motivations for defenders in ruinous information warfare strategies:

- ▶ The information warrior is a *legitimate defender* and is acting in an official military defense capacity of a constituent nation or ally that is being attacked by an unprovoked aggressor.

- ▶ The information warrior is *defending the aggressor nation* against a retaliatory ruinous information warfare strategy to halt the actions of aggressor.

The legitimate defender protecting a constituent nation or ally that is being attacked by an unprovoked aggressor will be able to rally the support of an alliance of nations as well as the resources of private sector companies and public communications providers of the attacked state. They will be able to mobilize technical, political, and economic support that is available through government and commercial channels that could be negatively impacted by the ruinous attack. Working under stress, they may be granted considerable leeway in their interpretation of protocols providing they do not take actions that directly result in damage to their allies or innocent nations. They may not be able to completely stop attacks, but they will be able to gain support to sever communications links and temporally halt computing activities in the attacked nation or region. They will also have a broad base of diplomatic support and aid from allies to stop attacks or mount a counterattack against the aggressor.

The information warrior that is defending the aggressor nation against a retaliatory defensive ruinous information warfare attacks is at a severe disadvantage. They will have more limited support, supplies, and personnel than the retaliators who will most likely be an alliance of nations that can gain support from technology companies and communications providers. These defenders were most likely acting as attacking forces when the aggressor nation first launched a ruinous attack. They are probably more qualified as attackers than they are as defenders, and they will not be able to hold their ground over a long period of time without voluntarily isolating systems to prevent retaliators from gaining entry and damaging systems. They will end up in a long period of economic embargoes and political isolation.

Potential Unwanted Consequences of Ruinous Information Warfare

Being the victim of a ruinous information warfare attack will likely result in extensive economic damage as well as disruption of commerce, banking, and international trade. However, the nation, region, or population that is the target of a ruinous information warfare attack will probably not be the only victim. Any government or unofficial illegitimate attacker that would be foolish or desperate enough to attempt a ruinous information warfare attack will also be careless enough to do damage to innocent states that share communications resources or have some economic dependency on the attacked nation or region. Those who launch ruinous information warfare attacks are also likely to use self-replicating viruses and malicious code against their target, which will inevitably spread itself to other areas of the world.

Ruinous information warfare attacks will be designed to inflict the maximum damage in the shortest period of time. The most aggressive information warriors who launch ruinous information warfare attacks may also attempt to keep other nations from coming to the aid of their target. This means the attacker may use whatever means they can think of to slow down the response of allies or major global alliances who will act to halt the attack or are likely to participate in retaliatory attacks of some type.

Offensive and Responsive Containment Information Warfare Strategies and Tactics

Offensive containment information warfare is an organized deliberate military effort to cripple or disable military information capabilities, halt industrial and manufacturing information activities, and disrupt information technology-based civilian and government economic activity to leverage a strong negotiating posture for an aggressor over a target nation, region, or population. This strategy is a limited destructive effort with a desire to leave infrastructure intact while temporarily disabling systems. When implementing the strategy there is regard for human life and the interlocking economic, social, or political relationships that the target has with neighboring states. The goal of strategy is to hinder the use of communications and computer systems in a manner that is similar to a blockade of a seaport.

A related strategy is defensive responsive containment information warfare. This strategy is an organized deliberate military effort to cripple or disable military information technology capabilities, halt industrial and manufacturing information technology activities, and disrupt information technology-based civilian and government economic activity to leverage a strong negotiating posture over an aggressor nation, region, population, or military/terrorist force. As with defensive ruinous information warfare, this strategy would be used as a response to an aggressor and is designed to aid in stopping the actions of the aggressor.

Complexity and Expense of Containment Information Warfare Strategies

To execute a successful containment information warfare strategy is far less complex and expensive than the efforts required to launch ruinous strategies. The complexity and expense are directly related to the size and the location of the target nation, region, or population. Achieving a successful military impact of a containment information warfare strategy is directly related to how dependent the target nation, region, or population is on communications and information systems. Table 5-2 shows the relationship between target characteristics, complexity and expense of the attack, and potential military outcomes.

Table 5-2: Complexity, Expense, and Potential Military Impact of Containment Information Warfare Attacks

Target Characteristics	Complexity and Expense	Potential Military Impact
Small nation, region, or population geographically close to attacker	Very low	Very low
Large nation, region, or population geographically close to attacker	Moderate	Moderate
Small nation, region, or population geographically far from attacker	Moderate	Low
Large nation, region, or population geographically far from attacker	High	Moderate

If the target is a small nation, region, or population geographically close to the home or resource bases of an attacker, the complicity and cost of launching a containment information warfare attack is very low. Because of the size of the target, the military impact is also likely to be very low unless the target has strategic value related to other political, economic, or war efforts of the attacker. A small island nation is certainly dependent on communications, as is any modern state, but is probably somewhat less dependent on computer systems with the exception of air and seaport traffic control and management. Thus it would be fairly easy to disable or hinder the use of the information and communications infrastructure because there is so little work that would need to be done, and there will likely be little, if any, military defense capability in place. However, the military impact would also be very low because there is likely to be little in the way of an organized military, and the small island state will likely have very little strategic value.

To launch a containment information warfare attack on a large nation, region, or population geographically close to the attacker has a moderate level of complexity compared to launching a ruinous strategy. In the case of containment, the size of the nation and the higher density of communications and computer systems provide more opportunity to hinder the use of critical systems. Costs are moderate because not all systems need to be hit in order to achieve success. The potential military impact, however, also remains moderate because when all systems are not hit alternative systems can be put into place more quickly.

To launch a containment attack on a small nation, region, or population geographically far from the attacker would have moderate, but relatively higher costs than hitting a small nation in closer proximity. As with a small nation, region, or population geographically close to the home or resource bases of an attacker, the value of success will also remain low. The exception is that the small nation, region, or population has other political, economic, or military value.

To launch a containment attack on a large nation, region, or population geographically far from the attacker will, as in all warfare, have higher costs and be relatively complex. With few exceptions, larger nations are likely to have more complex and dense communications systems that make for greater opportunity to hit systems and disrupt economic or military activity. In addition, the general defensive capabilities of a larger nation will be more sophisticated, but information warriors will be able to pick and choose systems to hit that are convenient and perhaps not the best protected systems. This allows for high impact with lower costs and lower risks.

The Perspective of the Attacker in Containment Information Warfare

The perspective, resources, actions, and tactics of an attacker in a containment information warfare attack will be similar to those of the attacker in a ruinous information warfare attack as previously discussed. The legitimate retaliator who is retaliating against an aggressor on behalf of their constituency or on behalf of an ally will have the same military, political, and economic advantages in containment attacks as they do in a ruinous attack. The key similarity is legitimization of their work. However, a containment attack regardless of whether it is defensive or offensive is the equivalent to any limited military action. Again, all of the protocols and expectations of any type of warrior acting on behalf of the sponsoring nation or alliance will also bind the information warrior in this situation.

The legitimate unprovoked aggressor in a containment information warfare attack has more advantages than the attacker in a ruinous information war. Their actions may take more time to detect, and it may be more difficult to prove that the containment action is occurring and actually causing damage or disruption. The aggressor in this scenario will probably be more careful about violating international protocol as well as being more careful not to cause damage to other nations or regions through the careless use of information warfare tools compared to their lack of concern when launching a ruinous information warfare attack.

The illegitimate attacker who is not acting on behalf of any legitimate government, but is using the military capabilities and resources of a nation to launch an unprovoked containment attack will probably still be the most unpredictable information warrior that may utilize this strategy. However, they will be able to leverage some of the same advantages as the legitimate unprovoked aggressor because of the lower profile of a containment attacked compared to a ruinous attack. However, the illegitimate attacker will still have fewer resources and will not be able to garner widespread support for their actions.

The Perspective of the Defender in Containment Information Warfare

The perspective, resources, actions, and tactics of a defender in containment information warfare attacks differ from the defender in a ruinous attack in several ways. In containment attacks, they will have a lower profile and the defender may have difficulty obtaining resources and convincing allies that the attacks are occurring. This, in turn, will hinder the ability of the legitimate defender to mount a thorough defense.

The information warrior that is defending the aggressor nation against a responsive containment information warfare attack is at a severe disadvantage just as they are when defending against defensive ruinous attack. They will have very limited support, supplies, and personnel compared to the retaliators who will most likely be an alliance of nations that can gain support from technology companies and communications providers.

Potential Unwanted Consequences of Containment Information Warfare

It is likely that there will be fewer unwanted consequences during containment information warfare attack than in a ruinous information warfare attack. When a nation exercises blockade strategy or other embargo methods, it is important that they maintain a high level of caution and not irritate their allies or other innocent parties. Thus, information warriors launching containment attacks will need to be more careful in their approaches and exercise far greater precession in their tactics. If the information warrior launching containment information warfare attacks gets sloppy and causes damage to global or regional systems, they will certainly face political and diplomatic consequences.

There is still the potential of disruption to regional communications systems and perhaps even the possibility of the accidental release or overuse of malicious code. It is important that information warriors conduct very careful analysis of the systems they plan to hit during containment attacks. They must make sure they are not going to damage neighboring countries or disrupt communications their allies may rely on in their own pursuit of economic or political activity in a region or nation. Close coordination with allies is thus essential to successfully utilize containment information warfare strategies.

Defensive Preventive Information Warfare Strategies and Tactics

The most complex activity for information warriors is to build defensive barriers against attacks. This has become more complicated with the growth of computer networks in general and especially with the growth of the Internet. There are now more systems to protect and more ways to get into systems than ever before. In addition, relaxed export restrictions on the part of the United States has made more sophisticated computer technology available to more people around the world. This includes networking technology such as switches and routers as well as workstations and software that can be analyzed for weakness or turned into information warfare weapons.

In addition to building strong systems, defensive preventive information warfare strategies also require ongoing intelligence work and analysis of the capabilities of other nations or potential attackers. In addition to technical challenges, defense builders also face the same political and economic issues in building defenses for communications and computer systems as they do in getting approval and funding for other types of national defense initiatives. The concept of information warfare is new to many policy makers and legislators, and many remain unconvinced that there is a real threat and that defensive preventive information warfare strategies should be funded. These combined circumstances make the job of the defense builder very difficult and will continue to keep defensive capabilities alarmingly weak.

Complexity and Expense of Defensive Preventive Information Warfare Strategies

To execute a successful defensive preventive information warfare strategy is by far the most complex and expensive of all information warfare efforts. The complexity and expense are directly related to the number of systems, geographical disbursement of systems, and the number of possible entryways into the systems. In addition, as the risk factor increases so does the necessity for strong defenses. Table 5-3 shows the relationship between target characteristics, complexity and expense of the defense, and potential military advantages for implementing a level of defense.

Table 5-3: Complexity, Expense, and Potential Military Impact of Defensive Preventive Information Warfare Strategies

Target Characteristics	Complexity and Expense	Potential Military Impact
Military communications and weapon systems	Very high	Very high
Government communications and computer systems	High	High
Industrial communications and computer systems	Very high	Very high
Commercial communications and computer systems	High	Moderate
Private citizen computer systems	Moderate	Low

The complexity and expense of securing all military communications and weapons systems from information warfare attacks are very high. The cost and complexity are increasing as the military deploys more off-the-shelf computing products that have a reputation for not being easy to secure. In addition, the military use of email and the Internet has also increased vulnerabilities. However, the potential military benefit for securing all military systems is very high.

The complexity and expense of securing all government communications and computer systems are high for many of the same reasons that the military faces high levels of complexity and expense. Governments rely heavily on commercial products and are using the Internet to serve and communicate with the citizenry. The military benefit of securing government systems is high, but not as high as securing military systems. One of the key roles of any military is to help protect civilian government interest, installations, and facilities during conflicts. The military can benefit from a well-functioning government, but again, it is not as essential as secure military systems.

The complexity and expense of securing all industrial communications and computer systems are very high. This is partially due to the widespread use of commercial computing products and software and is also related to the geographic disbursement of industrial sites and the fact that there are so many workers in industry who could pose a security threat. The military does have a vested interest in the security and defense of its suppliers in the event of information warfare attacks just as it has in the past during conventional conflicts. Thus the military benefit of strong defenses for industrial systems is very high.

The complexity and expense of securing commercial communications and computer systems are rated as high because of the proliferation of systems and the fact that so many people have access to the systems. However, the military benefit derived from defending such systems is only moderate because the military is not as dependent on these systems as they are on industrial systems and even government systems. Thus, there is less interest on the part of the military to protect these systems, which is really not to the benefit of the companies that rely on the systems. Without high levels of protection, these systems are extremely vulnerable during information warfare attacks, especially ruinous and containment attacks designed to hinder or stop economic activity.

The complexity and expense of securing private citizen computer systems such as home computers and communications devices are moderate, and there are many products available to help protect the systems. However, the military benefit of defending these systems is low because of general lack of dependence on the systems. The exceptions would of course be those that are related to industrial workers who are essential for continued military operations. Their importance still remains low because in the event of conflict industrial workers would be required to change their habits and curtail telecommuting, for instance, in order to improve security.

The Perspective of the Attacker in Defensive Preventive Information Warfare

The perspective of the attacker when facing a defensive information warfare strategy will depend on the attack strategy. If attackers were deploying an offensive ruinous or an offensive containment information warfare strategy, their perspectives would be the same as previously explained under those two strategies. Random and sustained terrorist information warfare strategies are examined later in this chapter. The perspectives of attackers using sustained and random rogue information warfare strategies and the perspectives of amateur rogue attackers are also examined later in this chapter.

The Perspective of the Defender in Defensive Preventive Information Warfare

The perspective of the defender in a defensive information warfare strategy will depend somewhat, but not completely, on the attack strategy. The perspectives of defenders facing attackers using various attack strategies are explained within those sections in this chapter. However, defenders who are working to develop defensive strategies are only partially concerned with the motivations or political and military goals of attackers. The job of the defender is to be able to defend against any type of attack. The analysis of the attackers perspectives are helpful in deciding what level of security to build for what type of system, but the primary guidance in developing defensive strategies is more dependent on the military value of systems, as illustrated in Table 5-3.

It is important to recognize that developers of defensive strategies face the widest variety of challenges and unknowns of any information warrior. Attackers will hit systems that they can successfully damage or disable. Attackers have the freedom to move from system to system looking for weaknesses. Defenders must be prepared for this behavior and are required to cover more ground, or protect more systems, than the attacker needs to successfully hit. Attackers can fail and move on to other systems. Defenders must succeed every time they defend. Thus the defender is under far more pressure than the attacker.

Potential Unwanted Consequences of Defensive Preventive Information Warfare

There are two major potential unwanted consequences of defensive preventive information warfare. First, the response of systems users to security measures that may make systems more complex to use. Second, the public and political perception of the intelligence gathering and monitoring activities that should accompany the technical and procedural methods used to secure systems.

The response of users to the complexity that may accompany a secure and defensible system is a social consequence of defensive preventive information warfare strategies. The use of complex passwords and multiple or layered login procedures tends to irritate system users. In most cases, users attempt to make their work as simple and as easy as possible. There is defiantly a lack of discipline on the part of users to maintain good security practices. This is probably due to a lack of education as to the importance of security and the level of threat that exists.

The public and political perception of the intelligence gathering and monitoring activities which defenders should undertake is not favorable. The FBI's use of Carnivore, for example, raised a public outcry. Surveillance of any type will always irritate a certain segment of the civilian population. Surveillance and spying also tends to irritate the governments of other nations, allies and non-allies alike. However, to be thorough and to be prepared with good defensive preventive strategies, it is necessary to understand the abilities of a potential enemy or attacker. Inventory and assessment methods of other countries and terrorist and rogue criminal groups are explained in Chapter 7. The processes of inventory and assessment are logical steps in developing adequate defensive strategies, but they come loaded with political and social consequences.

Random and Sustained Terrorist Information Warfare Strategies and Tactics

Random terrorist information warfare strategies are centered in the sporadic efforts of an organized political group or individuals against the military, industrial, civilian, and government information infrastructures or activities of a nation, region, organization of states, population, or corporate entity. Random attacks are among the favorite strategies of terrorists in general because they can hit and run and often avoid capture. Sustained terrorist information warfare strategies are the ongoing deliberate efforts of an organized political group against the military, industrial, civilian, and government economic information infrastructures or activities of a nation, region, organization of states, population, or corporate entity. Sustained attacks can last for days or months and can be turned off and on at the will of the terrorists. A sustained attack may not necessarily be directed at a single system or a single type of system, as was illustrated in the PH2 scenario in Chapter 3.

Complexity and Expense of Random and Sustained Terrorist Information Warfare Strategies

To execute successful random and sustained terrorist information warfare strategies is by far the least complex and least expensive of all information warfare efforts. The complexity and expense are impacted by two factors. First, the number of systems and geographical disbursement of systems targeted for attack and the level of security that is maintained on the systems. Second, the number of people staffing the attack and the equipment and communications systems used in the attack. The goal of a terrorist in launching an information warfare attack is to achieve either political or economic impact. Table 5-4 shows the relationship between target characteristics, complexity, and expense of the attack scenario and the potential gain derived by terrorists for attacking systems.

Table 5-4: Complexity, Expense, and Potential Gain in Terrorist Information Warfare Strategies

Target Characteristics	Complexity and Expense	Potential Military Impact
Military communications and weapon systems	High	Moderate
Government communications and computer systems	Moderate	High
Industrial communications and computer systems	Moderate	High
Commercial communications and computer systems	Low	Moderate
Private citizen computer systems	Low	Low

The complexity and expense of mounting random and sustained terrorist information warfare attacks of military communications and weapons systems are very high. It requires a high level of sophistication to successfully attack, damage, or disable a military system relative to attacking other types of systems. The increasing use of off-the-shelf computing products has made the business systems of the military more vulnerable, and Internet connectivity has provided more entry points for terrorists to attempt to hit military systems. However, the gain that terrorists can achieve even if they do succeed in damaging or disabling a military system is at best moderate. The types of gains achievable are mostly centered in public relations for a terrorist and an opportunity to grab headlines if they do succeed. If the random and sustained terrorist information warfare attack on a military system is done in conjunction with other terrorist activities, a terrorist group could achieve a momentary advantage in a physical attack of a military installation.

The complexity and expense of launching random and sustained terrorist information warfare attacks of civilian government communications and computer systems are moderate for a terrorist group. However, the potential gain is high if the attack is successful because government operations can be disrupted. This in turn may cause disruption in central banking systems or the disbursement of government funds. Again, terrorists can gain a higher profile for attacks on government systems and become a greater irritant to specific governments.

The complexity and expense of launching random and sustained terrorist information warfare attacks on industrial communications and computer systems are also moderate. This is partially due to the widespread use of commercial computing products and software, but is also dependent on the geographic disbursement of industrial sites, which provides more entry points into systems. In general, there is potentially high gain for a terrorist to hit industrial systems because of the possibility of extortion or the theft of trade secrets. If the industrial site is tied into the military, there is potentially higher gain for a terrorist because information on military supplies or weapons could be gained.

The complexity and expense of implementing random and sustained terrorist information warfare attacks on commercial communications and computer systems is rated as low because many systems are not well secured. The potential gain is classified only as moderate because, short of disruption, a commercial enterprise has little that a terrorist would be interested in. The potential gain could be higher if the attack were a subpart of a ruinous or containment attack launched by an illegitimate attacker as previously described.

The complexity and expense of random and sustained terrorist information warfare attacks on the computer systems of private citizens are low, but the potential gain is also low. Such efforts would probably best be accomplished by the use of viruses or malicious code as described in the PH2 scenario in Chapter 3. The gain could be escalated to moderate if the attacks were sustained, because consumers would be hindered in their efforts to conduct online purchases or stock trading. Hitting the systems of private citizens in this way is a good method of indirectly causing economic disruption without facing the challenge of attacking commercial or industrial systems.

The Perspective of the Attacker in Random and Sustained Terrorist Information Warfare

The perspectives of terrorists as information warfare attackers is examined in depth in Chapter 7, which covers information warfare from the terrorist perspective, and in Chapter 10, which examines the emergence of the new technologically literate terrorists. Briefly, terrorist information warriors are one of the biggest future threats to the information infrastructure and the new digital economy. The technological terrorist will act in the name of one religion or another and support or be supported by one or more outlaw nations. Once the skill sets are developed among terrorists, their methods of spreading terror will evolve.

The key to understanding the terrorist's viewpoint in their information warfare efforts is to recognize that they are very dedicated individuals who will work for long periods of time to accomplish their goals. Most terrorists are motivated by passion and belief, and generally hold a high level of hate for the country or group on which they focus their efforts. It is important also to recognize that although terrorists may find it difficult to successfully attack military systems, they also, by their very nature, will find such attacks a challenge and dedicate themselves to the process.

The Perspective of the Defender in Random and Sustained Terrorist Information Warfare

Beyond what has already been stated about the perspectives of defenders, the necessity to defend military systems from terrorists is something that most military planners recognize as being absolutely necessary. However, defending military systems against terrorist attacks is frustrating for military personnel. The military mission is to fight other military organizations. War, when clearly defined as war, is the focal point of military activity. It is what the military does best, and it is what members of the military are trained to do. Many members of the military view terrorists who hit, run, and hide as cowards at best—and we will forgo the colorful adjectives used by military staff as they describe the frustration of dealing with terrorist attacks.

However, the military is well aware of the motivation of terrorists, and many military units have suffered casualties in physical attacks conducted by terrorists. It is reasonable for the military to have a general disdain for terrorist activity. The process of fighting terrorists is riddled with diplomacy, politics, and posturing. This adds to the frustration of the military defenders who would just as soon seek and destroy the terrorist groups and skip the global rhetoric that is inherent in the fight against terrorism of all types.

Potential Unwanted Consequences of Random and Sustained Terrorist Information Warfare

Terrorists generally like to do damage, and they will do damage in any way they possibly can. This makes random and sustained terrorist information warfare strategies especially dangerous to the military as well as to government, industrial, commercial, and private systems. In the PH2 scenario in Chapter 3, the activities of the ad hoc terrorist group were not focused sorely against a specific organization. Once terrorists do start practicing information warfare on a wider basis, they will likely use any and all weapons they can get their hands on or create. This includes viruses and worms that indiscriminately move from system to system. Terrorists do not care who they hurt; their goal is simply to hurt and cause damage. This means that random and sustained terrorist information warfare strategies will probably have the most unwanted and widespread consequences of any type of information warfare.

Sustained and Random Rogue Information Warfare Strategies and Tactics

The probability of rogue criminals attacking military information systems is very high, but not for the political or religious reasons that may inspire terrorists to strike. Rogue criminals work for money, not salvation or political recognition. They steal money and steal information to sell to the highest bidder. Rogue criminal information warriors will also strike systems on a for-hire basis and will work as mercenaries for those who are willing to pay.

Random rogue information warfare is the sporadic efforts of an organized nonpolitical, criminal, or mercenary groups or individuals against the military, industrial, and civilian and government information infrastructures or activities of a nation, region, organization of states, population, or corporate entity. Sustained rogue information warfare is the ongoing deliberate efforts of an organized nonpolitical, criminal, or mercenary group against the military, industrial, and civilian and government economic information infrastructures or activities of a nation, region, organization of states, population, or corporate entity.

Complexity and Expense of Random and Sustained Rogue Information Warfare Strategies

Executing successful random and sustained rogue strategies is moderate in complexity and expense compared to most other information warfare efforts. The complexity and expense are impacted by two factors. First, the type of systems targeted for attack and the level of security that is maintained on the systems. Second, the number of people staffing the attack and the equipment and communications systems used in the attack. The goal of a rogue in launching an information warfare attack is to achieve financial gain—either directly by stealing money or indirectly by stealing information they can sell—or, as hired guns, to do damage to target systems. Table 5-5 shows the relationship between target characteristics, complexity, and expense of the attack scenario and the potential gain derived by rogue criminal for attacking systems.

Table 5-5: Complexity, Expense, and Potential Gain in Random and Sustained Rogue Information Warfare Strategies

Target Characteristics	Complexity and Expense	Potential Military Impact
Military communications and weapon systems	High	Moderate
Government communications and computer systems	Moderate	High
Industrial communications and computer systems	Moderate	Very high
Commercial communications and computer systems	Low	Very high
Private citizen computer systems	Low	Moderate

The complexity and expense of mounting random and sustained rogue information warfare attacks of military communications and weapons systems are very high, just as they are for any other military or terrorist organizations that attempts to hit a military system. To successfully attack, damage, or disable a military system requires a high level of sophistication relative to attacking other types of systems. Thus, only a well-equipped rogue group is going to be successful. The gain that a rogue group can achieve when and if they do succeed is likely to be only moderate because what they can gain from hitting a military system will probably be of little direct use to a rogue criminal. Thus, a rogue group will probably be hired by another party if they are going to bother hitting a military system.

The complexity and expense of launching random and sustained rogue information warfare attacks of civilian government communications and computer systems are moderate for a rogue just as they are for a terrorist group. However, the potential gain is high if a third party has hired the rogues to damage a specific system or obtain specific information. If there is not a third party involved, rogues will probably have little interest in striking government systems.

The complexity and expense of launching random and sustained rogue information warfare attacks on industrial communications and computer systems are also moderate. In general, there is potentially very high gain for a rogue to hit industrial systems because of the possibility of extortion or the theft of trade secrets. The rogue has a better chance of profiting from such activity than do terrorists, who tend to work for political or religious reasons and who may lack the contacts of the rogue groups to market stolen information. If the industrial site is tied into the military, there is potentially higher gain for a rogue because information on military supplies or weapons can bring a high price from the right buyer.

The complexity and expense of implementing random and sustained rogue information warfare attacks on commercial communications and computer systems are rated as low because many systems are not well secured. Again the potential gain is classified only as very high because the rogue will focus on ways to steal money or to steal competitive information that can be sold.

The complexity and expense of random and sustained rogue information warfare attacks on the computer systems of private citizens are low, but the potential gain for rogues could be at least moderate. The main reason a rogue would hit systems of private citizens is either for hire or to collect information that could be used to extort or coerce individuals or groups into specific actions. It is also possible that a rogue would be hired to merely harass individuals or groups of people. In this case, the potential gain would probably be low to moderate depending on the goals of the funding source.

The Perspective of the Attacker in Random and Sustained Rogue Information Warfare

The perspectives of rogue criminals as information warfare attackers is examined in depth in Chapter 7, which covers information warfare from the terrorist and rogue criminal perspective. Briefly, rogue criminal information warriors are one of the biggest future threats to the private companies. The technological criminal is motivated by monetary gain. The key to understanding the rogue criminal's viewpoint is to recognize that they are diligent in their actions and can work as individuals, in small groups, or as members of large criminal organizations. Rogue criminals use information warfare strategies as specific approaches to steal or extort money or to steal information for resale.

It is also likely that rogue criminals will use information warfare attacks in conjunction with other strategies or as tools in the process of intimidation or their efforts to dominate particular industries or geographical markets.

The Perspective of the Defender in Random and Sustained Rogue Information Warfare

The perspective of the defender in random and sustained rogue information warfare attacks will probably vary by the type of system they are defending. Military defenders view rogue criminals in much the same way they view terrorists. However, those individuals responsible for protecting industrial or commercial systems are likely to take rogues more seriously than they do terrorists. The terrorist will be viewed as a zealot and the rogue as a thief or saboteur who has selected information and communications systems for specific reasons and has a goal in mind. The defender may not be able to determine the goal, but their job is to protect the systems from harm, intrusion, and theft. Their reputations—and in the case of for-hire security firms, their contract—could be jeopardized if the rogue succeeds.

Potential Unwanted Consequences of Random and Sustained Rogue Information Warfare

There are probably fewer unwanted consequences from rogue information warfare attacks than any other type of attack. Rogues are not political, unless hired to be so, and they are not looking for headlines or drama like terrorists. Rogues, by the nature of their work, are going to be low key and focus on theft more so than destruction—unless of course they are being paid to destroy. Although rogues are one of the worst possible groups to hit industrial or commercial systems, they are also likely to be the most tidy of all information warriors.

Amateur Rogue Information Warfare Strategies and Tactics

Amateur rogue information warfare is the sporadic efforts of untrained and nonaligned individuals or small groups against the military, industrial, and civilian and government information infrastructures or activities of a nation, region, organization of states, population, or corporate entity. From a military perspective, amateur rogues tend to be more of a menace than a strategic or tactical threat. Amateur rogues tend to be under equipped and far less capable than terrorists or professional rogue criminals.

Amateur rogue strategies barely qualify as information warfare, but there have been cases when amateurs have intruded into systems and done damage. The military takes all attacks seriously and has apprehended and prosecuted amateur rogues in the past. Amateur rogues are trainees, but they also serve to provide training for military personnel who are tasked with defending systems. An amateur rogue hits military systems to gain experience and bragging points.

The main problem with amateur rogues is that they could very likely end up becoming professional rogue criminals and maybe terrorists. The best possible outcome is that they join the military and become defenders instead of attackers. Of course, not everyone in the military would agree with this proposition.

Conclusions and an Agenda for Action

The complexity, expense, and military advantage of deploying information warfare strategies have only recently become apparent to policy makers and legislators. For several years, military planners have attempted to educate policy makers and legislators and have worked hard to convince them that funds are necessary to adequately deal with information warfare threats. Military planners have also worked hard to develop offensive information warfare capabilities. Unfortunately, this struggle will likely continue for years to come. In addition to a lack of understanding on the part of policy makers and legislators, the perspective that the world has achieved a high level of peace and that major threats have deteriorated is widespread. Such a perspective is self-deceptive and dangerous to the future of peace.

Conclusions on Information Warfare Arsenal and Tactics of the Military

The complexity of information warfare has yet to be understood by policy makers and legislators. Security managers in private industrial and commercial firms clearly see the need to deal with attacks, as do those responsible for protecting military systems. The following conclusions are drawn from the analysis of information warfare strategies from a military perspective:

▶ The ten information warfare strategies show that there are considerably different motivations for attackers. The different types of strategies will vary in their direct impacts as well as their indirect impacts.

▶ Military supported information warfare attacks are likely to be directed at specific targets and cause fewer unwanted consequences than the attacks perpetrated by terrorists.

▶ Rogue criminals will attack systems for completely different reasons and with different approaches than military units or terrorists.

▶ Military systems may be the primary target of many attackers, but others will focus their efforts on industrial and commercial systems.

▶ Amateur rogue information warriors are more of a menace than a national security threat, but their attacks should still be taken seriously.

An Agenda for Action for the Information Warfare Arsenal and Tactics of the Military

Policy makers and legislators as well as military planners need to take several actions to ensure that military systems are protected. It is also important that the military is capable of assisting government agencies, industrial companies, commercial firms, and the citizenry at large in identifying threats and protecting systems. The following agenda for action is recommended:

▶ Military organizations should establish a systematic process to record information warfare incidents by type and correlate the success level of the attack with the countermeasures employed to counter the attack.

▶ The tactics used in the ten information warfare strategies should be analyzed to determine where there is commonality and which type of groups is likely to utilize similar tactics to profile attack scenarios and plan effective defensive measures.

▶ Military organizations should establish and support intelligence-gathering efforts to identify potential sources of threats to military systems as well as civilian government, industrial, and commercial systems.

▶ Military organizations should create a system of profiling that enables them to identify and categorize information warriors by the type of tactics they use and their motivations as attackers.

▶ Policy makers and legislators should consider all attacks on military systems, regardless of their source and known motivation, as a serious national and international security threat.

▶ Policy makers and legislators should support military efforts to deal with information warfare attacks and make the protection of military, government, industrial, and commercial systems a high national priority.

Chapter 6

Information Warfare Strategies and Tactics from a Corporate Perspective

Private sector companies have focused their communications and computer systems protection efforts on securing systems from intrusion, misuse, fraud, and abuse. This is certainly a logical approach given the overall social and political context in which the majority of corporate systems have been developed. Over the last two to three decades there has been an expectation that large massive wars would not occur. This has held true with few exceptions. However, victory in the Gulf War has also helped to foster a sense of military superiority and security prevails in the NATO alliance and the United States. Although these social political conditions are favorable, it is dangerous to assume that they will continue to exist and that peace will prevail.

When the demographics of systems developers and managers are examined, it is clear that the majority of IT professionals entered the profession, and many began their lives, in a post-cold-war environment. They do not expect war and they are not prepared for war. This is in contrast to the 1940s when war was a reality, and the 1950s and 1960s when war and potential nuclear destruction presented a scenario people were familiar with. If war had occurred in those times, nobody would have been surprised. Military decisions and even business strategies were developed with the assumption that there was going to be more massive war and that there were enemy forces waiting for the opportunity to conquer the world using any means at their disposal.

The relative peace of the last 40 years has been a welcome social condition, but it has also led to a complacent attitude toward the preparation for war. This chapter covers information warfare from a cooperate perspective. Preparation and planning for information warfare are examined along with guidelines for responding to information warfare attacks.

Overview of Defensive Strategies for Private Companies

Strategies to defend corporate systems in an information warfare environment must go beyond the process of making systems secure from intruders, hackers, virus attacks, fraud, and abuse. Although information warriors may well use all of these tactics, the broader context of war and how and when information warfare strategies may be deployed should be taken into consideration when designing security management approaches. What this means in practical terms is that corporate protectors should view their efforts in a broader context and be able to respond to a set of information warfare scenarios or strategies.

Information warfare defensive strategies also involve more than system-based security efforts. Only in the last few years has there been a movement toward integrating communications and computer security efforts with overall corporate security efforts. There has certainly been a prevailing perspective that there is little relationship between the security guards at the front desk and the people who issue passwords for the computer systems or pin numbers for the telephone system. Integration of these functions is important, but it is only a first step.

However, planners should not confuse shifts in organization structure with improved security and war preparation. This means that just because the password and pin number purveyors are assigned to the corporate security department, not all of the potential problems of information warfare attacks have been addressed.

Information systems security needs to be placed into as broad a context as corporate security has long been accustomed to dealing with. Planned responses to threats need to encompass physical as well as cyber security. This means that security of information and communications systems needs to be approached in a broader manner, just as physical and financial management security is dealt with to ensure business continuation. Security efforts designed to address information warfare attacks must be aligned with the real-world behavior of the various types of people who will employ different information warfare strategies. In practical terms, security developers should recognize that many attackers might have supporters or aides inside the organizations they attack, so systems protection means more than just keeping the hordes from breaking down the gates.

When dealing with security issues and preparing for information warfare attacks, information and communications need to be viewed differently than they were during the 1990s. Specifically, there has been a movement toward the deployment of enterprise-wide, highly integrated information systems, including applications such as enterprise resource planning suites. These systems have a certain appeal. They allow everyone in the organization, regardless of location, to work on the same platform, access the same data sets, communicate with peer groups and teams, share resources, and collaborate across the organization in a matrix manner to leverage all of the intellectual and management assets of the enterprise. This is a wonderful thing when organizations can make it work properly.

It is important, however, especially in global enterprises, to examine the downside of the enterprise-wide information utility. Such global systems may make a company's operations run smoother, but they are also an information warrior's dream come true. When these systems are designed to support a global organization with operations on all continents and in multiple countries, they create numerous entryways, which can be exploited by enemies well before any security alarms are set off. There are also more ways to have direct physical contact with terminal or server devices that are directly attached to the global system, which can provide for easier access and more opportunity to do damage to systems.

The development of supply chain systems, enterprise resource planning systems, integrated accounting systems, and management decision systems is setting the stage for easier attacks on corporate systems. Add to this trend the use of the Internet as a corporate communications tool and customer service access route, and the typical corporation has become an inviting opportunity for terrorists, rogue criminals, and professional information warriors of today, as well as of the future.

The key point that system designers and security managers need to address in dealing with information warfare is that it will happen. Without paranoia there will not be caution, and many software developers are not paranoid enough. U.S.-based software companies are an excellent example of developers having a lack of paranoia. Microsoft, for example, has established dominance in the personal computer operating system realm and for the most part in office desktop software, but the software the company produces has long been riddled with security weaknesses. The products, although user friendly, were developed focusing on providing users with more functionality and ease of use, not withstanding malicious attacks. The final test of the commercial off-the-shelf (COTS) computer product is whether consumers buy them, not their ability to withstand information warfare attacks.

Most private companies and government organizations use off-the-shelf products. This is a matter of practicality—the products are relatively cheap and much of the labor force knows how to use them. However, to be prepared for information warfare and to develop stronger system defenses in general, the weaknesses of commercial products much be dealt with in a realistic manner. In addition, popular system design approaches such as supply chains, enterprise-wide systems, or global corporate communications systems need to be carefully examined from the ground up to ensure they can be defended when attacked.

Participating in Defensive Preventive Information Warfare Planning

In addition to addressing their own security efforts, organizations should participate in national and global efforts to fight computer crime and secure systems against information warfare attacks. The establishment of the National Infrastructure Protection Center (NIPC) is one step that the U.S. government has taken to aid in this process. The role of the NIPC is to facilitate and coordinate federal government efforts to respond to incidents and attacks on infrastructures considered critical to the economy, including telecommunications, energy, banking and finance, water systems, government operations, and emergency services. For the NIPC to be successful in their efforts, cooperation of all parties with an interest in protecting these systems is necessary.

The Training, Outreach, and Strategy Section (TOSS) of the NIPC provides support and training to federal, state, and local law enforcement agencies, as well as security personnel in the public and private sector who work to protect the information technology infrastructure. The TOSS also works to coordinate outreach efforts between government agencies, industry, and academia, to encourage the sharing of information about foreign and domestic threats, vulnerabilities, and technological developments.

The Analysis and Warning Section (AWS) of the NIPC works to assess threats as well as vulnerabilities of critical technology infrastructures. The AWS provides analytical support for computer investigations and is a clearinghouse for research and analysis. The AWS is designed to be the primary hub for public/private sector information sharing and analytical work. It also staffs a 24-hour, 7-days-a-week Watch Operations Center that works with partner organizations in the private sector, intelligence community, defense establishment, and law enforcement area to identify threats and disseminate assessments, alerts, and advisories. The NIPC and AWS work within a legal framework established by several relevant federal laws, regulations, and executive orders including:

- ► The National Information Infrastructure Protection Act of 1996

- ► The High-Performance Computing Act of 1991

- ► The Computer Fraud and Abuse Act of 1986

- ► The Electronic Communications Privacy Act

- ► The Computer Security Act of 1987

- ► The Information Technology Management Reform Act of 1996

- ► Executive Order 13130, National Infrastructure Assurance Council, July 14, 1999

- Executive Order 13103, Computer Software Piracy, October 1, 1998

- Executive Order 13103, Computer Software Piracy, September 30, 1998

- Executive Order 13011, Federal Information Technology, July 16, 1996

- Management of Federal Information Resources, OMB Circular, A-130, February 8, 1996

- Security of Federal Automated Information Resources, Appendix 3 to OMB Circular, A-130, February 8, 1996

- Federal Information Processing Standards (National Institute of Standards and Technology)

In January 2001, the FBI and the NIPC unveiled the National Infra-Gard Program as a national protection initiative. The NIPC, with help from representatives of private industry, the academic community, and government agencies, developed the InfraGard initiative to share information about cyber intrusions, exploited vulnerabilities, and infrastructure threats. All 56 field offices of the FBI have established an InfraGard chapter, with more than 500 company members across the United States. The National InfraGard Program provides four basic services to members:

- An alert network using encrypted email

- A secure website for communication about suspicious activity or intrusions

- Local chapter activities and a helpdesk for questions

- Secure communications to allow industry to provide information on intrusions to the local FBI field office

Federal agencies that work with the NIPC include the Departments of Defense, State, Commerce, Treasury, and Transportation, the Environmental Protection Agency (EPA), and the Central Intelligence Agency (CIA).

General membership in InfraGard is open to all parties interested in supporting the purposes and objectives of InfraGard. On the local level, InfraGard is organized into 56 chapters, each of which is associated with a field office of the FBI. InfraGard members are responsible for promoting the protection and advancement of the critical infrastructure, cooperating with others in the interchange of knowledge and ideas, supporting the education of members and the general public, and maintaining the confidentiality of information obtained through involvement.

Locations of local InfraGard chapters are: Albany, Albuquerque, Anchorage, Atlanta, Baltimore, Birmingham, Boston, Buffalo, Charlotte, Chicago, Cincinnati, Cleveland, Columbia, Dallas, Denver, Detroit, El Paso, Honolulu, Indianapolis, Jackson, Jacksonville, Kansas City, Knoxville, Las Vegas, Little Rock, Los Angeles, Louisville, Memphis, Miami, Milwaukee, Minneapolis, Mobile, Newark, New Haven, New Orleans, New York, Oklahoma City, Omaha, Philadelphia, Phoenix, Pittsburgh, Portland, Richmond, Sacramento, Salt Lake City, San Antonio, San Diego, San Francisco, San Juan, Seattle, Springfield, St. Louis, Tampa, and Washington, D.C.

The NIPC is also working with organizations in other countries to raise awareness about threats and help countries address threats through substantive legislation. In addition, the NIPC provides advice to other countries on how to organize to deal with the threats. Countries that have formed cooperative relationships with the NIPC include Canada, Denmark, France, Germany, Israel, Japan, Norway, the United Kingdom, and Sweden.

One of the concerns that any private corporation that participates in InfraGard (or a similar program) has is that any information about their company needs to be kept confidential. The bylaws of InfraGard address this in that it requires members to maintain confidentiality and not use information obtained through their participation in Infra-Gard as a competitive analysis tool. Although the InfraGard requirements are clear, it may be difficult to ensure that such confidentiality is maintained and that participants do not gain a competitive advantage by using information to which they have been provided access. For InfraGard to work, information clearly has to be shared. This in turn increases the general knowledge base of representatives of the member organizations, which in turn makes them inherently more capable of being competitive. The process will likely hold together as long as there is not an instance of blatant use of specific information about another InfraGard member. However, corporations do need to be careful about the types of information representatives share during the course of their work with other InfraGard members.

Participation in efforts and activities such as those provided by InfraGard are certainly a good step for companies to take in working to build stronger defenses against information warfare attacks. However, just because a company is participating in these initiatives does not mean that they have successfully and thoroughly addressed all of the potential problems they face. A strong internal effort with cooperation between all of the divisions and business units in a company is still required to ensure they have adequate levels of protection in place. These issues and processes will be examined in more detail in the following sections.

Surviving Offensive Ruinous and Containment Information Warfare Attacks

The most severe information warfare situation that a company will face is a ruinous attack, which is an organized deliberate military effort to totally destroy the military information capabilities, industrial and manufacturing information infrastructure, and information technology-based civilian and government economic activities of a target nation, region, or population. In ruinous attacks, nothing is to be left intact and the attackers intend to cause the maximum amount of damage possible.

For defense planning purposes, the possibility of ruinous attacks needs to be put into a global perspective. The countries that are presently the most capable of launching an all-out ruinous attack are not likely to do so, because of their economic and political dependence on the rest of the world. In addition, these countries are often the home base of a global conglomerate that would probably be damaged in such an attack no matter where the geographical focal point of the ruinous attack is located. Be cautioned that present day capability will not remain the determining factor in the future of information warfare. Information warfare capabilities are being developed around the world by many countries that at present do not have such capabilities.

The second most severe information warfare situation that a company will face is a containment information warfare attack. This type of attack is defined as an organized deliberate military effort to cripple or disable military information capabilities, halt industrial and manufacturing information activities, and disrupt information technology-based civilian and government economic activity to leverage a strong negotiating posture for an aggressor over a target nation, region, or population.

Containment attacks are more likely to happen than ruinous attacks because they take far less effort and they can be used less overtly than an all-out ruinous information warfare strategy. Because a containment attack does not need to be as thorough and it does not require the sophistication of a ruinous attack, it is easier to execute and thus, more countries or organizations are capable of a containment attack. The key planning point is to determine where and under what conditions a containment attack may occur.

The first questions that arise are whether the geographical territory of the United States and that of major economic and political allies is susceptible to all-out ruinous attacks or more limited containment attacks, and whether companies should be prepared for such attacks. The probability at this time is low that a ruinous or even a sophisticated containment attack would be launched. Bear in mind, however, the capability of launching such attacks is not altogether impossible to develop.

Given this conclusion, why then should a company be concerned about developing capabilities to protect against such attacks? There are two main reasons. First, many large companies have a global presence with subsidiaries, divisions, or offices located around the world and in places where such attacks would be easier to launch and probably more effective in their impact. Second, the nature of information warfare attacks, and the tactics used during such attacks can have unanticipated consequences for companies that are not directly in the line of fire.

The practical implication of these two reasons may best be illustrated in an example. A small but industrialized nation in Asia suffers a ruinous or containment information warfare attack by a regional superpower. The smaller nation is the home of manufacturing facilities and regional offices of global corporations. The goal of the aggressor is to cause severe economic impact and disrupt manufacturing operations, banking, commerce, and the functioning of international transportation facilities. This scenario puts global companies in the direct line of fire as well as indirectly impacting many other companies that may be dependent on the small Asian nation's industrial output. There are several types of damage that could be incurred, including:

▶ Manufacturing systems that are integrated into a global design, production, and control infrastructure could be severely damaged locally as well as other parts of the global system disabled for periods of time.

▶ The management, marketing, and sales processes that are supported by local offices could be disrupted and sensitive corporate data on local systems could be compromised.

▶ The integrated global systems that support worldwide management, marketing, and sales processes could be indirectly compromised or disabled for periods of time.

▶ If malicious code or virus attack tactics were employed in the ruinous or containment attack, systems to which local servers and client devices are attached could be infected and disabled for a period of time.

▶ Management of local financial assets of global corporations could be severely disrupted and perhaps even totally compromised and lost during the attacks.

▶ Local personnel could be put into dangerous situations because of manufacturing malfunctions or accidents resulting from the attacks.

▶ Communication with personnel at local facilities could be disrupted for long periods of time.

▶ Information regarding the global architecture of corporate systems could be compromised, allowing attackers to do more damage to systems outside the geographic areas that are under direct attack.

▶ Intellectual property and trade secrets relating to the local operations, manufacturing processes, or products of the global corporation could be compromised.

Stopping such information warfare attacks is probably impossible for an individual company to accomplish. Well-organized information warriors will design such attacks to be swift and to cause as much damage as possible in a short period of time. Attacks will be sustained as long as possible, making rebuilding or returning to normal operations a major challenge. Local operations will certainly be disrupted and it is not likely that such disruption can be totally avoided. However, there are several steps that corporations can take to help protect their assets, maintain their global operations, and minimize the long-term damage of ruinous or containment information warfare attacks that are targeted at places where the corporation has facilities or operations. These include the following:

- ▶ As part of the overall business continuity plan, develop specific steps that global information systems managers should take if a ruinous or containment information warfare attack is launched against a country where the corporation has operations or offices.

- ▶ Also develop specific steps that local information systems managers should take if such information warfare attacks are launched against their country.

- ▶ Maintain a liaison with local authorities to coordinate responsive efforts and later, if necessary and if possible, assist in investigative activities.

- ▶ Be prepared to sever connectivity with systems in the attacked nation to minimize penetration into global systems and to stop the movement of malicious code.

- ▶ Maintain backups of all system configurations, applications, and data sets in other parts of the world.

- ▶ As a matter of local security, ensure that all people with access to in-country systems have had adequate security checks.

- ▶ Have in place alternative communications that enable global mangers to maintain contact with local personnel to aid in facilitating the predeveloped steps that should be taken in such an event and to monitor the impact of the attack.

- ▶ If and when possible, conduct a comprehensive assessment of damage and any intellectual property or trade secrets that were possibly compromised during the attacks.

- ▶ Be prepared to provide local authorities, as well as law enforcement and military personnel in other countries, information about the damage that occurred during the attack and any forensic evidence that may be helpful during subsequent investigations.

Most large companies that have been in business for several decades are well aware of the perils of war or civil unrest in countries in which they have had operations or business partners. These companies have security and systems staff that probably have some experience in dealing with disruption in locations in which they operate. However, there are many fast -growing companies developing a global reach that do not have the knowledge or past experiences of dealing with local disruptions. For the company seasoned by age and experience, it is advisable to assess the levels of protection that are in place for global information systems and ensure that business continuity plans take into account the possibility of information warfare attacks. For the younger company, it is advisable that they conduct a very thorough assessment of their in-house capabilities and skills in the event that they are ever confronted with ruinous or containment information warfare attacks. If necessary, they should seek outside assistance to develop better response capabilities.

Surviving Terrorist Information Warfare Attacks

There are two types of terrorist information warfare attacks that corporations need to be prepared to deal with—both of which have a high probability of occurring. The first is a random terrorist information warfare attack, which is the sporadic efforts of an organized political group or individuals against the military, industrial, and civilian and government information infrastructures or activities of a nation, region, organization of states, population, or corporate entity. Random terrorists have done damage to corporate properties around the world many times in the past. This includes damage to data centers and communications facilities.

The second type of terrorist action is more severe than a random attack. A sustained terrorist information warfare attack is an ongoing deliberate effort of an organized political group against the military, industrial, and civilian and government economic information infrastructures or activities of a nation, region, organization of states, population, or corporate entity. If an area of the world in which a company has operations becomes the target of a sustained terrorist information attack, the outcomes could be very similar to those of a containment information warfare attack. However, if a corporation becomes the specific target of a sustained terrorist information warfare strategy, a different defensive approach will be required.

If terrorists target a region, a nation, or perhaps even a city, global corporations as well as local business entities face many of the same perils as they would under a ruinous or containment attack. The consequences and potential damages that are discussed in the previous section are applicable, as are the steps that global corporations should take to respond to such attacks.

If a corporation becomes the specific target of a terrorist group, there are other issues that must be dealt with in addition to those discussed in the previous section. Corporations have become the targets of terrorists groups, militant advocacy groups, and even paramilitary organizations in the past. In the information age, the tactics of these groups are likely to change as they move away from physical actions such as bombings or burning facilities as well as other types of sabotage that have been the favorite tools of such groups in the past.

On one hand, being attacked by a terrorist group may be easier to deal with than being in the line of fire when an entire army of information warriors attacks a region or nation. The attacks may be less severe and the terrorist may not be as sophisticated or have access to as much technology as an army does. However, if the corporation is the only target of an information warfare attack, it may be far more difficult to get any support from local authorities to help stop attacks. In addition, a single corporation will not be able to muster the defenses of global alliances or even leverage diplomatic responses to the attacks.

In other words, when a single corporation is attacked they will largely be on their own to defend themselves unless the attacks are specifically directed at systems that are in countries that are capable of responding in an organized and effective manner. Thus, the best possible situation for a company under attack by terrorist information warriors is if the systems that are attacked are located in the United States or one of the other countries that have established relationships with the NIPC.

There are several steps that corporations can take to help protect their systems from random or sustained terrorist information warfare attacks. It is important that these steps be taken within the framework of those steps recommended in the previous section and that protection against terrorist information warfare attacks be an integral part of a company's overall security efforts. The steps to specifically deal with terrorist information warfare attacks include the following:

▶ As part of the overall business continuity plan, develop specific steps that global information systems managers should take if random or sustained terrorist information warfare attacks are launched against a country where the corporation has operations or offices or if the corporation is specifically targeted by a terrorist group.

▶ Information system security staff should collect and assemble information and data that can help track the sources of the terrorist attacks and identify the individuals involved in the attacks.

▶ The security departments of companies should maintain a list of people or organizations suspected of attacking corporate information systems or other property in the past and as much information about the attacks or the individuals responsible for the attacks should be kept on file in the security office.

▶ The security departments of companies should also maintain a list of people or organizations that in some way may pose a security threat to the corporation. The list should be comprehensive and include groups in all of the countries in which the company does business. The list should include individuals or groups that have general political or social views that may result in them targeting a company as well as individuals or groups that have specific issues with the company.

▶ Be prepared to provide local authorities as well as law enforcement agencies in other countries with information about the damage that occurred during the attack and any forensic evidence that may be helpful during subsequent investigations.

The probability of future terrorist attacking information systems is very high for several reasons. First, the next generation of terrorist is likely to be far more computer literate than the terrorist who has launched attacks during the last several decades. The Internet provides opportunities for terrorists to access systems around the world without incurring the expense of travel or recruiting and training local operatives to strike targets. Third, terrorists are starting to realize that it is more effective to damage communications and computer systems when they desire to have high levels of economic impact than it is to use car bombs that cause damage only to small areas. Finally, not all terrorists want to take part in suicide missions. They will find information warfare strategies are a far more attractive alternative than the almost-guaranteed death they face when using a tactic like a car bombing attack.

The terrorist is going to add a new dimension to information warfare, which so often in the past has been viewed as solely a military option. Thus, corporations are going to be faced with a new foe that is less predictable but equally as dangerous as an organized army of information warriors. Terrorists are also very dedicated to their missions and have an incredible sense of pride about their accomplishments. Those individuals who have successfully struck a blow at what they view as the American or European imperialist oppressors become heroes in their communities. It seems that terrorism is here to stay, and the only safe assumption that a corporation can make is that they will someday face terrorist attacks on their information systems. Global corporations are well aware that the more countries they do business with, the more enemies they will likely have.

Countering Rogue Information Warfare Attacks

Another new member of the information warrior elite is the rogue criminal who has the ability to break into computer systems to deliberately do damage or to steal information or money. The rogue criminal information warrior is mistakenly viewed as an individual who commits computer crimes such as altering or destroying databases or disabling computer systems. Such a definition may be adequate to cover some rogue criminal activity, but is far too limited to address the entire scope of potential rogue information warfare activity.

Random rogue information warfare is comprised of sporadic efforts of organized nonpolitical, criminal, or mercenary groups or individuals against the military, industrial, civilian, and government information infrastructures or activities of a nation, region, organization of states, population, or corporate entity. Sustained rogue information warfare is the ongoing deliberate efforts of an organized nonpolitical, criminal, or mercenary group against the military, industrial, and civilian and government economic information infrastructures or activities of a nation, region, organization of states, population, or corporate entity.

Rogue criminals who attack information systems should not be confused with terrorists. Their motivations are different and their goals are different. Rogue criminals are not considered politically oriented unless they are paid by a government or politically motivated organization to act in a mercenary fashion on behalf of their employers. Rogue criminals do not work for glory or patriotism—they work for money. Unlike terrorists, rogue criminal information warriors are not seeking headlines; their rewards are purely financial. Rogue criminals that employ information warfare strategies are likely to have one of many different objectives, including:

▶ Stealing money by manipulating databases or records on corporate computer systems.

▶ Stealing financial tools such as credit card numbers and bank account numbers or making fraudulent transfers of cash, bonds, or stocks.

▶ Obtaining trade secrets or business plans of corporations for sale to or on behalf of competitors or other intelligence-gathering entities.

▶ Sabotaging or threatening to sabotage corporate communications or computer systems in order to extort money from system owners.

▶ Sabotaging corporate communications or computer systems on a for-hire basis in order to impede the ability of a corporation to conduct business or compete in a certain marketplace or geographical location.

▶ Sabotaging government communications or computer systems on a for-hire basis in order to impede the ability of a government to conduct official business.

▶ Sabotaging communications or computer systems to act as a cover for other simultaneous or related criminal activities.

▶ Breaking into the computer systems of private citizens to obtain information about individuals that can be used to steal identities or extort money for disclosing private information.

One factor that is important to bear in mind when dealing with rogue criminals is that most often they work from both inside and outside a company when they are perpetrating a crime. Embezzlement involves an insider, and there is absolutely no reason to think that because computer systems are involved that the equation of insider operatives working with outside criminals will change. Corporate security needs to watch people inside the organization as much as they may watch those outside the organization.

Another important factor to consider about rogue criminals is that their allegiances can shift quickly. One week they could be working with the CIA and the next week they could be working to help terrorist organizations in the Middle East steal money. The key point is that rogue criminals work for money and whoever is willing to pay them will very likely get services that no other organization is capable or willing to provide.

There are several steps that corporations can take to help protect their systems from random or sustained rogue criminal information warfare attacks. As with dealing with other types of information warfare attacks, it is important that these steps be taken within the framework of those steps recommended in previous sections and that protection against rogue criminal information warfare attacks be an integral part of a company's overall security efforts. The steps to specifically deal with rogue criminal attacks include the following:

► As part of the overall business continuity plan, develop specific steps that information systems managers should take if random or sustained criminal information warfare attacks on corporate information systems are suspected or observed.

► Corporate security should run routine background checks on individual employees who have access to information systems, especially those with high-level skills who are readily capable of working with rogue criminals groups or who are capable of individually perpetrating information system-based crimes against the company.

► All employees who have remote access to corporate systems should be thoroughly briefed on the steps they should take to ensure that passwords and other information about corporate information systems are not deliberately or accidentally compromised. This includes the unauthorized use of corporate mobile computing devices such as notebooks and laptops or home computers that are used to access corporate systems.

► Information system security staff need to collect and assemble information and data that can help track the source of the rogue criminal attacks and identify the individuals involved in the attacks just as they would to help track the source of terrorist attacks.

► Corporate security departments should maintain a list of individual criminals or criminal organizations that are suspected of stealing or attempting to steal corporate information or assets in the past. As much information about the incidents or the individuals responsible should be kept on file in the security office.

► Be prepared to provide local authorities as well as law enforcement agencies in other countries with information about the damage or any theft of information that occurred during the attack and any forensic evidence that may be helpful during investigations.

As unpleasant as it may seem to hold all employees and their families in suspicion, it is important to understand that rogue criminal attacks on corporate systems will be much easier to accomplish if they have inside help or obtain critical information about access from an employee. In many cases, employees will deliberately aid outside criminal organizations. In other cases, they may inadvertently aid the criminal by careless computing habits.

Rogue criminals are not out to prove that they have hacking skills. Hack attacks can be rather quickly identified and dealt with. The rogue criminal has a specific goal when they hit a corporate system. They are not there as a tourist looking around to see what they can do, like many amateur rogues (discussed in the next section). Another important point about the activity of rogue criminal information warriors is that criminal activity will go far beyond simple crimes of fraud or embezzlement. This is why the classification of rogue criminal information warfare strategies was added to the analysis of strategies and why it should be considered an actual warlike threat.

Rogue criminals may be acting on their own behalf that, in many cases, could downgrade their actions to a mere crime. However, with the continued growth of organized crime, along with the internationalization of organized crime, the actions of the rogue attacker need to be upgraded to a warrior level. When rogue criminal information warriors sell their skills to politically motivated groups or to governments, and when they damage or disable systems through ruinous or containment information warfare attacks, then the rogue criminal is a warrior, not a petty thief.

Dealing with Amateur Rogue Information Warfare Attacks

Amateur rogues have various skill levels, from the beginner to highly skilled computer professionals. Amateur rogue information warfare is defined as the sporadic efforts of untrained and nonaligned individuals or small groups against the military, industrial, and civilian and government information infrastructures or activities of a nation, region, organization of states, population, or corporate entity.

Amateur rogues need to be taken seriously in the fight against information warfare attacks for many reasons. First, although amateurs in this analysis are not paid for their work and are not aligned with any political group, they can inflict serious damage on information systems. Second, amateurs like to brag about their exploits and, to show proof of their conquest, tend to post information about how they cracked into systems on various websites that are used for sources of information by rogue criminals, terrorists, and the information warriors of less than friendly nations. Third, once amateurs refine their skills, they can turn to professional crime and become members of the rogue criminal or terrorist information warrior class.

An argument can be made that amateurs, through their various attempts at skill development, provide a beneficial service by testing the security of systems and providing training exercises for information systems security professionals in the private sector as well as in the military. The argument has merit from a social and perhaps an ecological point of view, but law enforcement agencies, private corporations, and the military are not at all amused by the concept.

Companies need to take the actions of any intruder or saboteur seriously and should respond to what they may think is an amateur attack in the same manner as they would any other attack. Information system security staff should collect and assemble information and data that can help track down amateurs in the same way they would work to track down rogue criminals or terrorists. There is little choice—the defenders of information systems will likely be able to tell the skill level of attackers by their actions, but they will not be able to accurately determine the motivation of the attackers until they are fully investigated and apprehended. Prudence therefore demands that all attackers be treated as a serious threat.

Another serious point about amateurs that cannot be overlooked is that they may be part of a fledgling gang or criminal group, which if allowed to continue, could later cause more serious incidents or launch serious waves of information warfare attacks. Chapter 10 deals with the process of the curious nerd moving into more serious criminal or political activities and many of the social pressures that may push them in that direction.

There are certainly many pitfalls in dealing with the amateur class of information warriors. Government agencies as well as corporations who end up tracking down a 14-year-old and prosecuting him can face a high level of public skepticism. But it is important to point out that it was a juvenile offender who disabled a key telephone company computer servicing the Worcester, Massachusetts, airport in March 1997.

The juvenile identified the telephone numbers of the modems connected to the loop carrier systems operated by the telephone company providing service to the Worcester airport and the community of Rutland, Massachusetts. The juvenile impaired the integrity of data on which the system relied, thereby disabling it. As a result of the outage, both the main radio transmitter, which is connected to the tower by the loop carrier system, and a circuit, which enables aircraft to send an electric signal to activate the runway lights on approach, were not operational for about six hours.

It is doubtful that anyone was paying the young person who attacked the airport, but it was clearly a tactic that could be used by terrorists or military information warriors who had political reasons to take such an action. Thus, the Worcester attacker remains in the amateur class, but certainly demonstrated the type of skills that military planners and trainers would like to see in all of their information warriors. When dealing with amateur attackers, there are several things that corporations should keep in mind, including:

- ▶ The same level of diligence must be maintained when the company is pursuing an investigation of an attacker—and the same level of cooperation must be maintained with law enforcement authorities, as explained in previous sections—regardless if the attacker is viewed as an amateur or a terrorist.

- ▶ In the event that the amateur attacker ends up being a juvenile, it is advisable that the public relations department of the company assign staff to deal with media inquiries and work to mitigate any possible bad press that arises from the situation.

- ▶ It is important to reinforce the importance of the case to anyone in the corporation who may be involved; so often there is an attitude of soft-heartedness that sets in once it is discovered that the perpetrator is a juvenile.

- ▶ As in all cases, it is important that company representatives are careful about public comments they make about the attack or the attacker, but this is even truer if the attacker is a juvenile. Although it is important not to negatively impact the prosecutor's case, it is even more important to protect the reputation and public image of the company, and prosecuting a juvenile is never going to be universally popular.

Conclusions and an Agenda for Action

Although the world is enjoying a relatively high level of peace, the preparation for war remains a social, political, and economic necessity. The new face of war, information warfare, poses challenges for governments, military organizations, and private corporations. War has always impacted private companies. They have had to deal with disruption of their operations and loss of facilities and personnel in war-torn areas. They have also had to provide support to their government and their military protectors. All of these things remain true when dealing with information warfare attacks.

However, what is more true in information warfare than in any war in the past is that distant targets can be hit and damaged without sending vast armies and navies around the world to invade a foreign land. The global communications infrastructure has put every corporation on an enemy's map as a potential target for an information warfare attack. No company is safe, and all companies need to support national efforts to protect the information infrastructure as well as their assets and livelihood.

Conclusions on Information Warfare Strategies and Tactics from a Corporate Perspective

Corporations need to prepare for information warfare attacks. We would all be better off if such attacks never occur. But to hope that information warfare does not come and thus not prepare for it is foolish. Conclusions from this analysis of information warfare strategies and tactics from a corporate perspective are as follows:

- ► Information warfare is not solely a concern of the military or federal law enforcement agencies. All organizations with computer systems that are networked together across the country or around the world are vulnerable to information warfare attacks.

- ► Corporations will mutually benefit from participating in and supporting organizations like the NIPC as well as other regional or international efforts to prepare for information warfare attacks.

- ► The integration of physical security and information systems security efforts can help in the preparation for information warfare from an enterprise perspective and ensure that all parts of the company are working as a single unit toward the goal of protection.

- ► Companies need to prepare for many types of information warfare attacks, including ruinous and containment military-led attacks as well as very serious attacks by terrorists and rogue criminals.

- System designers and application developers should be more aware that major threats loom in the future and assume that any systems they build need to be constructed in the best manner possible to withstand information warfare attacks.

- Corporations should not assume that all attacks will originate outside the company without the support or cooperation of people inside the company. It is important that individuals who work in the information infrastructure of the company should have their backgrounds checked.

An Agenda for Action on Information Warfare Strategies and Tactics from a Corporate Perspective

Preparation for information warfare is not only the responsibility of the military. It requires cooperation from both the public and private sectors in the United States as well as governments around the world. In the face of information warfare, there is a lot at stake, including economic and political stability, and perhaps even the very future of many companies that are not prepared to withstand attacks. The following agenda for action is essential in the preparation for information warfare:

- Those corporations that support the NIPC and have become members of InfraGard should continue their support of the process. Those who are not yet members should join immediately.

- Corporations need to develop well-integrated business contingency plans that address how they will respond in the event of information warfare attacks on countries in which they have facilities and operations or attacks specifically directed toward the company.

- Corporate security departments should maintain lists of people or organizations that in some way may pose a security threat to the corporation. The list should be comprehensive and include groups in all of the countries in which the company does business.

- Information security professionals need to be trained to collect and assemble forensic evidence that can help investigators identify and track down those who attack information systems.

- All attacks on information systems should be taken seriously. Every effort should be made to identify and apprehend attackers regardless of their age, geographical location, or political and religious affiliations.

Chapter 7

Strategies and Tactics from a Terrorist and Criminal Perspective

The Internet is giving terrorist and rogues easier access to all types of systems around the world. Information warfare may well become the preferred tool of terrorists in the future. Rogue criminal organizations that work for hire will also pursue information strategies for profit. Alarming thoughts, perhaps, but evidence is quickly stacking up in favor of the proposition as was discovered through interviews with prosecutors, law enforcement personnel, and corporate security planners. Many expressed grave concerns about the future information warfare and computer crime activities of outlaw groups around the world.

It seems that information warfare is either an opportunity or a threat for all types of groups. The military perspective and the corporate perspective on information warfare were examined in Chapters 5 and 6, respectively. This chapter covers information warfare from the perspective of the terrorist and rogue criminal, including why terrorists and rogues have an advantage in information warfare, how outlaw groups will work from both inside and outside organizations to attack systems, and how these groups will obtain funding for their efforts.

Why Terrorists and Rogues Have an Advantage in Information Warfare

A fundamental dynamic of information warfare is that defenders must always succeed in protecting systems, whereas if attackers do not succeed, they can try again later or move on to another target that may be easier to steal information from, damage, or disable. Attack scenarios that reflect this reality have been (and will be) played out again and again. It is the defenders that are at risk in information warfare. They must succeed in order to keep systems up and running, to protect vital information, to maintain their jobs, or to comply with the terms of a security contract. Attackers have the easy side of information warfare, and terrorists and rogue criminals have the advantage of being able to come back many times and attempt an attack.

A second dynamic that favors the outlaw attacker is the growth of computer networks and the increase in Internet connectivity. There are many systems connected to so many other systems in numerous ways. It has become almost impossible to tally the number of systems that are connected, and many people have concluded that any further counting is a mute point. A conversation with a director of computer security at a large telecommunications firm revealed the magnitude of this problem. When asked, "Are all of the computers in your company secure?" the answer was straightforward: "They will be when I find out where they all are." This problem has become more widespread as corporations and military units build out their networks at an incredible rate and attach more and more devices to the networks every day. Network engineers and communications technicians in organizations around the world are building networks as fast as they can, many of which lag way behind in having adequate security.

A third dynamic that favors the attacker is that they have access to all of the same technology the defender has as well as all of the technical information about systems, including weaknesses in hardware and software. Although the companies that produce information technology products put forth considerable effort to conceal the weaknesses of their systems and software, it is virtually impossible to hide this information from people who really want to gain access. There are many websites, user manuals, bug reports, and books that provide a continuous flow of information about how information technology products work and what kinds of weakness are present in the products.

Another area where attackers have an advantage is that they can use the Internet and become members of the same clubs, chat rooms, bulletin boards, and email lists that defenders use to help them obtain information about products or confer with their peers. This anonymity is inherent in the wired world. Individuals can easily assume identities and remain anonymous as they wander the World Wide Web seeking out information that helps them develop information warfare attack tactics. The openness of the Internet and the freedom to publish almost any type of information in numerous countries has resulted in the Web becoming a huge repository of information for those who know how to find it and have the patience to do so.

Attackers can also gain an advantage in that they can work their craft from almost anywhere in the world. The Internet and the global telecommunications networks transform many of the tactics used by information warriors into casual telecommuting experiences. The global nature of communications also lets attackers from many different countries collaborate by exchanging information or working together as virtual teams in their attack efforts. This allows attackers to have the same sort of support network that defenders have established over the years.

Finally, attackers have an advantage in information warfare because they can easily outnumber defenders. In an organization with an information systems staff of 300 people, there are perhaps 30 people assigned to network engineering and administrative duties. There are maybe 10 people directly responsible for security efforts, many of whom perform basic functions such as password administration. This size of staff will be responsible for providing information systems services to 6,000 or more users who may be located in offices or factories around the world. The network and security staff generally uses commercial products, about which attackers have a full range of information. The defenders are likely to be working with limited resources, especially when technology budgets are tight. It is relatively easy to organize an information warfare attack force of dozens of people with the same or superior skill levels as the defenders in this example. Such situations can quickly put defenders at a severe disadvantage.

The combination of these dynamics has helped set the stage for successful terrorist and rogue criminal information warfare attacks. It also broadens the appeal for many organizations to adopt information warfare strategies.

Frankly, things do not look too good for system defenders. With all of the advantages that attackers can easily achieve they will be able to mount successful information warfare attacks with small budgets and a limited amount of equipment. When these advantages are paired with the strong motivations that terrorists have to serve their country or political group, they will quickly develop the skill sets and recruit the personnel necessary to be successful in their information warfare efforts. When these advantages are combined with the greed and outlaw tendencies of rogue criminal groups, these groups will also find information warfare strategies appealing. They will employ these strategies to attack systems on a for-hire basis, to steal corporate information for resale, or use attacks to steal money or in the support of extortion efforts.

The Future Computer-Literate Terrorist and Criminal

It is the information age. Computer literacy is on the rise around the world. Universities in many countries now offer advance degrees in computer science and telecommunications. Students from all reaches of the globe travel to the United States and European countries to become educated in computer sciences, systems design, and software development. Information technology industries are growing rapidly in Japan, India, China, Ireland, Brazil, Malaysia, South Korea, and Spain. Just a few decades ago these countries were well behind the United States in their use of information technology, their ability to manufacture information technology products, and the development of an internal industrial structure necessary to support the growth of an information technology sector. These conditions have changed rapidly and will continue to change as the world becomes more connected and more dependent on information technology.

In addition to formal education in information technology, advanced training necessary to install and maintain computers and networking equipment is being provided on a global basis. Many technology producers, such as 3Com, Cisco, Compaq, Hewlett-Packard, IBM, and Lucent, must provide training to their customers in order to facilitate the sales process and expand their installed base of customers around the world. These companies provide a level of sophistication in their training offerings that is unmatched in any university anywhere in the world. This training, like university education programs, adds to the global skill base of information technology workers.

As information technology knowledge and skills become more widespread there will be a greater opportunity for those prone to terrorism or criminal activity to develop proficiencies necessary to become information warriors. Thus, it is inevitable that future generations of terrorists and criminals will have skills that will make them a serious threat to the global information infrastructure. They will also be able to direct these skills to attacking government, military, and corporate information systems. This means that in ten to twenty years the threat of information warfare strategies being employed by less than friendly forces will increase dramatically.

It is also likely that criminal families and terrorists will deliberately educate their children in information technology fields. These groups have always and will continue to seek and develop skill sets that are appropriate for the economic, political, and social conditions in which they operate. They are going to respond to the needs of the information technology in step with the rest of the world, and they will patiently and diligently create their own armies of information warriors dedicated to fulfilling the goals of their culture and social groups.

Selecting Information Warfare Targets

The success of any type of information warfare attacks is going to be highly dependent on the skill levels of the information warriors executing the attack. While inside information and the support of an internal operative in a target organization will be helpful to rogue criminal and terrorist information warfare strategies, these groups still need trained information warriors if they are going to achieve success. As previously discussed, criminal families and terrorist communities are certainly willing to put forth the effort and resources to train members of their social groups. These groups may also focus attention on recruiting outside expertise.

Although rogue criminals and terrorists may not be too particular about their targets, they will eventually recognize that some targets are more economically or politically valuable than others. Thus it is important that terrorist and criminal groups develop expertise about the information infrastructures of various industry sectors. It is also important to select a target that is consistent with the overall goals of the criminal gang or terrorist group.

To determine which industry or business sectors terrorists and rogue criminals may be most interested in attacking, more than 500 industry classifications were reviewed by the author. If there was some record of known historical interest in the sectors, the interest level of both terrorist groups and organized criminal groups was rated considering several factors. For criminals, known past or present involvement was the key factor in the rating process, tempered by the level of financial gain that could be obtained through successful attacks. For terrorist groups, past activities were considered as well as financial gain and the potential dramatic impact that a terrorist group could achieve by successfully attacking a target organization in the sector. Interest was then rated from low to high. Sectors that were rated of low interest to both terrorists and criminals were then eliminated from the final list. The results of the analysis are shown in Table 7-1.

Table 7-1: Interest Level of Terrorist and Criminal Groups in Launching Information Warfare Attacks Against Organizations in an Industry Sector

Sector/Industry	Terrorist Group Interest Level	Rogue Criminal Interest Level
Accounting, tax preparation, bookkeeping, payroll services	Low	Moderate
Aerospace product and parts manufacturing	High	Moderate
Air traffic control	High	Moderate
Aircraft manufacturing	High	Moderate
Airport operations	High	Moderate
Ambulance services	Low	Moderate
Amusement, gambling, and recreation industries	Low	High
Apparel, piece goods, and notions wholesalers	Low	High
Armored car services	High	High

Table 7-1 Continued: Interest Level of Terrorist and Criminal Groups in Launching Information Warfare Attacks Against Organizations in an Industry Sector

Sector/Industry	Terrorist Group Interest Level	Rogue Criminal Interest Level
Automobile dealers	Low	Moderate
Automobile manufacturing	Moderate	Low
Automotive parts, accessories, and tire stores	Low	Moderate
Beer and ale wholesalers	Low	High
Beer, wine, and liquor stores	Low	Moderate
Boat dealers	Low	Moderate
Book publishers	Low	Moderate
Breweries	Low	Moderate
Cable networks	High	Moderate
Casino and casino hotels	Low	High
Cellular and other wireless telecommunications	High	Moderate
Chemical manufacturing	High	Moderate
Clothing and clothing accessories stores	Low	Moderate
Commercial banking	High	High
Communications equipment manufacturing	High	Moderate
Commuter rail systems	High	Moderate
Computer and peripheral equipment and software wholesalers	Moderate	Moderate
Computer and electronic product manufacturing	High	Moderate
Computer and peripheral equipment manufacturing	High	Moderate
Computer and software stores	Low	Moderate
Computer facilities management services	High	High
Computer storage device manufacturing	High	Moderate
Computer systems design and related services	Moderate	Moderate
Computer systems design services	Moderate	Moderate

Table 7-1 Continued: Interest Level of Terrorist and Criminal Groups in Launching Information Warfare Attacks Against Organizations in an Industry Sector

Sector/Industry	Terrorist Group Interest Level	Rogue Criminal Interest Level
Construction	Low	Moderate
Construction machinery manufacturing	Moderate	Moderate
Consumer lending	Moderate	Moderate
Convenience stores	Low	Moderate
Correctional institutions	Low	Moderate
Courts	Moderate	Moderate
Credit bureaus	Low	Moderate
Credit card issuing	High	High
Credit intermediation and related activities	Moderate	High
Credit unions	Moderate	High
Custom computer programming services	Moderate	Moderate
Data processing services	Moderate	Moderate
Database and directory publishers	Low	Moderate
Deep sea, coastal, and Great Lakes water transportation	High	Moderate
Depository credit intermediation	Moderate	High
Distilleries	Low	Moderate
Electric power generation	High	Low
Electric power transmission, control, and distribution	High	Low
Electron tube manufacturing	High	Moderate
Electronic shopping and mail order houses	Low	Moderate
Electronics and appliance stores	Low	Moderate
Engine, turbine, power transmission equipment manufacturing	Moderate	Moderate
Executive government offices	High	Moderate
Fabricated metal product manufacturing	Moderate	Moderate

Table 7-1 Continued: Interest Level of Terrorist and Criminal Groups in Launching Information Warfare Attacks Against Organizations in an Industry Sector

Sector/Industry	Terrorist Group Interest Level	Rogue Criminal Interest Level
Fiber optic cable manufacturing	Moderate	Low
Financial transactions processing, reserve, clearinghouse activities	High	High
Fire protection	High	High
Food manufacturing	Low	Moderate
Footwear wholesalers	Low	High
Gambling industries	Low	High
Gasoline stations	Low	Moderate
Grocery and related product wholesalers	Low	High
Grocery stores	Low	Moderate
Guided missile and space vehicle manufacturing	High	Moderate
Hardware stores	Low	Moderate
Hardware wholesalers	Low	High
Hazardous waste collection	Low	Moderate
Heavy duty truck manufacturing	Moderate	Low
Hospitals	Moderate	Low
Hotels (except casino hotels) and motels	Low	Moderate
Industrial machinery manufacturing	Moderate	Moderate
Industrial truck, tractor, trailer manufacturing	Moderate	Moderate
Inland water transportation	High	Moderate
Insurance carriers	Low	Moderate
International affairs	High	Moderate
International trade financing	High	Moderate
Investment banking and securities dealing	High	High
Jewelry and silverware manufacturing	Low	Moderate

Table 7-1 Continued: Interest Level of Terrorist and Criminal Groups in Launching Information Warfare Attacks Against Organizations in an Industry Sector

Sector/Industry	Terrorist Group Interest Level	Rogue Criminal Interest Level
Labor unions and similar labor organizations	Low	High
Legal counsel and prosecution	Low	Moderate
Legislative bodies	High	Moderate
Light truck and utility vehicle manufacturing	Moderate	Low
Machinery manufacturing	Moderate	Moderate
Marine cargo handling	Low	High
Men's and boys' clothing and furnishings wholesalers	Low	High
Military armored vehicle, tank, and component manufacturing	High	Moderate
Mining	Low	Moderate
Monetary authorities—central bank	High	High
Mortgage and non-mortgage loan brokers	Low	High
Motion picture and sound recording industries	High	Moderate
Motor vehicle body manufacturing	Moderate	Low
Motorcycle dealers	Low	Moderate
National security and international affairs	High	Moderate
Natural gas distribution	High	Low
Navigational services to shipping	High	Moderate
Navigational, measuring, and control instruments manufacturing	High	Moderate
Newspaper publishers	Low	Moderate
Non-depository credit intermediation	Moderate	High
Nuclear electric power generation	High	Low
Online information services	Moderate	Moderate
Paging	High	Moderate
Payroll services	Low	High

Table 7-1 Continued: Interest Level of Terrorist and Criminal Groups in Launching Information Warfare Attacks Against Organizations in an Industry Sector

Sector/Industry	Terrorist Group Interest Level	Rogue Criminal Interest Level
Periodical publishers	Low	Moderate
Pipeline transportation	High	Moderate
Police protection	Moderate	High
Political organizations	High	Low
Port and harbor operations	High	High
Portfolio management	High	High
Primary metal manufacturing	Moderate	Moderate
Public finance activities	High	Moderate
Racetracks	Low	High
Radio, television, wireless communications equipment manufacturing	High	Moderate
Radio networks	High	Moderate
Radio stations	High	Moderate
Rail transportation	High	Moderate
Railroad rolling stock manufacturing	High	Moderate
Sales financing	Moderate	Moderate
Satellite telecommunications	High	High
Savings institutions	Moderate	High
Scheduled air transportation	High	Moderate
Scheduled passenger air transportation	High	Moderate
Search, detection, navigation, guidance, aeronautical, and nautical system and instrument manufacturing	High	Moderate
Secondary market financing	Moderate	Moderate
Securities and commodity exchanges	High	High
Securities brokerage	High	High

Table 7-1 Continued: Interest Level of Terrorist and Criminal Groups in Launching Information Warfare Attacks Against Organizations in an Industry Sector

Sector/Industry	Terrorist Group Interest Level	Rogue Criminal Interest Level
Security guards and patrol services	Low	Moderate
Security systems services	High	High
Semiconductor and other electronic component manufacturing	High	Moderate
Ship and boat building	High	Moderate
Software publishers	High	High
Software reproducing	High	High
Space research and technology	High	Moderate
Spectator sports	Low	High
Taxi and limousine service	Low	High
Telecommunications	High	Moderate
Telephone call centers	Low	Moderate
Television broadcasting	High	Moderate
Textile mills	Low	Moderate
Tobacco and tobacco product wholesalers	Low	High
Tobacco manufacturing	Low	Moderate
Truck transportation	High	Moderate
Trusts, estates, and agency accounts	Low	Moderate
Uranium/radium/vanadium ore mining	High	Moderate
Urban transit systems	High	Moderate
Vending machine operators	Low	Moderate
Warehousing and storage	Low	High
Waste collection	Low	High
Waste treatment and disposal	Low	Moderate
Wholesale trade, durable goods	Low	High

Table 7-1 Continued: Interest Level of Terrorist and Criminal Groups in Launching Information Warfare Attacks Against Organizations in an Industry Sector

Sector/Industry	Terrorist Group Interest Level	Rogue Criminal Interest Level
Wine and distilled alcoholic beverage wholesalers	Low	High
Wineries	Low	Moderate
Wired telecommunications carriers	High	Moderate
Wireless telecommunications carriers (except satellite)	High	Moderate

Targets that Appeal to Both Terrorists and Rogue Criminals

Of the potential information warfare targets that were evaluated for their level of appeal to terrorists and rogue criminals it is important to examine which targets may be in the greatest danger. It is not surprising that terrorists and rogue criminals would have some common interest in targets. Among the types of organizations that both may decide to strike are armored car services, commercial banking, and credit card issuing firms. Stock exchanges and brokerages are also on the mutual favorites list of terrorists and rogue criminals. Targets that were rated of high interest for both the terrorist and rogue criminals are shown in Table 7-2.

Table 7-2: Targets that Appeal to Both Terrorists and Rogue Criminals

Sector/Industry	Terrorist Group Interest Level	Rogue Criminal Interest Level
Armored car services	High	High
Commercial banking	High	High
Computer facilities management services	High	High
Credit card issuing	High	High
Financial transactions processing, reserve, clearinghouse activities	High	High
Fire protection	High	High
Investment banking and securities dealing	High	High

Table 7-2 Continued: Targets that Appeal to Both Terrorists and Rogue Criminals

Sector/Industry	Terrorist Group Interest Level	Rogue Criminal Interest Level
Monetary authorities—central bank	High	High
Port and harbor operations	High	High
Portfolio management	High	High
Satellite telecommunications	High	High
Securities and commodity exchanges	High	High
Securities brokerage	High	High
Security systems services	High	High
Software publishers	High	High
Software reproducing	High	High

Targets that Appeal to Terrorists, but Not Rogue Criminals

Of the potential information warfare targets that were evaluated for their level of appeal to terrorists and rogue criminals, there are several that were rated as highly appealing for terrorists but less attractive to rogue criminals. Most of the targets that have high terrorist appeal and lower rogue criminal appeal are public and national infrastructure targets, including electric power, government organizations, and major manufacturing companies. Targets that were rated of high interest to terrorists, but lower interest to rogue criminals are shown in Table 7-3.

Table 7-3: Targets Rated of High Interest to Terrorists, but Lower Interest to Rogue Criminals

Sector/Industry	Terrorist Group Interest Level
Electric power transmission, control, and distribution	High
Natural gas distribution	High
Nuclear electric power generation	High
Political organizations	High

Table 7-3 Continued: Targets Rated of High Interest to Terrorists, but Lower Interest to Rogue Criminals

Sector/Industry	Terrorist Group Interest Level
Aerospace product and parts manufacturing	High
Air traffic control	High
Aircraft manufacturing	High
Airport operations	High
Cable networks	High
Cellular and other wireless telecommunications	High
Chemical manufacturing	High
Communications equipment manufacturing	High
Commuter rail systems	High
Computer and electronic product manufacturing	High
Computer and peripheral equipment manufacturing	High
Computer storage device manufacturing	High
Deep sea, coastal, and Great Lakes water transportation	High
Electron tube manufacturing	High
Executive government offices	High
Guided missile and space vehicle manufacturing	High
Inland water transportation	High
International affairs	High
International trade financing	High
Legislative bodies	High
Military armored vehicle, tank, and component manufacturing	High
Motion picture and sound recording industries	High
National security and international affairs	High
Navigational services to shipping	High

Table 7-3 Continued: Targets Rated of High Interest to Terrorists, but Lower Interest to Rogue Criminals

Sector/Industry	Terrorist Group Interest Level
Navigational, measuring, and control instruments manufacturing	High
Paging	High
Pipeline transportation	High
Public finance activities	High
Radio networks	High
Radio stations	High
Radio, television, wireless communications equipment manufacturing	High
Rail transportation	High
Railroad rolling stock manufacturing	High
Scheduled air transportation	High
Scheduled passenger air transportation	High
Search, detection, navigation, guidance, aeronautical, and nautical system and instrument manufacturing	High
Semiconductor and other electronic component manufacturing	High
Ship and boat building	High
Space research and technology	High
Telecommunications	High
Television broadcasting	High
Truck transportation	High
Uranium/radium/vanadium ore mining	High
Urban transit systems	High
Wired telecommunications carriers	High
Wireless telecommunications carriers (except satellite)	High

Targets that Appeal to Rogue Criminals, but Not Terrorists

Of the potential information warfare targets that were evaluated for their level of appeal to terrorists and rogue criminals, there are several that were rated as highly appealing for rogue criminals but less attractive to terrorists. Most of the targets that have high rogue criminal appeal and lower terrorist appeal are those that have traditionally held the interest of organized criminals. These include companies in the apparel industry, beer and liquor firms, casinos and hotels, and waste collection. Targets that were rated of high interest to terrorists and lower interest to rogue criminals are shown in Table 7-4.

Table 7-4: Targets Rated of High Interest to Rogue Criminals, but Lower Interest to Terrorists

Sector/Industry	Rogue Criminal Interest Level
Apparel, piece goods, and notions wholesalers	High
Beer and ale wholesalers	High
Casinos and casino hotels	High
Credit intermediation and related activities	High
Credit unions	High
Depository credit intermediation	High
Footwear wholesalers	High
Gambling industries	High
Grocery and related product wholesalers	High
Hardware wholesalers	High
Labor unions and similar labor organizations	High
Marine cargo handling	High
Men's and boys' clothing and furnishings wholesalers	High
Mortgage and non-mortgage loan brokers	High
Non-depository credit intermediation	High

Table 7-4 Continued: Targets Rated of High Interest to Rogue Criminals, but Lower Interest to Terrorists

Sector/Industry	Rogue Criminal Interest Level
Payroll services	High
Police protection	High
Racetracks	High
Savings institutions	High
Spectator sports	High
Taxi and limousine service	High
Tobacco and tobacco product wholesalers	High
Warehousing and storage	High
Waste collection	High
Wholesale trade, durable goods	High
Wine and distilled alcoholic beverage wholesalers	High

Working from the Inside of Information Warfare Targets

Criminals, and often terrorists as well, understand the benefit of having inside information on any organization that they wish to penetrate in order to more readily and effectively accomplish their goals. Financial crimes such as fraud and embezzlement are very often successful because of the joint efforts of an inside operative and an external person or group. Random and sustained rogue criminal information warfare strategies are very likely to employ a combination of an insider and an external team to perpetrate their crime. It has been a successful tactic in the past and it can help facilitate any type of information warfare attacks in the future.

An insider is sometimes planted in an organization as a mole. The education of the children of criminal families, as previously described, will certainly help to create an operative who is capable of securing employment as information technology professional. Once they have become employed, they can continue their career development while simultaneously aiding their family in the pursuit of criminal activity.

In other cases, employees of companies are blackmailed or intimidated into helping criminals or terrorists. As outlaw groups increase their corporate knowledge, they will be able to identify insiders that could be helpful to their efforts. Once these individuals have been identified, the historically successful tactics of payoffs, blackmail, or threats to self or family will be employed to coerce the cooperation of the victim.

Insiders will be able to provide essential information, including system and communications configurations and design, known weaknesses in security, and even passwords on corporate laptops, all of which can help criminals and terrorists penetrate information systems for whatever purpose they have in mind. This will reduce the efforts of criminal gangs and terrorist groups to gain access to systems and may allow them to have continued system access over long periods of time. The key to this tactic being successful is that the insider is capable of delivering the support necessary to accomplish a job or mission. The most likely candidate to work as an inside operative will

- ▶ Be able to gain access to essential information in a manner that is considered normal and standard operating procedure within the penetrated organization.

- ▶ Be capable of working for long periods of time as a mole in an undercover operation.

- ▶ Be dedicated to their cause either because of political or social ties to outside groups or because the outside group has gained substantial power over the individual through intimidation or blackmail.

Establishing an inside connection or planting an operative in an organization is not a difficult process. A highly trained information technology professional with ties to a criminal family or terrorist group who deliberately pursues employment with target organizations will likely have little difficulty obtaining a job because of the shortage of skilled professionals. It should be simple enough to obfuscate the background of any such individual to the point that they could pass the level of background checks that most organizations are willing to pursue.

Avoiding Pursuit and Capture

Information warfare attacks launched by military organizations do not always need to be cloaked, and any cloaking efforts will of course depend on the political status or military profile of the attack. In general, terrorists or criminals who launch information warfare attacks will probably want their identities and locations to remain obfuscated as much as possible. In addition to concealing their true location, terrorists and criminals may also need additional equipment and bandwidth to accomplish their attacks. There are several likely paths that such groups will take in order to accomplish these objectives.

If the groups are being supported or employed by a less than friendly government, they may also be aided in obtaining access to telecommunications services, Internet service providers, or government facilities in the sponsoring country. This will certainly help with the equipment and access requirements of the attack, but terrorists and rogues will also need to use every approach possible to assume identities and make it appear that their attacks are coming from other locations. This is a mid-level information warrior skill.

It is also probable that terrorists and rogue criminals will attempt to employ a network of attackers around the world who can work in a coordinated manner. It is easy to establish Internet access accounts under assumed identities that can be used from homes and offices available to the attack force. At present, law enforcement agencies in most countries are so under-trained and have so little interest in these attacks, it is possible for attackers to work from a location for at least several hours—if not several days—before the police finally arrive.

Another approach that terrorists and criminals will rely on is the unauthorized use of computers and connections that belong to private companies, government agencies, individual citizens, and perhaps even military organizations to launch attacks. This can also allow for significant blocks of time for attackers to work without being physically pursued. Another resource that terrorists and criminals can exploit is university computer systems that often lie idle much of the time, especially on holidays and during vacation periods. All of these systems can be used on a hands-on basis for extended periods of time. Alternatively, they can be programmed as drones or robots to execute commands at prescheduled time or be triggered remotely by a controller.

Other tactics that terrorists and criminals can employee include physically taking over a branch office of a company and using the company's own systems to access and download information, manipulate records, or plant malicious code. This would be easy enough to accomplish in several countries through the use of force, bribes, or both. In addition, it is fairly easy for terrorists and criminals to engage the support of affiliates who can accomplish specific tasks from computers in their company, school, or home. This support can be gained through payment, coercion, blackmail, or intimidation. In many cases, it may be easy for terrorists to recruit help through political, cultural, and emotional persuasion.

Bear in mind that not all information warfare attacks require the sophisticated skill levels of a senior computer programmer. Military tactics in information warfare include the physical destruction of communications systems as well as computer systems and monitoring and control devices. Terrorists, of course, just love to blow things up and can take fairly simple approaches to causing disruptions in global information and communications systems. It is not fancy, but it is still an information warfare tactic that will remain valid for eternity.

Fund Raising for Terrorist and Rogue Criminal Information Warriors

To prepare for the effective use of information warfare strategies, terrorists and rogue criminals will need financial resources to pay their information warriors and obtain appropriate equipment and other resources. This is certainly the case in any organization that needs to defend against information warfare attacks or use offensive information warfare strategies. Thus, terrorist groups and rogue criminal organizations need to allocate the necessary funds to meet their development objectives.

One reason that financial services and banking organizations were rated as high interest targets for both terrorists and rogues is that both criminal groups have historically robbed, embezzled, or otherwise stolen much of the money they use to operate. The tradition is expected to continue in their development of information warfare skills and their preparation for using information warfare strategies. A high level of funding would allow these organizations to establish their own training programs and develop the highly skilled workforce they will need to effectively launch information warfare attacks. If these groups are going to sell their services on the open market, they will need to show that they have the skill base and demonstrate that they also have a successful track record in accomplishing attacks. They must also be able to provide competitive pricing for their work.

One option that terrorists and rogue criminals have that law enforcement agencies and military units do not have is that they can steal computer systems, software, and communications services to use in their information warfare efforts. Using stolen technology can help terrorists and criminals lower their overall cost of operations and free funds for recruitment and training of personnel. Their lower overhead can certainly be translated into a competitive advantage as competing terrorists and rogue criminals attempt to market their information warfare services.

Conclusions and an Agenda for Action

Terrorists and rogue criminals will embrace information warfare strategies in the future. In the meantime, they have a lot to do in terms of developing skill sets, recruiting qualified information warriors, and developing adequate funding sources for their information warfare activities. They also must learn how to properly plan and manage information warfare attacks and how to select targets that meet their overall political or financial goals.

In many ways, information warfare is an ideal strategy for terrorists and rogue criminals. Terrorist can inflict considerable damage and cause extensive economic disruption without necessarily getting themselves killed. This will certainly appeal to a large number of terrorists. Bear in mind that there will always be terrorists who are willing to die for their cause, and just because terrorists get more sophisticated in their tactics does not mean that the days of suicide bombers are over.

Rogue criminals are also likely to find information warfare attractive for a similar set of reasons. They won't be shot at all the time, they can probably get paid for breaking into systems and damaging them or stealing information, and they can also use information warfare attacks as a means of intimidating companies or individuals. It looks like information warfare strategies are also ideally suited for criminal organizations.

Conclusions on Information Warfare Strategies and Tactics from a Terrorist and Rogue Criminal Perspective

To thoroughly prepare to launch effective information warfare attacks, both terrorist groups and rogue criminals have considerable work to do in order to develop their skill sets. As these capabilities are developed, target selection is key to both terrorists and rogue criminals aligning their information warfare efforts with other goals. The following conclusions were drawn from the analysis of information warfare strategies and tactics from a terrorist and rogue perspective:

- ▶ The rapid growth of computer networks and expansion of Internet connectivity has created more entryways into systems. Security efforts do not always keep pace with the network building efforts.

- ▶ Attackers have many advantages in information warfare, including access to technical information about systems, the ability to collaborate on a global basis, and the ability to strike systems from many different paths.

- ▶ Terrorists will need to focus their target selection efforts on organizations that can help meet their political goals, while rogue criminal information warriors will choose targets that help meet their financial or organizational goals. Random attacks launched against any company at any time will do little to help these groups meet their goals.

- ▶ There are information warfare targets that have high appeal to both terrorists and rogue criminals, but there are also targets that have higher appeal to terrorists than rogue criminals and vice versa.

- ▶ Rogue criminals and terrorist groups are very likely to use an insider to obtain information that makes it easier for them to penetrate or attack the information systems of a company.

- ▶ Terrorists and rogue criminal groups also need to develop good skill sets and recruit qualified information warriors before they can leverage information warfare strategies as a viable approach to accomplishing their goals.

An Agenda for Action on Information Warfare Strategies and Tactics from a Terrorist and Rogue Criminal Perspective

Terrorist groups and rogue criminals need to accomplish several things before they are fully prepared to employ information warfare strategies. The following agenda for action is applicable to these groups. Law enforcement agencies and military organizations should monitor the progress of terrorists and rogue criminals in accomplishing this agenda and be prepared to counter their attacks.

- ▸ Terrorist groups and rogue criminals need to take a methodical approach to developing their information warfare abilities, and they should start soon if they want to effectively compete with other groups in the future.

- ▸ They should rely on stolen technology to keep their costs down and allow for sufficient funds to pay personnel costs associated with developing their information warfare abilities.

- ▸ Terrorist groups and rogue criminals should establish their own comprehensive training programs in order to develop a cadre of highly skilled information warriors.

- ▸ As in any business, terrorist groups and rogue criminals should start developing their track record and show success in their information warfare efforts in order to justify their internal budgets and to attract business from outside funding sources.

Chapter 8

The Arms Dealers and Industrial Mobilization in Information Warfare

There has been considerable debate over which information technology products are defensive tools in information warfare and which are offensive tools. In reality, all information technology products can be used as either defensive or offensive tools in information warfare. What distinguishes whether a product is defensive or offensive is not what the product was designed to do, but rather how it is being used and by whom and under what circumstances.

Another important point to recognize is that the companies that create and market information technology products and services will all play a role in information warfare. Each company is certainly responsible for informing their users how to properly use their products and how to protect those products from misuse, abuse, or attack. This makes all technology producing companies part of the defensive information warfare establishment.

It has also been a long-standing tradition that industrial companies cooperate with the militaries of their home countries by providing either products or manufacturing capability to support the country's defensive or offensive military goals. Information technology producing companies have certainly worked with their militaries in developing, designing, and implementing systems that can serve those military goals. Information warfare will be no exception to the rules or to that tradition.

This chapter examines the process by which all information technology producing companies become parts of the information warfare machines of their nations. This includes cooperation in the defense of the information infrastructure, and when and if it becomes necessary to assist their government and military in launching information warfare attacks on their enemies or their attackers.

Mobilization Requirements for Technology Companies in Information Warfare

The history of war is also the history of industrial mobilization. As nations prepare for war or respond to an aggressor, it is clear that they need supplies, materials, and expertise to fight their wars. The process of industrial mobilization is the transformation of industry from peacetime activity into a program to support national military objectives. This includes the mobilization of materials, labor, capital, production facilities, and contributory items and services essential to the requirements of the military in meeting their national objectives. There has been considerable study of the process and the outcome of industrial mobilization, much of it focused on World War II. Subsequent to World War II, a quasi-permanent military/industrial establishment emerged to support the military objectives of the Cold War, much of which has been mothballed as the world moves away from the Cold War mentality. However, there are still examples of industrial mobilization in place in many nations.

Industrial mobilization also entails converting existing transportation capacity to support industrial production and wartime logistical requirements to move supplies, materials, and personnel in a manner that is necessary to meet military objectives. As a result of this need, the United States established the National Defense Reserve Fleet (NDRF) under Section 11 of the Merchant Ship Sales Act of 1946, to serve as a reserve of ships which can support national defense purposes. These ships could be activated to meet shipping requirements during national emergencies. The Maritime Security Program (MSP), which is now part of the U.S. Department of Transportation (DOT), facilitates the conversion of the privately owned, U.S.-flagged, and U.S.-crewed liner fleet in international trade. During a time of war, this fleet becomes available to support the Department of Defense (DOD).

In addition, there is the Civil Reserve Air Fleet Program, in which the DOD uses aircraft owned by a U.S. organization or citizen to meet the military needs of the nation. The aircraft are allocated by the DOT to augment military airlift capability. These aircraft are allocated in accordance with DOD requirements to such tasks as international long-range and short-range cargo missions or to move troops to locations.

Another example of how civilian properties can be dedicated to the support of national objectives is the Emergency Alert System (EAS). In 1994, the EAS replaced the Emergency Broadcast System (EBS) as a tool that the president of the United States and others may use to warn the public about emergency situations. Through the EAS, the president would have access to thousands of broadcast stations, cable systems, and participating satellite programmers to transmit a message to the public. The new EAS uses digital technology that also enables state and local officials to quickly send out local emergency information targeted to a specific area. The information can be sent through a broadcast station and cable system even if those facilities are unattended. The EAS digital signal is the same signal that the National Weather Service (NWS) uses on NOAA Weather Radio (NWR) which allows NWR signals to be decoded by the EAS equipment at broadcast stations and cable systems. Broadcasters and cable operators can then retransmit NWS weather warning messages almost immediately to their audiences.

These mobilization programs have served the United States through several wars and conflicts. However, they were designed to help meet national defense needs in an age when warriors fought against warriors on a field that was dedicated to the purpose of battle. Information warfare brings a new twist to the standing need of being able to mobilize industrial resources for the purpose of defending a country. Within the context of information warfare several questions about industrial mobilization need to be addressed:

- ▶ How can the laws that provided for mobilization during more traditional warfare efforts be modified to meet the needs of information warfare?

- ▶ Under what conditions will the resources of information technology manufacturers, software producers, and information technology service companies and consulting firms be mobilized for national defense?

- ▶ How broad will the scope of mobilization of the information technology industry be and what resources will they be required to provide the military?

- ▶ Will private data, competitive information, and customers' use of information technology companies be accessible by the military during mobilization?

- ▶ Will the national telecommunications infrastructure, especially that related to the Internet, be mobilized or restricted in use during industrial mobilization to respond to information warfare attacks?

- ▶ Will technology companies be required to disclose trade secrets about their products to information warriors during mobilization?

The U.S. Congress has not yet addressed these issues, and the process by which they will be addressed will become a matter of massive public debate. Private industry did not respond well to the calls for mobilization in the early days of World War II. It was not until after the attack on Pearl Harbor that the full cooperation of private industry was secured. It may take the launch of an extensive information warfare attack before these issues are addressed. But however long it may take to resolve these questions, it is important that they be addressed.

The Top Technology Companies that Can Provide Information Warfare Expertise

The largest information technology companies in the United States have ongoing government contracts and supply products to military organizations. The importance of this relationship has long been recognized by the military, which in cooperation with the Department of State has worked to curtail the export of the most powerful and sophisticated technology products. There are many information technology companies that have become critically important to the military in the United States and will likely become even more important as information warfare becomes a reality. There are also many companies that utilize computers to design products or as component parts of their products, including key players in the weapons and space industries.

Many of the technology companies that will serve very important roles in defending against information warfare attacks and contributing to developing abilities to launch offensive information warfare attacks are shown in Table 8-1. These companies are familiar to most people, but not all are readily viewed as part of the traditional military/industrial complex. However, as the face of warfare changes the military must rely on companies that have products or high levels of expertise in strategies or tactics that are relevant to the times. That is why these companies are essential to the future information warfare abilities of the United States.

Table 8-1: The Top Technology Companies that Will Play a Key Role in Information Warfare

3Com	Dell
Allied Telesyn	Eastman Kodak
Amdahl	Electronic Data Systems
Apple Computer	EMC
AT&T	Emerson Electric
BMC Software	Ericsson
Boeing	General Dynamics
Cisco Systems	General Electric
Citrix Systems	Harris
Compaq	Hewlett-Packard
Computer Associates	Hitachi Data Systems
Computer Sciences Corp	Honeywell International
Cray	IBM

Table 8-1 Continued: The Top Technology Companies that Will Play a Key Role in Information Warfare

Informix	Rolls-Royce Allison
Intel	RSA Security
Lockheed Martin	SAP
Lucent Technologies	Sikorsky Aircraft
MCI WorldCom	Silicon Graphics
Microsoft	Sprint
Motorola	Storage Technology
NCR	Sun Microsystems
NEC	Sybase
Network Associates	Symantec
Nortel (Northern Telecom)	Tektronix
Northrop Grumman	Teradyne
Oracle	Unisys
PeopleSoft	United Technologies
Raytheon Company	

Aerospace and Defense Companies that Can Provide Information Warfare Expertise

Information warriors will have a variety of needs, including the type of aerospace and defense technology that these highly specialized companies can provide. There are already strong ties between these companies and defense organizations around the world. It is likely that as information warfare becomes practiced as a routine strategy, defense organizations will turn to their long-standing suppliers to provide new technologies for both offensive and defensive information warfare tactics. Table 8-2 shows many of the well-established aerospace and defense companies that can provide information warfare technology and support. Military organizations have many advantages in relying on their traditional aerospace and defense contractors for this critical support, including:

- ▶ These companies can provide specialized technologies that cannot be purchased off the shelf by non-defense organizations.

- ▶ Most of these companies have business units and personnel that are cleared for security purposes, which allows military organizations to have a less cumbersome development relationship with the companies.

- ▶ Developers in many of these companies have an understanding of defense and warfare needs that is unique to their historical involvement in defense contracting.

- ▶ These companies do not have a vested interest in protecting their own information technology products or having weaknesses about such products revealed.

Table 8-2: Aerospace and Defense Companies that Can Provide Information Warfare Technology and Support

Advanced Aerodynamics & Structures	BF Goodrich
Aerosonic	B/E Aerospace
Airbus Industries	B.V.R. Systems
Alcatel Space	Bae Systems Canada
Alliant Techsystems	Ball Aerospace & Technologies
Alvis PLC	Banner Aerospace
American General	Bay Star Satellite Communications
Antcom	BBC Technology
Applied Analogue Systems	Boeing
Argo-Tech	Butler National
Asia Satelli	CAE
Aviall	Calian Communications Systems
Aviation General	Canadian Satellite Communications
Aztek Satellite	Celsius

Table 8-2 Continued: Aerospace and Defense Companies that Can Provide Information Warfare Technology and Support

Challenger Unicom	Finmeccanica
CIC International	Galaxy Aerospace
Cidera	GE American Communications
CLA SatCom	GenCorp
Cobham PLC	General Dynamics
Columbia Communications	General Electric
Comptek Research	General Motors
Curtiss-Wright	Gilat Satellite
Daimler Chrysler	Gulfstream Aerospace
Danby Satellite & Aerial Systems	Harris
Dassault Aviation	Herley Industries
Digisat	Honeywell International
DRS Technologies	Hughes Space And Communications
ECC International	Indra Sistemas
EchoStar Communications	International Mobile Satellite Organization (Inmarsat)
Eclipse Aviation	Intersat Space Communications
EDAC Technologies	Intertechnique
EDO	Kellstrom Industries
Elbit Systems	L-3 Communications Satellite Networks
ElecSys	LAU Technologies
EMS Technologies	Litton Industries
Esterline Technologies	LMI Aerospace
European Aeronautic Defence and Space Company	Lockheed Martin
Eutelsat	Magellan Aerospace
Fairchild Dornier	Motorola

Table 8-2 Continued: Aerospace and Defense Companies that Can Provide Information Warfare Technology and Support

National Aeronautics and Space Administration	Rolls-Royce Allison
Northrop Grumman	Scott Technologies
Orbital Sciences	Sikorsky Aircraft
PanAmSat	TAT Industries
Pemco Aviation Group	Teleflex Incorporated
Pratt & Whitney	United Defense Industries
Radyne ComStream	United Industrial
Raytheon Company	United Technologies
Remote Control	Woodward Governor Company
Rockwell International	WorldSpace

Computer System Manufacturers that Can Provide Information Warfare Expertise

There are also numerous companies that design, develop, and produce computer systems that can play a role in creating information warfare tools and provide expertise to military organizations. There are existing relationships between many of these companies and military organizations, but the process of converting their expertise and technologies into information warfare tools is really just beginning. There are business opportunities these companies should explore in order to expand their product offerings and revenue base. Table 8-3 shows many of the computer system manufacturers that can provide information warfare technology and support. Military organizations have many advantages in working with established or growing computer technology companies in developing information warfare tools, including:

▶ The established companies that have been developing computer systems for many years have considerable expertise in system design and have extensive knowledge about the computers that are used in business and manufacturing environments around the world.

▶ Developers in many of the newer companies have innovative ideas that could add to the arsenal of information warfare tools, and they are looking for new markets for their technologies and their expertise.

▶ Information warriors need to have as broad an understanding as possible about all types of computer systems if they are going to be effective in defending or attacking systems.

Table 8-3: Computer System Manufacturers that Can Provide Information Warfare Technology and Support

3Dlabs	Apple Computer
Actel	Applied Microsystems
Aculab	Arca Technologies
Adaptec	AST Technology Labs
ADE	Asyst Technologies
Advanced Micro Devices	ATI Technologies
Advanced Power Technology	Atmel
Aeroflex	Axiom Technology
Agere Systems	AXT
Alliance Semiconductor	Badger Technology
Alpha Industries	Bridgewater Systems
Altera	BroadSoft
AMCC (Applied Micro Circuits)	Brooks Automation
Amdahl	Bull HN Information Systems
American Power Conversion	CADTEL Systems
Amkor Technology	Canoga Perkins
ANADIGICS	Catalyst Semiconductor
Analog Devices	C-Cube Microsystems
Anicom	CDMA Development Group

Table 8-3 Continued: Computer System Manufacturers that Can Provide Information Warfare Technology and Support

Celeritek	Integrated Silicon Solution
Cirrus Logic	Intel
Citrix Systems	Intergraph
Compaq	International Microcircuits
Conexant Systems	Lexmark
Cray	Lightchip
Dataram	LSI Logic
Dell	LTX
Dense-Pac Microsystems	Maxtor
DSP Group	Micrel
Eastman Kodak	Microchip Technology
Elantec Semiconductor	Micron Technology
eMagin	MIPS Technologies
EMC	National Semiconductor
Emerson Electric	nCube
ESS Technology	NEC
Exabyte	Peregrine Systems
Fairchild Semiconductor	Pitney Bowes
Gateway	Rambus
General Semiconductor	Ramtron International
Genesis Microchip	Sage Instruments
Hewlett-Packard	Sanyo
Hitachi Data Systems	Seiko Epson
IBM	Silicon Graphics
Integrated Circuit Systems	Silicon Storage Technology

Table 8-3 Continued: Computer System Manufacturers that Can Provide Information Warfare Technology and Support

Spirent	Trident Microsystems
Storage Technology	Unisys
Sun Microsystems	Virage Logic
Tektronix	Virata
Teradyne	Wyle Laboratories

ZiLOGComputer Networking Product Companies that Can Provide Information Warfare Expertise

Another key area that information warriors need both knowledge and expertise in is computer networking products. Most of the computers in large organizations around the world are networked in order to allow for Internet access, the deployment of enterprise applications, and centralized management of systems. These computer networks and the technology that supports them provide critical pathways into the systems which information warriors can use as a mean of attack. However, information warriors must be able to navigate all types of networks and utilize the networks as an attack tool. They must also understand computer networks in order to develop defensive measures and tools. Table 8-4 shows many of the computer networking product manufacturers that can provide information warfare technology and support. Military organizations have many advantages in working the companies that produce computer networking technologies in developing information warfare tools, including:

▶ The established companies have been developing computer networking technology for many years and have considerable expertise in network design and operations.

▶ The companies that produce networking technology also have extensive knowledge about networks that are used in business and manufacturing environments.

▶ Military organizations will be able to acquire and test networking technology to determine better defensive measures as well as developing effective attack procedures.

Table 8-4: Computer Networking Product Manufacturers that Can Provide Information Warfare Technology and Support

3Com	Elastic Networks
Aerodyne Communications	eSoft
Alcatel Optronics	F5 Networks
Allied Telesyn	FiberCore
ARESCOM	Floware Wireless Systems
Avocent	Harmonic
BATM Advanced Communications	Leitch
Bookham Technology	Lucent Technologies
Cisco Systems	Luminent
Comtrol	Microsoft
Comverse Technology	Novell
Corvis	Omnitron Systems Technology
Digi International	ONI Systems
Digital Technology	Optical Cable
D-Link Systems	Sonus Networks
	Sorrento Networks

Telecommunications Systems Companies that Can Provide Information Warfare Expertise

It is also important that military organizations have an understanding of telecommunications technology and systems. Attackers can use telecommunications systems to access remote computer systems or can attack the telecommunications systems in an effort to disrupt communications services. Thus information warriors must be able to defend telecommunications systems as well as use them for attack scenarios. Table 8-5 shows many of the prominent telecommunications equipment manufacturers that can provide information warfare technology and support. Military organizations can gain several advantages by working with the companies that produce telecommunications technologies, including:

▶ The established companies that have been developing telecommunications technology for many years have considerable expertise in telecommunications system design and operations.

▶ The companies that produce telecommunications technology also have extensive knowledge about the numerous telecommunications systems that have been built around the world. They know how systems are designed and understand the strengths and weakness of the systems.

▶ Military organizations will be able to test telecommunications technology to determine better defensive measures as well as developing attack procedures.

Table 8-5: Telecommunications Equipment Manufacturers that Can Provide Information Warfare Technology and Support

Acclaim Technology	Brooktrout Technology
ACT Networks	C-COR Electronics
ADC	Celotek
ADDvantage Technologies Group	Ceragon Networks
ADTRAN	Clarent
Advanced Switching Communications	CNT
Airspan Networks	Com21
Allgon AB	Comdial
AltiGen Communications	Compel
American Technology	ComTelco International
AMTELCO	Control Cable
Anaren Microwave	Controlware
Andrea Electronics	Cyclades
Applied Signal Technology	Datamarine International
Bluestreams Communication	Dataprobe

Table 8-5 Continued: Telecommunications Equipment Manufacturers that Can Provide Information Warfare Technology and Support

Datron Systems	Matsushita Communication Industrial
Decision Data/NLynx	Mitel Semiconductor
Ditech Communications	NetSolve
DMC Stratex Networks	Network Equipment Technologies
ECI Telecom Business Networks	Nokia
Eicon Networks	Perle Systems
Elcotel	PictureTel
Endwave	RAD Data Communications
Ericsson	RADware
Exalink	Sonoma Systems
Finisar	SpectraLink
Fortress Technologies	Spectrian
Foundry Networks	Sync Research
General DataComm Industries	TC Communications
General Microwave	TCI International
Globecomm Systems	Telaxis Communications
HT Communications	Telco Systems
Hypercom Network Systems	Telmax Communications
IMC Networks	Tiara Networks
International Data Sciences	Triton Network Systems
Litton Network Access Systems	TTI Newgen
Loral Space & Communications	Verilink
Lucent Technologies	ViaSat
Luxcom	VIR Linear Switch
LXE	Western Multiplex
Mariposa Technology	

Telecommunications Service Providers that Can Provide Information Warfare Support

In addition to understanding the underlying technology in telecommunications systems, information warriors must have a thorough understanding of the telecommunications systems that exist in the world. There are literally thousands of small telephone and wireless communications systems and hundreds of major systems now in service. It is probably not necessary to be able to defend or penetrate all of the systems, but the larger systems are certainly of high military interest. Telecommunications is a regulated industry with strong government controls over how systems are built and the rates and tariffs the service providers are allowed to charge. Telecommunications are of critical importance to the economies of all nations. Table 8-6 shows many large telecommunications service providers that can provide information warfare support. Military organizations have many advantages in working the companies that provide telecommunications services when creating or executing information warfare plans and strategies, including:

▶ Much of the world's telecommunications services are provided by large companies which dominate the global telecommunications services and operations.

▶ Telecommunications services providers are the best source of information about how their systems are built and can relate important design and construction details to military organizations.

▶ Military organizations must develop a thorough understanding of the global telecommunications infrastructure in order to develop adequate defensive measures as well as use the systems for offensive tactics.

Table 8-6: Telecommunications Service Providers that Can Provide Information Warfare Support

Access International	Air2Web
ACT Teleconferencing	AirCell
ACTEL Enterprises	AirGate Wireless
Acterna	AirNet Communications

Table 8-6 Continued: Telecommunications Service Providers that Can Provide Information Warfare Support

AirTouch	Apollo Communications
AirTrac Chicago	Arianespace
Alcatel Submarine Networks	Ascom Transmission
Aleron	Asia Access Telecom
Allegiance Telecom	Asia Global Crossing
Allen Tel Products	Asia Pacific Cellular Infrastructure Group
ALLTEL	Asia Satellite Telecomms (AsiaSat)
Aloha Networks	AT&T
Alpha-Tel	Audiovox Communications
AMCI Wireless Data Solutions	Authentix Network
Amdocs	Avance en Telecomunicaciones, Avantel (Mexico)
American Samoa Telecom Authority	Avaya Communication
American Tower	Bandwidth Asia
American Wireless	Bartley RF Systems
Ameritech	BayCom
Anacom	BCT.TELUS Mobility
Aneco Communications	BECET (Kazakhstan)
Angstrom Networks	Bechtel Telecommunications
Anritsu Company	Belgacom
Antedo	Belkin Components
Antenna Plus	Bell Atlantic
Antennas America	Bell Atlantic NYNEX Mobile
Antennas for Communications	Bell Canada
APA Optics	Bell Mobility
APCC	Bell Mobility (Canada)

Table 8-6 Continued: Telecommunications Service Providers that Can Provide Information Warfare Support

BellSouth	Cellular Company (Russia)
BellSouth Ecuador	Cellular One Group
BellSouth International Wireless Services	Cellular South
BellSouth Mobility	Cellxion
BellSouth Nicaragua	Celumovil (Colombia)
BellSouth Peru	Centigram Australasia
BellSouth Wireless Services	Central Tower
Berkeley Varitronics Systems	Centurion Wireless Technologies
BizTone	CenturyTel
Blue Sky Communications	Certicom
Brience	China Quantum Communications
British Telecom	Chomerics, division of Parker Hannifin
Cable & Wireless	Chunghwa Telecom
Cal-North Cellular	Cibernet
Canon	Cincinnati Bell Wireless
CANTV (Venezuela)	Cingular Wireless
Catapult Communications	Clarity International
Catena Networks	Classwave Wireless
CBCS Global	CLDS (Columbia Long Distance Services)
Cedetel (Mexico)	Clearnet Communications
Cellemetry	CLP Telecom
Cellerita	CMG Telecommunications
CellPort Systems	CMT Communications
CellStar	Coastel Communications Company

Table 8-6 Continued: Telecommunications Service Providers that Can Provide Information Warfare Support

Comcast	Globalstar
Comcel (Colombia)	Globe Telecom
Crosswave Communications	GlobeSpan
CSA Wireless	Glowlink Communications Technology
CTI Movil	GN Nettest
Deacon Communications	Group Telecom
Deutsche Telekom	GST Telecom Hawaii
Digitel	GTE
Dobson Cellular Systems	Hughes Network Systems
Douglas Telecommunications	iAsiaWorks (Hong Kong)
DST Communications	Ibridge Network
Eastern Telecoms Philippines	ICG Satellite Services
ECtel	Ichina Global.Com
Extended Systems	Illinois Supercondutor
FiberGlobe	Intelsat
FINTEL (Fiji International Telecommunications)	International Telecommunications Data Systems
Flash Networks	Intersil
France Telecom	IPirion
General Telecom	Iridium
Global Access Limited	ITT Industries
Global Communication Services	ITXC
Global Crossing	Iusacell (Mexico)
Global One Communications	Kensar Telecommunications
Global Telecom	Korea Telecom
Global Wireless Data	Leap Wireless

Table 8-6 Continued: Telecommunications Service Providers that Can Provide Information Warfare Support

Level 3 Communications	SBC Communications
Lightbridge	Siemens Telecom
Lockheed Martin Global Telecommunications	SignalSoft
MACH Americas	SK Telecom
Marconi Communications	Space Communications
MCI WorldCom	SpectraCom
Metawave Communications	SpectraSite Communications
Motorola	Sprint
Movicom BellSouth Argentina	Swisscom
Movilnet (Venezuela)	TE.SA.M. (Argentina)
mPhase Technologies	Tadiran Microwave Networks
Next Level Communications	Telcel Radiomóvil (Mexico)
Norcel (Mexico)	Telcordia Technologies
Nortel (Northern Telecom)	Telecom Cook Islands
North Atlantic Tower	Telecom Fiji Limited
NTT (Japan)	Telecom Italia
Nynex	Telecom New Zealand Limited
Pan Asia Telecom	Telecom Services Kiribati
Panasonic	Teledesic
Philippine Communications Satellite	Telefonia Bonairiano
Powerwave Technologies	Telefonica de Argentina
PrivaSys	Telefonica de Espana
Prodelin	Telefonica del Peru
Qwest Communications	Telefónica Moviles de Espana
Remec	Telefonos de México, Telmex

Table 8-6 Continued: Telecommunications Service Providers that Can Provide Information Warfare Support

Teleglobe Communications	TRW Space and Electronics Group
Telekom Austria	U.S. Cellular
Telekom Malaysia	Verizon Wireless
Telemedia Networks International	VoiceStream Wireless
Telesat Canada	WesTower
Tellabs	WorldSpace Asia

Software Producers that Can Provide Information Warfare Expertise

It is critical that information warriors understand as many operating, utility, and application software packages as possible. The primary reason is that there will be times when information warfare tactics call for the intrusion into systems to acquire or manipulate data rather than destroying the entire computer system. This tactic often requires far more advanced skills than are required to attack and disable a computer system. Table 8-7 shows many of the important software producers that can provide information warfare expertise and support. Military organizations can gain many advantages by working with the companies that produce software packages that are used by businesses and governments, including:

▶ Most medium to large organizations use a wide variety of software packages for accounting, process management, inventory control, and sales force support. Those packages are best understood by the companies that produce them.

▶ Information warriors may be called upon to enter systems and acquire data to help support other warfare operations or to manipulate the data to cause disruption in organization operations.

▶ Software producers can provide information warriors with the necessary training and technical support to accomplish data acquisition or manipulation assignments.

▶ Software producers also have access to many of their customers' systems, which can aid information warriors in system entry and monitoring.

Table 8-7: Software Producers that Can Provide Information Warfare Expertise

Accrue Software	BETA Systems Software
Active Software	BindView Development
Active Voice	Blaze Software
Actuate Software	Blue Martini Software
Acxiom	Bluestone Software
Adaytum Software	BMC Software
Adobe Systems	BPA Systems
Amdocs	Bradmark Technologies
Anteon	Breakaway Solutions
Aonix	Broadbase Software
Apple Computer	Bull Worldwide Information Systems
Applied Terravision Systems	Business Objects
Applix	Cadence Design Systems
Aprisma Management Technologies	Caere
Apropos Technology	Calico Commerce
AremisSoft	Camstar Systems
Ariba	Candle
Artemis Management Systems	Catalyst International
Aspen Technology	Centura Software
Astea International	Chain Link Technologies
Attachmate	Check Point Software Technologies
Autodesk	Cincom Systems
Baan	Citation Computer Systems
Baltimore Technologies	Citrix Systems
BEA Systems	Clarus
Bentley Systems	Cognizant Technology Solutions

Table 8-7 Continued: Software Producers that Can Provide Information Warfare Expertise

Cognos	Digital River
Command Data	DocuCorp International
Compaq Computer	E.piphany
Computer Associates	Eagle Point Software
Computer Horizons	Eclipsys
Computron Software	Edgewater Technology
Compuware	Elron Software
Comshare	EMC
Concero	Entrust Technologies
Concord Communications	Environmental Systems Research Institute
Concur Technologies	Epicor Software
Constellation Software	Excalibur Technologies
Continuus Software	Gensym
Corel	Global Software
Corporate Management Solutions	Glovia International
CorVu	HarrisData
Crystal Systems Solutions	Heroix
CSG Systems	Hewlett-Packard
CSI-Maximus	Hitachi
Cyrano	HNC Software
Dataforce	Hummingbird
DataMirror	Hyperion Solutions
Dataware Technologies	i2 Technologies
Demand Management	IBM
Dendrite International	IFS Industrial & Financial Systems
Descartes Systems Group	ILOG

Table 8-7 Continued: Software Producers that Can Provide Information Warfare Expertise

Indus International	Microsoft
Industri-Matematik International	Microware Systems
Inference	Mobius Management Systems
Informatica	Multiactive Software
Information Builders	NaviSys
Informix	NCR
Infosys Technologies Limited	NEON Systems
Inprise	Net Perceptions
IntelliCorp	NetManage
Intergraph	NetObjects
Interlink Group	NetPro Computing
Interlinq Software	NetScout Systems
Isogon	Lawson Software
J.D. Edwards	Logility
Jasc Software	Macola Software
Kanbay	Macromedia
Keane	Network Associates
Landmark Systems	Nexgenix
MapInfo	Novadigm
Marathon Technologies	Novell
MathSoft	NOVO
Mechanical Dynamics	Omtool
MEDecision	ON Technology
Mentor Graphics	Ontrack Data International
Mercury Interactive	Onyx Software
Micrografx	Open Market

Table 8-7 Continued: Software Producers that Can Provide Information Warfare Expertise

Optika	QNX Software Systems
Optimal Networks	QSP
Optio Software	Quality Systems & Software
Optum	Quest Software
Oracle	Rainbow Technologies
OSI Software	Rational Software
OTG Software	Red Hat
PDS	Remedy
Pegasystems	ROI Systems
PeopleSoft	Sagent Technology
Percussion Software	Samsung
Peregrine Systems	SAP
Pervasive Software	Sapient
Phoenix International	Saratoga Systems
Platform Computing	SAS Institute
PowerCerv	ScanSoft
PowerQuest	SCH Technologies
Precise Software Solutions	SCO (Santa Cruz Operation)
Primavera Systems	SCT
Prime Response	SDRC
Primus Knowledge Solutions	Seagate Software
Progress Software	Seagull
Provia Software	Segue Software
Proxicom	Selectica
Puma Technology	Serena Software
QAD	Siebel Systems

Table 8-7 Continued: Software Producers that Can Provide Information Warfare Expertise

SilverStream Software	Trimax
Silvon Software	UniComp
Spyglass	Unify
StarBase	Unisys
Sterling Commerce	USData
STS Systems	USinternetworking
Sun Microsystems	Vastera
SunGard Data Systems	VenturCom
Sybase	Veritas Software
Symantec	Verity
Synopsys	Versata
Syspro Impact Software	Viant
Systar	Viasoft
System Software Associates	Viewlocity
Systems Xcellence	ViryaNet
Tangram Enterprise Solutions	Wipro Limited
TCSI	Witness Systems
Timberline Software	Wonderware

Computer Services and Consulting Firms that Can Provide Information Warfare Expertise

Computer services and consulting firms are also a potential wealth of information and expertise for military organizations. Many of the large consulting and services firms have undergone a series of mergers and acquisitions during the last five years, and that trend will probably continue. These services and consulting firms are familiar with how many companies around the world use computers. They also have considerable expertise in information technology. Table 8-8 shows many of the largest consulting and services firms that can provide information warfare expertise. Military organizations can gain many advantages by working with these companies, including:

- ▶ Access to large areas of expertise in a wide variety of information technologies, communications, and networking systems.

- ▶ Information about how companies around the world are using information technology and what kind of systems they are using.

- ▶ Many of these firms have routine access to customer systems that can provide information warriors with alternative routes into the systems.

Table 8-8: Consulting and Services Firms that Can Provide Information Warfare Expertise

A.T. Kearney	Delphi Consulting Group
Aberdeen Group	EDS
Accenture	Emergent
ACT Systems	Forrester Research
Alliance Consulting Group	Gartner Group
ARIS	Hewlett-Packard
Arthur Andersen	IBM Global Services Consulting Group
Arthur D. Little	International Data Corporation (IDC)
Booz Allen & Hamilton	Kennedy Information
Boston Consulting Group	KPMG Peat Marwick
Cambridge Technology Partners	McKinsey & Company
Cap Gemini Ernst & Young	Mercer Consulting Group
Comdisco	Mitchell Madison Group
Computer Economics	PricewaterhouseCoopers
Computer Sciences Corporation	RLG International
Coopers & Lybrand	RSA
Decision Consultants	Unisys Federal Systems Division
Deloitte & Touche	Yankee Group

Internet Service Providers that Can Provide Support to Information Warriors

Although many Internet service providers have come and gone, and many more will continue to move quickly in and out of the business, there are several companies that are staying in the business and have developed large customer bases. The larger and more stable companies can certainly provide support for information warriors. Table 8-9 shows many of the larger Internet service providers that can provide information warfare support. Military organizations can gain several advantages through working with these large Internet service providers, including:

► Access to large networks that can be used by information warriors to launch attacks and make tactical moves against specific targets.

► Information about how companies around the world are using the Internet and in many cases what kind of technology they have connected to the Internet.

► Access to email systems and Web hosting environments as well as other Internet services that can be targeted, monitored, or defended by information warriors.

Table 8-9: Internet Service Providers that Can Provide Information Warfare Support

America Online	InterPacket Networks
Asia Pacific Internet Company	InterSatCom
AT&T Global Network	Koral Communications
AT&T Worldnet	Loral Orion
CompuServe	MindSpring
Cybersurf	Pacific Internet
EarthLink Network	Palm.net
EUnet	Prodigy
Europe Online	PSINet Europe
FalconStream	Staedtenetz Vorarlberg
Global Access	Tachyon.net
Global One	UUNET Technologies
GlobeTrotter	World Online

Cooperation Between Governments and Technology Companies in Information Warfare

What may raise concerns for countries outside the United States is that they depend very heavily upon the products and services of many of the companies in the previous tables. Many government organizations and private companies around the world are part of the customer base of these technology companies. Because we are enjoying a relatively high level of global peace, the countries that have purchased products from these information technology producers and service companies may not consider themselves to be at risk. However, risk equations can change very quickly.

The long-term dominance of the United States in the field of computers has provided both an economic and military advantage. It is an information warfare asset that much of the world's expertise and information about computer and communications system design belongs to companies based in the United States. Because so many countries are using products created or designed in the United States, the country's information warriors can sustain somewhat of an edge in technology mastery. In a warfare situation, information warriors in the United States can also get information from technology producers that can provide a military advantage over the countries that are using technology produced by those companies with headquarters in the United States.

But advantages can cut both ways. One company listed is SAP, which is based in Germany. SAP has users around the world who now rely on its enterprise resource planing (ERP) software. Thus SAP has inside information on many of its customers and in some cases has legitimate access to their computer systems in order to help maintain the SAP software and the applications built on that software. During peace this is not viewed as a problem. But in the event of a war SAP, as well as many of the other companies listed in the previous tables, could aid their governments and militaries in attacking the systems that they sold to their customers in other countries. Other examples of why major information technology companies should be viewed as an asset during information warfare include:

- ▸ IBM has a global installed base of hundreds of thousands of customers. The company has provided maintenance services, consulting, and systems development work for many of these customers and has routine access to their systems.

- ► Cisco Systems, 3Com, and Nortel have provided tens of thousands of organizations with networking equipment and technology that enables them to connect their in-house systems to the Internet.

- ► Lucent Technologies and Ericsson have installed thousands of telecommunications switches around the world and provide maintenance services, support, and parts to a large part of the telecommunications industry in dozens of countries.

- ► RSA Security, Network Associates, and Symantec provide security products to thousands of companies that rely on those products to protect their systems and the integrity of their corporate data assets.

It is no question as to whether these companies are honest and have maintained a high level of integrity in their business dealings in the past. There is, however, a question as to how these companies will respond—or be required to respond—to governments of their home nations or host nations in the event of massive information warfare attacks. It is likely than most of these companies will have no choice but to cooperate with their governments when national and international security is at risk. This will definitely put the companies at odds with their customers.

Although much of this may sound theoretical in nature, the U.S. Department of Defense is clear on its position that it does not want to rely on products that have a substantial number of parts made by a company outside the United States. There are two clear reasons for this position. The first is security, which the DOD does not want to compromise by increasing the chance that hostile forces could gain a better understanding of how systems work and potentially devise ways to better attack systems that have been made outside the United States. The second is dependence, which the DOD also does not want to compromise by becoming dependent on a foreign supplier for parts and technical assistance. The same attitude should be expected on the part of defense departments around the world.

Conclusions and an Agenda for Action

Information warfare poses many new challenges to the military. But it also creates a new dynamic between the military and the companies that manufacture information technology and those companies that can provide technology and expertise to the military. Resolving the relationship between the military and information technology companies will take a long time to accomplish. It is going to be a complicated process that has global ramifications.

Conclusions on the Arms Dealers and Industrial Mobilization in Information Warfare

It is important that military planners and policy makers as well as information technology industry executives start addressing the complexities of information warfare. They must resolve any issues that stand between them so that their nations can better prepare for national defense against information warfare attacks. The following conclusions were drawn from the analysis of arms dealers and industrial mobilization in information warfare:

▶ What distinguishes whether a product is a defensive or offensive tool is not what the product was designed to do, but rather how it is being used and by whom and under what circumstances.

▶ The laws regarding industrial mobilization need to be modernized to ensure that the military is provided with the resources necessary to quickly respond to information warfare attacks.

▶ Information technology producers are inherently part of their national defense structure and have a role of providing military units with defensive and offensive tools, cooperating in the defense of the information infrastructure. When and if necessary, they must also assist their militaries in launching information warfare attacks against other countries even when they must risk alienating their customers in those countries.

▶ There are hundreds of information technology manufacturers, software producers, computer services companies, and consulting firms that have technical abilities, expertise, and technology that can aid the military in fighting information technology wars.

▶ The companies that own the information and communications technology patents and house the expertise about these systems are in a delicate position. If it appears they are overly willing to help the military in information warfare efforts, foreign customers may become alienated and seek other vendors to meet their needs.

An Agenda for Action for Arms Dealers and Industrial Mobilization in Information Warfare

There is much work to be done to align industrial capabilities with national and international defense issues in order to be prepared for information warfare. Legislation and government regulations that address military and private sector war-management activities are outdated and need to be modernized. The following agenda for action is recommended to move the processes forward:

▶ Military organizations need to conduct a comprehensive requirements analysis to determine what kind of support is needed from information technology manufacturers, software producers, computer services firms, and the consulting community to prepare for information warfare.

▶ Legislative bodies and government regulators need to devise and enact appropriate laws and regulations to ensure that industrial mobilization can be quickly accomplished to provide military organizations with adequate resources to deal with information warfare attacks.

▶ Information technology manufacturers, software producers, computer services firms, and the consulting community need to address the requirements and participate in the law making process. This will help to ensure that there is an appropriate balance between the needs of the military to prepare for information warfare and the needs of the technology producing companies involved to maintain viable relationships with their customers around the world.

Chapter 9

Civilian Casualties in Information Warfare

In the debates over military conduct during wartime, there has been substantial disagreement about inflicting civilian casualties. In an effort to modernize and humanize war, many arguments have emphasized that militaries should fight militaries and there should be no intentional harm done to civilian populations. In addition, special efforts should be made not to damage hospitals, schools, civilian neighborhoods, or populations who are generally unarmed and pose no threat to military activities.

Wars, however, are imperfect circumstances and tend not to bring out the best behavior in people. Those nations or groups that do inflict pain, suffering, and death on civilian populations are subject to considerable criticism and negative consequences once conflicts subside. This includes prosecution for war crimes for those who extremely violate the protocols of no violence against civilians. It also includes severe public reactions to all parties involved in even the slightest slip in behavior or miscalculations of targets.

Saddam Hussein, for example, worked very hard to convince the world that the coalition that formed to free Kuwait from occupation by Iraq was deliberately bombing elementary schools and indiscriminately killing the women and children of Iraq. Although this may have created some positive sentiment for the civilians in Iraq, Saddam Hussein had come to be viewed as such a brute and barbarian that there were not many people willing to believe his claims. There were even fewer who were willing to come to the defense of Iraq.

The forces of the coalition that worked to free Kuwait and those involved in Bosnia all faced high levels of scrutiny for their actions, and there was a definite expectation that those military forces manage their activities in a way that did not violate the protocols of not harming civilians. There have been many cases over time where civilians were used as shields against military actions, and cases where such tactics have slowed the movement of military efforts. Without a doubt, whether behavior of the military has been perfect or not, there is an expectation that modern military actions are not to result in massive civilian casualties.

Information warfare by its very nature, however, is largely directed at civilian populations. Each of the ten strategies discussed in this book will directly impact civilian populations. This is due in part to a high level of dependence on information systems and the massive numbers of civilian computers that are attached to networks. This makes damage to civilian populations in information warfare situations absolutely inevitable. In addition, all of the ten information warfare strategies can be directed at a nation, region, or population. This chapter examines why civilian populations are at risk in information warfare and the potential impacts that information warfare will have on individuals and groups of civilians.

Why the Cyber Masses Are at Risk

Each information warfare strategy has a set of potential consequences for nonmilitary organizations and private citizens. The impact that could be felt by nonmilitary organizations will depend on the type of attack strategies used as well as the duration of the attacks. The severity of attacks for private citizens will also depend on the scope and duration of information warfare attacks. Potential impacts that could be felt from the ten information warfare strategies include:

▶ Offensive ruinous information warfare and defensive ruinous information warfare attacks can result in extensive damage or disruption to corporate information systems. Investor value can be diminished because of such disruptions, and workers can be displaced from their jobs as companies cease operations during the conflicts. In addition, the assets of private citizens can be diminished because of lost stock values. Viruses or other destructive code launched during attacks could damage private citizen computers.

▶ During offensive containment and defensive responsive containment information warfare attacks, companies and private citizens can suffer similar consequences as those experienced during offensive ruinous and defensive ruinous information warfare attacks. However, the severity, geographical scope, and duration of the disruptions are likely to be far less than during ruinous attacks.

▶ The impact of random and sustained terrorist information warfare will be far less than those of the military-launched ruinous and containment attacks. It is likely that terrorists will target specific industries, companies, or government organizations. Thus the potential disruption of operations and the diminishing investor value will not be as widespread.

▶ Random and sustained rogue information warfare will also be narrower in scope than military-led ruinous or containment attacks. However, investor value could be diminished by destructive attacks on corporate systems, and private citizen computers could suffer some sporadic damage.

▶ Amateur rogue information warfare attacks will not have the same impact as military, terrorist, or rogue criminal attacks unless the amateur is extremely good as an attacker or extremely lucky in their attack efforts. Small numbers of corporations and government organizations could experience disruption, and private citizens could suffer from virus attacks.

▶ Defensive preventive information warfare strategies should have the least impact on computer users unless there is an accidental disruption of communications during the initiation of preventive measures.

▶ All information warfare strategies are potentially disruptive to public and emergency services, which could put individuals that are chronically or acutely dependent on services at risk while medical emergency, fire, police, or other security services are disrupted.

▶ All information warfare strategies are potentially disruptive to communications systems, including email, telephone, and banking-related services, which can cause delays in business and personal activities.

The most severe impact that information warfare attacks will likely have on private citizens is that their ability to manage their financial assets could be disrupted because online transactions of banks or stock brokerages are disrupted. In the case of ruinous or containment attacks, the disruptions could be very lengthy. However, in the case of terrorist attacks, the private citizen is likely to suffer little disruption unless specific financial services or banking companies are targeted. In addition, the electronic records of financial service companies and banks are backed up and usually secure. Although it can take days to recover information, private citizens should be able to have the status of their accounts restored relatively easily. The process of doing so may cause considerable distress to individuals, but the distress is far less of a consequence than losing all of their assets.

Circumstances with the Highest Potential Impact for Individual Citizens

Ruinous and containment information warfare attacks will have the greatest impact on the largest number of private citizens. The attacks, however, will not discriminate against or in favor of specific individuals, and there is likely to be widespread disruption and discomfort for private citizens. There could be a severe impact on selected groups of citizens or on specific individuals, if for some reason they are specifically targeted by terrorists, rogue criminals, or amateur attackers. Such targeted attacks could take place for political, religious, or economic reasons.

Take, for example, the actions of a militant group that has a social or political agenda. Anti-abortionists, instead of protesting and picketing, could start using information warfare strategies to further their cause. Such groups could attempt to hack into computers and steal confidential information about the patients of abortion clinics or of other medical groups and use that information to embarrass individuals or expose personal information. Other actions that could hinder the operations of an abortion clinic include the destruction of computer systems or the theft of email addresses of staff, associates, or patients, which could then be used to harass individuals. The potential list of tactics and dirty tricks is only limited by the imagination of fanatics.

Another example is an information warfare attack on a specific company or the officers and employees of a corporation that, for some reason, becomes the target of a terrorist group or rogue criminal gang. The trade secrets of the company could be stolen from computers and disclosed, company computers could be disabled or destroyed, and employees could have their email or other personal information disclosed by attackers. Corporate officers could have their homes burglarized and their computers stolen, and the personal information on their computers could be disclosed or used in extortion attempts. The goal of the attacks could run a continuum from harassment to disruption to destruction.

The possibility of a group of people or an individual being targeted under such circumstances is probably tied very closely to their jobs, political or religious affiliations, or some characteristic of their private lives. The potential combination of circumstances is probably close to infinite. Individuals with long lists of enemies or with something they would like to hide need to be very careful about computer security as well as the type of information they keep on their personal or company computers. In addition, they should also be careful about what they do in cyberspace. There are many traps on the Internet, and some are legitimate. For instance, law enforcement officers from many countries around the world have cooperated to monitor, track, and trap child pornographers in cyberspace. These same tactics can be used by any group that has the skill levels of law enforcement agents and the ability to organize their efforts.

Conclusions and an Agenda for Action

Private citizens can suffer disruption to their computing activities as well as their lives during information warfare attacks or when groups of terrorist or rogue criminals target their companies or them as individuals. Corporations as well as individuals need to be proactive in implementing good computer security practices in the office, on the road, and at home. The following conclusions and agenda for action are directed at companies and individuals to help protect themselves in the event of information warfare attacks.

Conclusions on Civilian Casualties in Information Warfare

There are several things that private citizens need to be prepared for in the event of information warfare. Their ability to manage their financial assets could be disrupted for periods of time and their cyber lives could literally be put on hold. This means they may not have the ability to work as telecommuters, send email, or use Internet sites that they depend on in their profession or daily lives. Several conclusions can be drawn from this brief review of civilian casualties in information warfare:

▶ Civilian casualties during the use of information warfare strategies are very likely to occur, including the loss of employment, destruction or damage to personal computers, and having personal data compromised.

▶ The personal wealth of individuals could be diminished if the companies in which they hold stock experience severe or long-term disruption of their operations because of an information warfare attack.

▶ Terrorists, rogue criminals, or even amateur information warriors who have a political, religious, or economic agenda could target specific companies or individuals.

▶ Individuals need to use caution about the type of information they keep on their computers, how they use the Internet for communications, and where they go and what they do on the Internet.

An Agenda for Action on Civilian Casualties in Information Warfare

Individuals can take several steps to better protect their personal information as well as preserve the integrity of their financial accounts in the event of information warfare attacks. Corporations can also help protect their employees and corporate officers from becoming targets in cyberspace. The following agenda for action is recommended:

▶ Corporations should brief their employees, from a general perspective, about risks they are exposed to in cyberspace. When necessary, employees should be kept informed of any known actions or intentions of terrorists or rogue criminals toward the company and what that may mean to individuals and how they use the Internet.

▶ Individual citizens need to practice good security and caution in their use of the Internet and the records they keep on their personal or work computers. This is especially true for those individuals who work for companies that are the potential targets of militant groups.

▶ Individuals should inform their employers if they think they have become the target of a terrorist or rogue criminal group because of the activities their employer is involved in.

▶ Private citizens need to keep copies of records regarding their financial accounts, especially those maintained in online environments, to ensure that all information and the status of their accounts are fully recovered in the event that their financial service companies or banks are hit by an information warfare attack.

Chapter 10

The New Terrorist Profile: The Curious Nerd Is Moving to the Dark Side

In the future, information warriors will emerge from a variety of sources. What will distinguish one type of information warrior from another are philosophy and purpose, not skill sets. To be an effective information warrior, individuals need superior computer skills, as well as an in-depth understanding of information technology architectures and telecommunications protocols and processes. Once the skill set is developed and individuals are trained in intrusion and destructive attack methods, they will be able to use those skills for either good or evil. This is one of the most disturbing aspects of information warfare.

As discussed in Chapter 1, the ability to implement different types of information warfare strategies is highly dependent on resources and organizational structure. Skilled information warriors will be readily available to military organizations and governments, but they will also become resources for terrorist groups and criminal gangs. The bright and shiny technological future thus has a high potential for becoming very tarnished. This chapter examines the nature of information warriors and the potential for the emergence of a new class of technological terrorists and criminals. Topics covered in the chapter include:

- ▶ The social nature of the emerging class of technological terrorists

- ▶ The education and training of a growing population of individuals capable of becoming information warriors

- ▶ What motivates information warriors to fight for either good or evil

- ▶ Societal issues that could lead to the alienation of computer scientists

- ▶ The existing affinity among computer geeks and how that could lead to more people becoming information warriors

- ▶ The social nature of Americans and how that will likely impact their decision to become technological terrorists and cyber soldiers of fortune

- ▶ The gender gap in information technology professions and how that will impact the future cadre of information warriors

- ▶ The racial gap in information technology professions and how that will impact the future cadre of information warriors

The New Techno-Terrorists and Criminals

The training of so many potential information warriors has some very serious implications. On one hand, computer-dependent nations will have a better chance to exploit the economic potential of information technology as well as defend against cyber-terrorism. On the other hand, it also means there is a new type of terrorist being bred and trained. They will be technologically savvy, they will know how computers and communications systems work, and they will know how to attack, disrupt, damage, and perhaps even destroy information technology infrastructures and computer-based economic activities. They will use sustained and random terrorist information warfare, sustained and random rogue information warfare, and amateur rogue information warfare strategies to attack nations and economies around the world. These people are the bad, the nasty, and the antisocial technological terrorists and criminals of the future. They will target military and government organizations as well as private companies that use electronic commerce to support their business operations and generate revenue.

If the world continues to sustain its path toward peace, it is not likely that any one of the technological nations will attack another technological nation in an all-out information war. The global economy has so entwined the fate of these nations and created interdependency that one technological nation cannot destroy another without doing substantial damage to itself. Terrorist and rogue information warriors are the biggest future threat to the information infrastructure and the new digital economy. The technological terrorist could act in the name of one religion or another and support or be supported by one or more outlaw nations. The rogue information warrior could be motivated by economic gain and practice the age-old crafts of extortion and theft.

The terrorist and the rogue information warrior requires that all technological nations that are computer dependent have strong defensive preventive information warfare capabilities and a cadre of warriors trained in defensive responsive containment information warfare tactics. Overall, terrorist methods will remain the same as always: they will attack anything that is vulnerable and will focus their attacks on headline-grabbing efforts to make civilian populations fearful and to embarrass government officials and organizations. Rogues will remain rogues and will bring information warfare skills to the highest bidder or work independently to extort or steal money through electronic means.

Naiveté in dealing with terrorists and rogue information warriors is as great a folly as being unprepared for car bombings and having lax security in civil aviation. The terrorist always strikes the weakest point, and the rogue always steals from those without adequate protection and security. A scenario as to how fast and how deep the terrorist and rogue can strike the digital economy was presented in Chapter 3, and the new terrorist profile is expanded upon in this chapter.

The population of terrorists—that is, the number of people who, if they were required to state a profession, would actually call themselves terrorists—has certainly varied over the last several decades. Understand, of course, that many people who the industrial nations view as terrorists do not see themselves as such, but rather as freedom fighters or (in a religious context) the instruments of one god or another. Their mission on earth is to fight some form or source of evil. Compared to terrorists, there are probably many more people who would likely declare themselves to be criminals. This is certainly true in the United States where about 1.5 percent of the population is imprisoned.

Just how many information warriors will become terrorists or criminals is obviously impossible to predict. The likelihood of terrorists or criminals becoming information warriors is something that absolutely must be prepared for by computer-dependent nations. According to the Uniform Crime Report in 1999, more than $463 million was lost as the result of robbery offenses. The average dollar loss of $1,131 per robbery reflects a 15 percent increase from the 1998 figure. In 1999, the average dollar loss ranged from $620 taken during robberies of convenience stores to $4,552 per bank robbery.

But robbery is not the only way people can steal money. The U.S. Federal Bureau of Investigation (FBI) defines white-collar crime as those illegal acts that are characterized by fraud, concealment, or a violation of trust and are not dependent upon the application or threat of physical force or violence. The FBI's Honolulu White-Collar Crime Program (WCCP) is one of many law enforcement units responsible for investigating federal crimes related to fraud, theft, or embezzlement occurring within or against the national and international financial communities. Individuals and organizations commit these crimes to obtain money, property, or services; to avoid the payment or loss of money or services; or to secure personal or business advantage. FBI financial crimes investigations target criminal activities such as money laundering, healthcare fraud, theft of intellectual property rights, bankruptcy fraud, insurance and securities fraud, telemarketing fraud, computer fraud, financial institution fraud, fraud against the government, and environmental crimes.

The FBI's White-Collar Crime Program is the largest and most diverse of all FBI criminal programs, which include Organized Crime/Drugs, Violent Crimes, and Civil Rights programs. The White-Collar Crime Program is growing and changing at a rapid rate due to the globalization of communications, travel, business activities, and crime. During fiscal year 1998, the White-Collar Crime Program consumed about 25 percent of FBI agent resources and achieved 36 percent of the FBI's total convictions.

White-collar crime comes in many shapes and sizes. The Little Rock FBI office has the authority to investigate all forms of fraud and abuse affecting both government-sponsored (Medicare and Medicaid) and private-insured health benefit programs. Nationally, it is estimated that Americans will spend more than $1 trillion a year on healthcare and that 10 percent or $100 billion is attributed to fraud or abuse.

Securities regulators estimate that securities and commodities fraud has reached approximately $40 billion per year. The North American Securities Administrators Association (NASAA) has estimated that Internet-related stock fraud is currently the second most common form of investment fraud. That same source estimated that investors lose $10 billion per year (or $1 million per hour) to this type of fraud.

The FBI defines a terrorist incident as a violent act or an act dangerous to human life, in violation of the criminal laws of the United States or of any state, to intimidate or coerce a government, the civilian population, or any segment thereof, in furtherance of political or social objectives. A suspected terrorist incident is a potential act of terrorism in which responsibility for the act cannot be attributed at the time to a known or suspected terrorist group or individual. Terrorism prevention is a documented instance in which a violent act by a known or suspected terrorist group or individual with the means and a proven propensity for violence is successfully interdicted through investigative activity.

The FBI classifies domestic terrorists as groups or individuals who are based and operate entirely within the United States and Puerto Rico without foreign direction and whose acts are directed at elements of the U.S. government or population. International terrorism is the unlawful use of force or violence committed by a group or individual who has some connection to a foreign power or whose activities transcend national boundaries. These acts are directed at persons or property to intimidate or coerce a government, the civilian population, or any segment thereof, in furtherance of political or social objectives.

On May 22, 1998, President Clinton signed Presidential Decision Directive 63 (PDD-63) on Critical Infrastructure Protection. The directive stated: "I intend that the United States will take all necessary measures to swiftly eliminate any significant vulnerability to both physical and cyber attacks on our critical infrastructures, especially our cyber systems." President Clinton continued to pursue the 1998 initiative and his fiscal year 2000 budget included requests for $2.849 billion for critical infrastructure protection, computer security, and domestic preparedness against a weapons-of-mass-destruction attack. As part of the effort of critical infrastructure protection and computer security, President's Clinton's fiscal year 2000 budget requested $1.464 billion for protection of critical infrastructure and computer security. This represents a 40 percent increase in the two budget years since President Clinton created the Critical Infrastructure Protection Commission. Included in the budget was $500 million for a critical infrastructure applied research initiative.

In November 1999, corporations in the United States were warned of cyber-terrorism by officials from the National Security Agency (NSA) and the U.S. Department of State (DOS) in a briefing of hundreds of representatives from multinational corporations and non-profit organizations. The officials also warned the representatives that their move into electronic commerce and the building of websites may provide terrorists with information about their companies that could be used to launch a cyber or physical attack. Companies such as Eastman-Kodak, Bristol-Myers-Squibb, Lucent Technologies, and the New York Stock Exchange were urged to examine their websites to determine how a terrorist could exploit the information posted on the sites to plan raids of corporate facilities.

Computer Crimes and Terrorist Attacks

Computer terrorist attacks and computer crimes really do happen, and the number of incidents is increasing. In 1996, the Defense Information Systems Agency (DISA) estimated that as many as 250,000 attacks on DOD systems might have occurred in 1995. DISA indicates that the number of attacks has been increasing each year for the past few years, and the trend is expected to continue. In fiscal year 1998, the FBI opened 547 computer intrusion cases, and in fiscal year 1999, the number of cases had jumped to 1,154. At the same time, because of the opening of the National Infrastructure Protection Center (NIPC) in February 1998, and the improving ability to fight cybercrime, more cases were closed. In fiscal year 1998, 399 intrusion cases were closed, and in fiscal year 1999, 912 such cases were closed. However, the number of pending cases increased by 39 percent, from 601 at the end of fiscal year 1998 to 834 at the end of fiscal year 1999.

Attacks on computer systems are not new and are not an invention of the Internet age. Terrorist groups in Europe have attacked many computer systems over the last three decades. Many of these attacks were old-style terrorist attacks, usually involving bombings. In 1976 through 1978, a group called the Red Brigade bombed eight computer centers in Italy, causing millions of dollars in damage. In 1969, an anti-war group attacked a chemical company's computer center in Midland, Michigan, destroying hundreds of data tapes. Computer centers at Boston University, Fresno State College in California, the University of Kansas, and Sir George Williams University in Montreal were also attacked during antiwar activities. Similar attacks occurred in Belgium, France, and Germany during the 1970s. Examples of computer-related crimes and cyber-terrorism in the late 1990s include the following:

▶ In October 2000, the Inspector General of the U.S. Postal Service announced that nine indictments were returned by a grand jury in Dallas, Texas, charging Robert Russell Sanford with theft and unlawfully obtaining access to computers belonging to the Postal Service, the state of Texas, the Canadian Department of Defense, and Glinn Publishing Company of Milwaukee, Wisconsin.

▶ In September 2000, a federal grand jury in Los Angeles indicted a Southern California man on charges of fabricating a press release that led a publicly traded company to temporarily lose more than $2 billion in market value. Mark Simeon Jakob of El Segundo, was named in an eleven-count indictment for causing numerous investors to suffer millions of dollars in trading losses because of his distribution of a false press release. The grand jury accused Jakob of nine counts of securities fraud and two counts of wire fraud for allegedly causing Internet Wire, Inc. and other news agencies to publish a false news report about Emulex Corporation. Jakob allegedly engaged in a series of trades of Emulex stock, through which he realized approximately $240,000 in profits when the stock lost more than half its value on August 25 after false news was circulated via several business news organizations.

▶ In September 2000, a Mission Viejo, California, man named Diekman was taken into federal custody after being charged with hacking into several NASA computers and using stolen credit card numbers to purchase electronic equipment. The NASA computer systems at Stanford contained sensitive satellite flight control software used to control NASA satellites. Diekman, who for the previous two years used the nicknames Shadow Knight and Dark Lord, allegedly gained unauthorized root-level access to at least three computer systems at the Jet Propulsion Laboratory (JPL). This hacking activity gave him control over all aspects of the computers, including the ability to modify files and alter security on the systems. According to the affidavit, Diekman used JPL's computers to intercept electronic communications on the JPL systems, launch attacks on other computer systems, and run Internet Relay Chat software. IRC, a form of real-time communications on the Internet, was used by Diekman to communicate with other hackers and to trade information. Diekman's IRC software allowed him to control his own channel that was running on JPL computers.

▶ In September 2000, Patrick W. Gregory, also known as MostHateD, was sentenced in federal court to 26 months imprisonment and three years supervised release, and was ordered to pay $154,529.86 in restitution for conspiracy to commit telecommunications fraud and computer hacking. Gregory was a member of an online computer hacker organization known as total-kaOs, and later was a member of another online computer hacker organization called globalHell. Gregory and Chad Davis, also known as Mindphasr, cofounded globalHell in February 1998.

▶ In July 2000, Andrew Miffleton of Arlington, Texas, was sentenced in federal court to 21 months imprisonment and ordered to pay a $3,000 fine as well as $89,480 in restitution to Verio, Inc., a national Internet service provider (ISP). Miffleton associated himself with a group known as the Darkside Hackers. From May 1998 to February 1999, Miffleton hosted a Web page for the Darkside Hackers on his home computer. In February 1999, Miffleton obtained a list of Verio's passwords. This password list contained root-level passwords that afforded the user complete control over a computer system. Miffleton trafficked in some of these passwords by giving them to the Darkside Hackers. He and others used the passwords to access computer systems throughout the country without authorization. Miffleton also obtained approximately forty individual user-level passwords for the ISP, twenty electronic serial numbers/mobile identification number pairs for cellular telephone service, one AT&T calling card number, and five credit card numbers. All of these were unauthorized access devices that were obtained by Miffleton with the intent to defraud the providers of the access devices.

► On April 19, 2000, Scott D. Dennis of Anchorage, Alaska, was indicted for allegedly interfering with a government-owned communication system. Dennis was the system administrator and computer security officer for the U.S. District Court for the District of Alaska. The indictment stated that he initiated at least one of five attacks on Judsys, a mail list server that runs on a computer owned and operated by the U.S. District Court for the Eastern District of New York. Judsys is a private mail list server whose subscribers are restricted to U.S. Court System computer system administrators. The indictment alleges that from December 1999, through January 7, 2000, Judsys was the victim of approximately five computer attacks. The method of attack was an electronic mail flood that impaired the availability of the Judsys system by overwhelming it with inappropriate electronic mail.

► In February 2000, Ikenna Iffih, of Boston, Massachusetts, was charged with using his home computer to illegally gain access to a number of computers. These included computers controlled by the National Aeronautics and Space Administration (NASA) and an agency of the U.S. Department of Defense (DOD), where, among other things, he intercepted login names and passwords, and intentionally caused delays and damage in communications. In April 1999, Iffih obtained unauthorized access to a corporate Internet account, which he then used to illegally access a computer controlled and operated by the U.S. Defense Logistics Agency. Iffih then concealed his actual computer address through a Telnet proxy, which created the appearance that his address was that of the government's computer. He accessed, without authorization, the website of Internet service provider ZMOS and recklessly caused damage to the ZMOS computer located in the state of Washington. As a result, ZMOS, which hosts corporate Web pages and provides Internet service for corporate customers, suffered a significant loss of business. Beginning in May 1999 and continuing until August 1999, Iffih obtained unauthorized access to the same corporate Internet account, this time using it to access the NASA computer research project Web server located in Maryland. He seized control of the NASA computer, allowing him to read, delete, or modify any files on the system. He then installed a sniffer program on the system to intercept and save login names and passwords of users that were transferred over to the NASA system for his own use later. The compromised NASA Web server did not contain classified or sensitive information and was not involved in any way with satellite command or control. Iffih also used the NASA computer as a platform to launch attacks on other computer systems, such as an attack on the U.S. Department of the Interior's Web server, where he defaced its Web page with hacker graphics.

▶ In November 1999, Eric Burns of Shoreline, Washington, who used the computer screen name Zyklon, was sentenced to fifteen months imprisonment and three years of supervised release, and ordered to pay $36,240 in restitution. Burns pled guilty on September 7, 1999, to intentionally hacking a protected computer and causing damage. He admitted that he had hacked and damaged computers in Virginia, Washington state, Washington, D.C., and London. These systems included computers hosting the United States Information Agency (USIA) and the North Atlantic Treaty Organization (NATO) Web pages, and the U.S. Vice President's Web page, 21stCentury.gov. The defendant also admitted that he had advised others on how to hack computers at the White House. Burns designed a program he called Web Bandit to identify computers on the Internet that were vulnerable to attack. These included the computer server in Reston, Virginia, that hosted the Web pages for USIA, NATO, and the Vice President. Between August 1998 and January 1999, Burns hacked the server four times. These attacks affected U.S. embassy and consulate websites, as well as others that were dependent on USIA for information. On one occasion, the attacks made thousands of pages of information unavailable and resulted in the closing down of the USIA website for eight days. Burns also attacked the Web pages of approximately eighty businesses whose pages were hosted by Laser.net in Fairfax, Virginia, the Web pages of two corporate clients of Issue Dynamics in Virginia and Washington, D.C., the Web page of the University of Washington, and the Web servers of the Virginia Higher Education Council in Richmond, Virginia, as well as an Internet service provider in London. The defendant usually replaced the attacked Web pages with references to himself as Zyklon, proclaiming his love for a woman named Crystal. In May 1999, the White House Web server was attacked, and there was an attempt to replace it with a page that had references to Zyklon and Crystal. The White House was alerted to the attempt and had to shut down its Web server, disconnect both the public and private computer networks from the Internet for two days, and reconfigure the computer system. During Internet chat sessions, Burns took credit for the attack, both before and after it was discovered, but he told the court that he had simply provided advice to others about how to do it.

▶ In September 1999, Corey Lindsly and Calvin Cantrell were sentenced in federal court for hacking into computer systems belonging to Sprint Corporation, Southwestern Bell, and GTE, illegally obtaining long distance calling card numbers and selling them. Lindsly and Cantrell are the major ringleaders in a computer hacker organization known as the Phone Masters. In addition to the numerous telecommunications systems that were penetrated, the group also penetrated computer systems owned by credit reporting agencies, utility providers, and systems owned by state and federal governmental agencies, including the Nation Crime Information Center (NCIC) computer. These hackers organized their assaults on the computers through teleconferencing and utilized the encryption program Pretty Good Privacy (PGP) to hide the data they traded with each other.

▶ In August of 1999, Kevin Mitnick, who pleaded guilty to a series of federal offenses related to a two-year computer hacking spree, was sentenced to 46 months in federal prison. Mitnick pled guilty to four counts of wire fraud, two counts of computer fraud, and one count of illegally intercepting a wire communication. Mitnick's hacking career made him the most wanted computer criminal in U.S. history. He was arrested in North Carolina in February 1995. In a global plea agreement filed in U.S. District Court in Los Angeles, Mitnick admitted that he broke into a number of computer systems and stole proprietary software belonging to Motorola, Novell, Fujitsu, Sun Microsystems, and other companies. He admitted using a number of tools to commit his crimes, including social engineering, cloned cellular telephones, sniffer programs, and various hacker software programs. Mitnick acknowledged that he had altered computer systems belonging to the University of Southern California and used these computers to store programs that he had misappropriated. He also admitted that he had stolen email, monitored computer systems, and impersonated employees of victim companies, including Nokia Mobile Phones, Ltd.

▶ In March 1998, Eugene E. Kashpureff, owner of AlterNIC, a commercial registration service for Internet domain names associated with Internet websites, was charged with interrupting service for tens of thousands of Internet users worldwide. Kashpureff hijacked Internet users attempting to reach the website for InterNIC, his chief commercial competitor. Thousands of Internet users trying to reach InterNIC were involuntarily rerouted to AlterNIC's website, and were impeded from registering or updating the registration of domain names. After launching his Internet attacks, Kashpureff boasted to the media about the effects of his scheme, claiming that he could divert all communications destined for China, the 100 most-visited websites in the world, and the White House website.

▶ In March 1998, federal criminal charges were unsealed against a computer hacker who disabled a key telephone company computer servicing the Worcester, Massachusetts, airport, disabling the FAA control tower for six hours in March of 1997. In the course of his hacking, he broke into a pharmacy computer and copied patient records. The juvenile hacker identified the telephone numbers of the modems connected to the loop carrier systems operated by the telephone company providing service to the Worcester Airport and the community of Rutland, Massachusetts. On March 10, 1997, the hacker accessed the system servicing the airport and impaired the integrity of data on which the system relied, thereby disabling it. Public health and safety agencies suffered the loss of telephone service as well, as did the FAA tower at the Worcester Airport, the Worcester Airport Fire Department, and other organizations. As a result of the outage, both the main radio transmitter, which is connected to the tower by the loop carrier system, and a circuit, which enables aircraft to send an electric signal to activate the runway lights on approach, were not operational for about six hours.

▶ Between January and March 2000, multiple ecommerce websites in the United States, Canada, Thailand, Japan, and the United Kingdom were attacked by a hacker known as Curador.

Curador broke into the sites and apparently stole as many as 28,000 credit card numbers, with losses estimated to be at least $3.5 million. Thousands of credit card numbers and expiration dates were posted to various Internet websites. After an extensive investigation, on March 23, 2000, the FBI assisted the Dyfed Powys (Wales, U.K.) Police Service in a search at the residence of Curador, whose real name is Raphael Gray. Gray was arrested in the U.K. along with a co-conspirator under the U.K.'s Computer Misuse Act of 1990.

▶ In 1994, foreign crime groups operating in several different countries were able to hack into the Citibank Cash Management System. The criminals compromised passwords to impersonate account holders worldwide, and attempted 40 transfers totaling $10 million. As a result of early detection by Citibank officials, and close cooperation between Citibank investigators, payee banks, foreign police, and the FBI, the perpetrators were tracked down and arrested, and actual losses were limited to $400,000.

Where Information Warriors Will Come From

Another key element in assessing the likelihood of the various information warfare strategies being implemented—and when and where they will be implemented and by whom—is to understand where information warriors will come from. Information warriors who are capable of high-level information warfare strategies such as offensive ruinous information warfare are very expensive people. It takes years to train highly capable information warriors. The United States has trained the greatest number of high-level information warriors and probably outnumbers those in other countries, even NATO allies, by at least 300 to 1. On the other end of the continuum, individuals capable of amateur rogue information warfare are more readily available and live around the world.

Knowing the potential sources of information warriors is important, but so is being able to estimate the number of people adequately trained to implement various types of information warfare. In addition, it's important to determine who among the entire pool of trained information warriors is willing to participate in the different types of information warfare. Examining training requirements and available skilled individuals, as well as potential political or ideological alignments of trained people, helped derive the information warrior population estimates in Table 10-1. The population counts in the various categories are not mutually exclusive and include both military and civilian employed individuals. Skill sets in several categories are transferable across different categories of information warfare and in several cases, especially in the existing military environment, information warriors are trained in more than one strategy. When properly compensated, information warriors—like any warrior—may decide to change allegiances.

Table 10-1: The Information Warrior Population Estimates

Type	Estimated Number of Capable Warriors in 2000	Estimated Number of Capable Warriors in 2005
Offensive ruinous	25,000	75,000
Offensive containment	20,000	60,000
Sustained terrorist	5,000	20,000
Random terrorist	15,000	50,000
Defensive preventive	40,000	65,000
Defensive ruinous	25,000	75,000
Defensive responsive containment	20,000	60,000
Sustained rogue	2,000	15,000
Random rogue	10,000	30,000
Amateur rogue	50,000	150,000

The most superior training in information warfare is being done by the U.S. military. Policy makers, business managers, and the general public should view this as an asset and a favorable condition. One thing that should be considered, however, is that by 2010 the U.S. military will discharge at least 20,000 well-skilled information warriors. Outside of the United States, formal training in information warfare is either nonexistent or scarce. NATO allies often share training with U.S. forces and just as often mold their training programs after those created in the United States. Most of the former military information warriors will find rewarding employment in information technology fields or as civilian employees of the United States government. Others may decide to sell their skills on the open market, including in the realm of espionage and soldier-of-fortune activities. These retiring personnel from military organizations in the United States and allied states are fully capable of participating in high-level strategies like offensive ruinous information warfare and offensive containment information warfare. They can easily, and in small groups, participate in sustained terrorist information warfare, random terrorist information warfare, sustained rogue information warfare, random rogue information warfare, and amateur rogue information warfare.

One of the wildcards in information warfare is former Soviet military and KGB personnel. Most of these retired or displaced workers who have a criminal bent have had no difficulty in finding work with local or regional criminal organizations. Others may have found employment, part time or full time, with the U.S. Central Intelligence Agency and other intelligence organizations in NATO countries. Rumors about their whereabouts and activities certainly fly through underground folklore, but it seems that former Soviet militarists have turned to what was most readily available, which includes quiet retirement, petty crime, or spying for their former enemies. Because of the expense and organizational structure associated with offensive ruinous information warfare and offensive containment information warfare, it is not likely that the former Soviets will independently participate in these high-level strategies. They could, however, readily participate in sustained terrorist information warfare, random terrorist information warfare, sustained rogue information warfare, random rogue information warfare, or amateur rogue information warfare.

The biggest overall threat, and the population that has the least to lose in terms of present or future economic comfort, are those individuals who are now capable of participating in random rogue information warfare and amateur rogue information warfare. The number is growing and will grow faster than in any other category of individuals capable of implementing information warfare strategies. By 2005, there will be more than 150,000 people capable of participating in these types of information warfare activities. The various hack attacks, denial-of-service attacks, worms, and viruses that have been unleashed by this category of information warriors have caused tremendous economic damage and disruption over the last decade.

It is clear that the number of people who are capable of implementing various types of information warfare strategies is growing. What is not clear is the global capability of preventing or responding to information warfare attacks. It is logical to conclude that the more people who are capable of information warfare, the more information warfare becomes a threat to both military and commercial infrastructure around the world.

Understanding Why People Become Cyberwarriors

The interest in career opportunities in information warfare and related areas such as computer crime investigation and computer security is growing, but it is growing slowly. Interviews with high school students, college students, and military personnel reveal a general interest in computer careers, but candidates at this age level usually have narrowed the areas in which they plan to work. According to the U.S. Bureau of Labor Statistics (BLS), the number of computer-related positions continues to grow and will increase by 117 percent by 2008. Computer systems analysts, engineers, and scientists held about 1.5 million jobs in 1998, including about 114,000 who were self-employed. Salaries for computer systems analysts and programmers range from the low $30,000s to a high of about $99,000, as shown in Table 10-2.

Table 10-2: Annual Salaries for Computer Systems Analysts and Programmers (from the U.S. Bureau of Labor Statistics)

Salary Levels	Computer Systems Analysts	Computer Programmers
1998 median	$52,180	$47,550
2001 median at 4% annual growth	$58,700	$53,490
1998 highest 10%	$87,810	$88,730
2001 highest 10% at 4% annual growth	$98,790	$99,820
1998 middle 50%	$40,570 to $74,180	$36,020 to $70,610
2001 middle 50% at 4% annual growth	$45,640 to $83,450	$40,520 to $79,440
1998 lowest 10%	$32,470	$27,670
2001 lowest 10% at 4% annual growth	$36,530	$31,130

There are several things that make computer security-related jobs attractive to information technology professionals, and higher salary is one of them. A survey of salaries conducted for this analysis shows that the median salaries for Unix security administrators are about $3,000 higher than for systems analysts and about $7,000 higher than for computer programmers. Computer security professionals working in consulting positions earned an average of $75,000 annually in the year 2000. This survey was based on limited cases, but the results were similar to those of other published surveys. In addition to better salaries, the late 1990s with the growth of the Internet resulted in an exciting time for computer security professionals. Computer security is an issue in almost all organizations. For computer security professionals, major virus attacks such as Melissa and the Love Bug were the "Big Ones" and had extensive news coverage. Protecting computer systems became a more glamorous career option in the late 1990s than programming or network administration.

Information technology jobs in the military have also become attractive to the men and women of the armed forces. These jobs are an excellent training ground for individuals who are planning for their civilian careers. The U.S. Army School of Information Technology, for example, has a complete training program comparable to what the civilian sector offers. Courses include Local Area Networks Concept and Configuration, Introduction to Routers, Web Page Design and Administration, Network Manager (IP Networks), Systems Administration for Solaris, Systems Administration for NT, and Systems Security. However, not counting special allowances or the value of a housing benefit, pay scales for enlisted personnel in the U.S. Army are rather dismal compared to civilians with comparable computer-related positions, as shown in Table 10-3.

Table 10-3: U.S. Army Enlisted Members Pay Scale for 2000

Pay Grade	Annual Pay After 10 Years of Service
E-9	$36,184
E-8	$31,219
E-7	$27,529
E-6	$24,566
E-5	$22,338
E-4	$19,127
E-3	$16,031
E-2	$13,529
E-1	$12,067

Overall, there is decent career potential for individuals in computer-related jobs. Civilian pay scales are relatively comparable to other professional positions, and the work is relatively clean. In addition, the electronic commerce boom has provided many computer professionals with new avenues in which to use their skills. People in the military find computer-related positions attractive because they can lead to well-paying civilian jobs after they are discharged from active service.

The decision to become an information warrior, from a career perspective, is far different from simply pursuing a computer-related job. The number of computer professionals who make the formal leap into information warfare careers is still relatively low. Of the 1.5 million people holding computer engineer, programmer, or analyst positions, less than 3 percent are qualified as information warriors. Of the 2.4 million people on active duty in the military or on military reserve status in the United States, less than 2 percent are qualified as information warriors. This makes information warfare-qualified people a relatively elite group. This elite status and the present glorification of technology are the factors most likely to attract people to the ranks of information warriors.

Motivations for Warriors in the New Frontier

Beyond being attracted to an elite cadre in the first place, the motivating influences of information warriors in their day-to-day work are also different from those of other computer professionals. This conclusion is supported by dozens of interviews conducted over a five-year period with professionals involved in these new frontier elite professions. Individuals interviewed included law enforcement officers investigating computer crime and terrorism, prosecutors working on computer crime cases, computer security professionals, and military personnel. These interviews were conducted for a variety of projects, including market analysis, product evaluations, and articles for journals and magazines written by the authors of this book.

It is important to note that during all of these projects the people interviewed did not compromise any sensitive material. Although their input helped to forge the perspectives that are the foundation of this analysis, the work in this book includes an independent perspective and is by no means to be considered an exposé of insider or confidential information regarding military or law enforcement operations. The common thread through all the interviews was that people who are working in information warfare or information security fields truly enjoy their work. They expressed feelings of satisfaction and even joy about being on the cutting edge of technology and being able to take on such massive challenges. All of the people interviewed and their entire cadre have earned the respect of the authors.

Information technology and the Internet have in fact presented a new frontier to societies and nations in many parts of the world. As with any frontier, the job of policing activity and protecting public assets and national security is a difficult one. To a certain extent, information warriors and their civilian counterparts are viewed as nerds and technoids, but in a way they seem to be proud of that. They have a deep-rooted feeling about their abilities, their intelligence, and their dedication to a very important cause. These feelings are probably true for the bad guys just as much as for the good guys. Hackers and computer bandits probably take as much pride in their abilities and accomplishments as do the people trying to stop them. Similar levels of pride have been noted for terrorists, especially those who have a religious basis for their actions. This should by no means be considered an endorsement of hacker or terrorist activity, but it is something the good guys need to understand. The bad guys are as driven as the good guys—and they have a skill set that often matches and sometimes exceeds that of the good guys.

These dynamics are interesting and a bit scary. The basic conclusion about information warriors, both guardian and attacker, is that they are highly intelligent people who are very motivated to demonstrate their skills and beat their opponents. For those who need their information technology infrastructures and assets protected, this is simultaneously the best and the worst news they can get. This does not mean all the bad guys are brilliant—in fact, many of them are blundering idiots and are readily apprehended. It does mean, however, that there are many bad guys who are very good at what they do. One of the social tasks in this century is to keep the good guys good. This means they need to be challenged, they need opportunities to exercise their skills, and they need to be appropriately compensated.

The Alienation of Computer Geeks

Information warriors, be they good guys or bad guys, seem to emerge from two ends of a continuum. They were either computer geeks who became warriors or they were warriors who became geeks. Please note that the term "geek" is used to describe an individual with a high level of computer skills—all other personality characteristics held constant for the moment. The computer geek has been made fun of in real life and in fiction, and has been the target of jokes, ridicule, and social heckling. This is and will remain a social issue and is a possible predictor as to why so many young geeks end up being hackers.

Many highly skilled computer professionals started their lives as geeky little kids. In the opinion of many people many of these kids who grew up to be computer professionals never outgrew their geekiness. Computer geeks, even as adults, are made fun of and ridiculed. It has become common to hear people make comments about their department geek or those geeks in the basement who take care of the computers. The social excommunication has been relentless and merciless. This is a problem and could become a bigger problem in the future.

The stereotypical teenage hacker has often been portrayed as an antisocial recluse. Behind that description is likely to be an isolated, alienated individual whose primary source of self-esteem is his or her ability to do what other people cannot do: hack, take systems down, and cause chaos and economic damage.

Beyond the obvious problem of social cruelty, there is another social problem brewing. Within the next five years, there will be more than 150,000 people capable of implementing some type of information warfare strategy. Many of these people are going to start out as young, isolated, alienated individuals who people think of as geeks and treat as geeks. This is not a good thing. Our society will suffer a backlash from the widely practiced social excommunication of geeks. This does not have to happen, but social mores are not likely to change, and it is not likely that geeks are going to become a protected class. However, without deliberate social action the probability of the young geek going to the dark side of the information warrior elite will continue to get higher. Standing on a social pillar of self-righteousness and condemning the antisocial behavior of geeks gone bad will not yield positive results.

Affinity Within the Pocket Protector Sect

Geeks growing up alienated and possibly moving to the dark side of information warfare are a problem that could well lead to yet another problem. Grown-up geeks can remain alienated and socially isolated and have difficulty forming relationships with people different from them. Although the alienation may start young, social attitudes toward geeks do not really change regardless of how old the geek is, and this can make it difficult for an extreme geek to mature. Adults can be as mean as children when it comes to ridicule, and the more different an individual is from others, the more likely he or she is to remain isolated. This can result in the geek becoming an outcast—and where the outcast finds companionship is with other outcasts.

This raises a concern because as the population of information warfare-capable individuals grows, those individuals need to be integrated into a social system that reinforces preferred behavior. The extremely intelligent geek will need to be with other extremely intelligent geeks. The geeks will gravitate, or more likely be pushed because of ridicule, to people he or she feels comfortable with and with whom they have common interests. If there are opportunities to enter information warfare careers on the side of the good guys, and there is a sense of community and feeling of camaraderie, they will gravitate there. On the other hand, if the positive opportunity does not exist, they are likely to seek community and camaraderie elsewhere. The problem this could create, as dramatically illustrated in the PH2 scenario in Chapter 3, is that they end up forming groups of alienated and socially isolated individuals whose only source of positive reinforcement is each other.

This could result in the emergence of gangs of geek renegades, terrorists, or rogue criminals capable of doing considerable damage by launching information warfare attacks. If this outcast scenario does play out, it is likely that such gangs will start by seeking a challenge and working to share their experience or impress each other. That, however, could quickly turn into a profit-seeking enterprise that does "hits for hire" or is involved in bank rip-off schemes or other revenue-generating activities. It is doubtful that these groups would become gun-toting hoodlums who machine-gun rival gangs having coffee in a cybercafé. But the economic damage they could do would be far greater than anything organized crime has managed to accomplish to date. There will never be an opportunity for social rehabilitation of these individuals. If these groups move toward crime or terror, it is likely they will not come back.

Why Cybercrime and Terrorism Can Be Fun and Profitable

Another force that can contribute to the emergence of terrorist or rogue information warfare or soldier-of-fortune activity is economics. Although computer programmers, security administrators, and other computer professionals make a fairly good annual income, it is still relatively low compared to the income of an investment banker or high-level stockbroker. In addition, the income of computer professionals, unless they are on options or stock programs or own a business, will not rise dramatically over their lifetime. If a computer professional gets a 5 percent increase in her annual salary, that places her in an average growth income category of all computer professionals. It can take years for a programmer to reach an annual income of $98,000. Combine the income barriers with issues of alienation and isolation and you have a recipe for disaster—at least, a cyber-disaster. The temptations of riches face many computer professionals who can readily see ways to steal money through computer systems. Many more may become tempted in the future.

Not all of the cybercrime of the future will involve the theft of money. Industrial spying and competitive intelligence have long been activities that corporations and nations have indulged in for profit and advantage. The Economic Espionage Act of 1996 made the theft and misappropriation of trade secrets federal crimes. The act added a new Chapter 90 to Title 18 of the United States Code and calls for a two-tiered approach to combat economic espionage and conventional forms of trade secret theft and misappropriation. Economic espionage, as described in Section 1831, refers to foreign power sponsored or coordinated intelligence activity, directed at the U.S. government or corporations, entities, or other individuals operating in the United States, for the purpose of unlawfully obtaining trade secrets. Section 1832 punishes the theft, misappropriation, wrongful conversion, duplication, alteration, or destruction of a trade secret as well as punishing the attempts and conspiracies.

Most of the cyber-terrorism attacks and cybercrimes prosecuted over the last several years had to do with illegal entry, modification of systems, harm to systems, or theft of money. What has probably gone largely unnoticed, at least to the general public, is stealth intrusion for theft of information. The FBI office in San Francisco has been actively investigating the actions of more than 20 countries and their efforts in the misappropriation of trade secrets from the high-tech companies of Silicon Valley. The growth of the Internet and the fact that many companies connect their internal networks or intranets to the Internet makes it easy for hackers to enter systems and copy documents on computers inside the organization without ever physically entering the building.

Information warriors who are involved in terrorism or cybercrime have considerably different motives from information warriors who fight in the name of their country. Their potential compensation and social rewards are also different. Military personnel who are involved in offensive ruinous information warfare, offensive containment information warfare, and defensive preventive, responsive, or containment information warfare are rewarded with their basic compensation and occasional bonus pay, and have a high sense of patriotic achievement.

Religious or politically motivated terrorists usually gain little in the way of financial compensation, but are often revered in their community and can die as heroes in their country. Criminal gang members or individual operatives who attack for profit only achieve financial compensation when they perpetrate a successful heist. Criminal gang members or individual operatives can also be compensated for stealing trade secrets and conducting competitive intelligence operations, but they need to be successful in order to be compensated. Individual hackers, petty thieves, or social clubs are rewarded through self-esteem building or claims to bragging rights. The motives and financial rewards for different information warriors involved in different types of strategies are shown in Table 10-4.

Table 10-4: Motives and Financial Rewards for Information Warriors

Type	Type of Information Warrior	Motives and Financial Incentives
Offensive ruinous	Mercenaries and active military personnel	Basic compensation, bonus programs, and patriotic motives
Offensive containment	Mercenaries and active military personnel	Basic compensation and bonus programs
Sustained terrorist	Religious or politically motivated attackers	Little if any compensation, but high social rewards
Random terrorist	Religious or politically motivated attackers	Little if any compensation, but high social rewards
Defensive preventive	Mercenaries and active military personnel	Basic compensation, bonus programs, and patriotic motives
Defensive ruinous	Mercenaries and active military personnel	Basic compensation, bonus programs, and patriotic motives

Table 10-4 Continued: Motives and Financial Rewards for Information Warriors

Type	Type of Information Warrior	Motives and Financial Incentives
Defensive responsive containment	Mercenaries and active military personnel	Basic compensation, bonus programs, and patriotic motives
Sustained rogue	Criminal gang members or individual operatives	High rewards when successful and résumé-building activities
Random rogue	Criminal gang members or individual operatives	High rewards when successful and résumé-building activities
Amateur rogue	Individual hackers, petty thieves, or social clubs	Self-realization and bragging rights

The motivation of terrorists and rogues is not that complicated, and it is not difficult to understand even though it may be difficult to accept. Terrorists usually have political or religious motivations and often the two are combined. In the United States, patriotism, God, and country are blended through years of social tradition, and there are other countries where similar blends have evolved over centuries. Political motivations are often supported by religious righteousness. Soldiers pray to their gods before they go to battle. So do terrorists. The soldier and the terrorist are the same in that they are dedicated patriots, and conclusions as to whether they are good or evil are in the eye of the beholder. Ethnocentrism, racism, and elitism are always ingredients in the judgment process.

Professional criminals have often been turned into folk heroes as well. In the history of the United States, this was often accomplished through a dramatic increase in name recognition. Pretty Boy Floyd and the Bird Man of Alcatraz were among the many popular criminal heroes of the past. Kevin Mitnick was a hero to some hackers during his day. Reomel Ramores, the student in the Philippines who was the primary suspect in the release of the Love Bug virus in May 2000, became, at least for a short time, a local hero for his alleged participation in one of the biggest computer virus attacks to date. Criminal types have their heroes and so do geeks, and this notoriety may be one of the primary motivations for many computer criminals, especially amateurs.

Whether they seek wealth, notoriety, fame, or fortune, the motivations of the computer criminal and rogue information warrior are going to be different from those of non-criminal computer programmers or computer systems analysts. Right or wrong, motivation is motivation, and investigators, prosecutors, and government officials need to adjust to the simple fact that society both creates and motivates criminal minds. If the motivated criminal has computer skills at a high enough level to engage in information warfare, he or she will become a greater threat to society.

Will Americans Make Good Terrorists and Cyber Soldiers of Fortune?

There are many possibilities for military personnel trained as information warriors when they are discharged. Some will retire and live happily ever after. Others will pursue second careers and go to work for software companies or find employment as computer security experts. But there is also the legacy of the soldier who can never quit fighting and who wants to always be a soldier. Most of the men and women who serve in the U.S. military are upstanding citizens. There are, however, some alarming statistics about people in the military. Alcoholism, drug abuse, spousal abuse, and child abuse rates are as at least as high in the military as they are in the civilian population as a whole.

In many ways, the pressures of military life are far more extreme than the pressures of day-to-day civilian life. Mobility requirements, family separation, danger, and the possibility of death are always looming in the background, and unfortunately, they bring the stability of military personnel into question. This is not a criticism of the military; these are merely the facts of military life. It also may contribute to the possibility that some of the people discharged from the U.S. military who are trained as information warriors could turn to cybercrime and terrorism, drifting to the dark side of the information warfare elite.

One stabilizing factor in this dilemma is that there is a high demand for well-trained and skilled information technology workers. This means that almost anyone who leaves the military with good computer skills can readily find gainful employment. The movement to commercial off-the-shelf product usage by the military also improves the employability of military-trained computer professionals because it improves the transferability of skills. The private sector, government agencies, and the military all now use many of the same commercial computer products. This is far different from 20 or 30 years ago when the military was using specialized single-purpose technologies to address communications and computing requirements. Given the overall demand for information technology workers, it is most likely that military-trained information warriors will move into comparable civilian careers and work in security-related positions. The BLS supports these prospects with its projected availability of information technology jobs through 2008.

However, there is still the 1.5 percent factor. That is, 1.5 percent of the population in the United States is imprisoned, which could lead to the conclusion that at least 1.5 percent of the population of the United States is willing to participate in criminal activity. If the ratios of criminal participation from the total U.S. population are applied to people discharged from the military, of the previously mentioned 20,000 trained information warriors that the military will discharge by 2010, about 300 of them could have criminal tendencies. A population of 300 highly trained information warriors with criminal tendencies may not seem like a large number, but as the examples of computer terrorist attacks and computer crimes previously described in this chapter show, one individual can cause considerable harm and economic damage.

The possibility of even a small number of highly trained information warriors turning to the dark side needs to be addressed. This can be done through several means. First, advanced screening of military personnel prior to entry into information warfare training programs could possibly prevent some personality types from being trained. Second, employment placement programs can be established to ensure that information warriors have ample opportunity to obtain gainful employment upon discharge. Third, programs to retain seasoned information warriors as trainers for the next generation of information warriors could be established, thus decreasing the possibility of highly trained information warriors going to the open market for mercenary employment.

The possibility of U.S. military-trained information warriors turning into bad guys doesn't really address the likelihood of them doing so. It also does not address the question of whether they would even make good terrorists or rogues. The answers to these questions remain elusive. The only safe bet is to let paranoia rule. If even a handful of military-trained information warriors decide to turn terrorist or criminal, the damage they could do would far exceed any of the examples previously mentioned in this chapter. Only the U.S. military can address this issue, and so far there is no solid indication that it has developed a comprehensive solution.

Gender, Race, and Nationality in Information Warfare Careers

To round out an examination of the new terrorist profile, participation by gender, race, and nationality needs to be explored. In the United States the National Science Foundation is supporting programs to attract women and minorities to information technology fields in the United

States. The purpose of these programs is twofold. First, the United States needs more information technology workers and cannot continue to rely on foreign workers to fill positions. Second, women and minorities are under-represented in information technology fields. The implications of this for the study of the information warrior population is that women and minorities are also likely to be under-represented in the information warrior population.

Another dynamic to consider in the study of the information warrior population is national origin and country of residence of potential information warriors. Several countries have made concerted efforts to train information technology workers and support the development of information technology-related industries. These countries include China, Finland, France, Great Britain, Germany, Ireland, Israel, Japan, Malaysia, the Netherlands, Spain, and Sweden. Computer-related training in these countries is very high quality, and university-level students often come to the United States for their college education or advanced training. In addition, most large U.S.-based technology companies are developing contractual relationships with companies in these countries. Some of these relationships involve the sale of technology, the licensing of patents and sharing of trade secrets, or the manufacturing of components or finished products.

Overall, most of these countries are facing the same sort of shortage of information technology workers as the United States faces. This shortage helps keep information technology workers gainfully employed and out of mischief. However, the relationships between companies operating in these countries and the technology producers of the United States means that the population that has access to information about the technologies is becoming more global in scope. U.S. military and State Department concern about expanding the knowledge base and skill level of other countries has long been reflected in the export restrictions that have been placed on powerful computer equipment. As these restrictions have eased over the last several years, more advanced technology has become available to more countries.

These trends impact the assessment of the sources of threats based on gender, race, or nationality. With lower participation in information technology fields by women and minorities in the United States, the odds are lower that either women or minorities would become terrorists or rogue information warriors. However, the threat of information warriors emerging from other countries is continually increasing. It remains doubtful that state-against-state information warfare will be waged by China, Finland, France, Great Britain, Germany, Ireland, Israel, Japan, Malaysia, the Netherlands, Spain, and Sweden. However, the possibility of terrorist or rogue information warfare activity from the population of technology workers in these countries is high and is getting higher every day.

In addition to information warfare attacks, the threat of economic espionage or industrial spying by governments, organizations, businesses, or individuals from this list of countries is also increasing. The Internet allows spies to readily travel around the world without ever leaving their office or home. As the NSA and DOS have warned, the move to electronic commerce and the creation of corporate websites have provided new doorways for spies to enter through.

Conclusions and an Agenda for Action

Information warriors will be both good guys and bad guys. In addition to dealing with the development of information warfare strategies and cooperation among nations, computer-dependent nations need to address the recruitment and training of information warriors. A better understanding of the information warrior mentality and personality needs to also be developed. Just as it is past time to come to grips with information warfare, the military, civilian governments, private industry, and international organizations around the world have a very busy agenda ahead of them in recruiting and retaining trustworthy computer professionals. It is critical that people with high-level computer skills are integrated into society and not ostracized to the point where they turn to criminal or terrorist activity for self-realization or financial gain. All of these factors present a significant social challenge. Basic conclusions from the analysis of information warriors and principles that can realistically guide the process of moving forward in dealing with information warriors are as follows.

Conclusions Drawn from the New Terrorist Profile

▸ The U.S. government has warned private companies and non-profit organizations that they are vulnerable to information warfare attacks.

▸ In the United States, the population of trained information warriors is increasing, as is the population of people capable of learning information warfare skills.

- ▶ The U.S. military trains the most highly skilled information warriors and will be discharging several thousand trained people during the next decade.

- ▶ There is already a well-established history of computer systems attacks by terrorists and criminals. Some of these attacks have been for money, others for political reasons, and yet others just so individuals could claim bragging rights to the accomplishment.

- ▶ People become information warriors for self-realization as well as for profit. Politics and religion also motivate terrorists who are involved in information warfare.

- ▶ Many terrorists and rogue information warriors are just as highly skilled as those who are defending the information infrastructure against attacks.

- ▶ Social alienation can help drive highly skilled computer professionals into small groups that could be motivated to attack information technology architectures and information assets as revenge for being ostracized or for financial gain.

- ▶ The pay levels of computer professionals, combined with their constant exposure to information systems that control money and financial assets, could increase their temptation to steal money using those systems.

- ▶ Women and minorities in the United States are under-represented in computer professions and will thus likely be under-represented in information warfare professions.

- ▶ Several countries have initiatives to expand their information technology sectors and have relationships with technology producers in the United States, which gives more people access to sophisticated equipment and skill-development opportunities. This will lead to more people around the world being capable of launching information warfare attacks.

An Agenda for Action to Deal with the New Terrorist Profile

The U.S. government needs to set an agenda for action to deal with the growing population of information warriors within this country as well as in other countries. Action steps should include, but not be limited to, the following areas:

▶ Programs should be established to help ensure that individuals trained as information warriors by the military, when discharged, do not drift into mercenary or criminal activities.

▶ Records of individuals trained as information warriors by the military need to be maintained with detailed information about their training. These records should be made available to federal authorities investigating computer-related crimes.

▶ Law enforcement records on known criminals and terrorists need to include information describing their computer skills and any attempts they have made to use computers to support their activities.

▶ Private companies and civilian agencies of the U.S. government need to apply strict hiring practices for information technology professionals and conduct background checks on new hires who will have access to government computers or documentation about government computers.

▶ Private companies, government agencies, and the military need to maintain a high level of confidentiality about their computer operations to reduce the possibility of terrorists and criminals gaining information that could be used to help launch information warfare attacks.

▶ U.S. military and civilian law enforcement need to be prepared to deal with a larger population of information warriors and develop a greater understanding of the personality types and motivations of terrorists and rogue information warriors.

▶ The development of information warfare capabilities and the training of information warriors on a global basis must be monitored. The U.S. military, intelligence-gathering organizations, and civilian law enforcement agencies need to closely monitor social and technological developments in countries that are expanding their high-tech sectors. These countries include China, Finland, France, Great Britain, Germany, Ireland, Israel, Japan, Malaysia, the Netherlands, Spain, and Sweden.

Chapter 11

Law Enforcement: Being Behind the Technology Curve and How to Change That

One of the key differences between information warfare and the warfare models of the past is how the wars will start and how a nation, region, or group will know it is actually at war. The military realizes it is in a warfare situation when its forces are physically attacked, when there are cyber or physical attacks on military installations, or when the Department of Defense or government officials (organization structure will vary by country) declare that a state of war exists. In an information warfare situation, attacks against a nation can start in the private sector and even against government installations, as illustrated in the PH2 scenario in Chapter 3, and the military would not necessarily have any direct involvement in countering the attacks. The military will only get involved when it is directly attacked or when directed to react.

The likelihood that attacks will be perpetrated by terrorist groups and rogue criminal gangs instead of the organized military forces of another country also leaves responsibility for dealing with information warfare attacks squarely on the shoulders of civilian law enforcement agencies. (The exception is when military systems are attacked.) In the United States, the separation of jurisdiction and legal responsibility excludes the military from being overtly involved in responding to information warfare attacks against civilian properties until directed to intervene by civilian powers. It will take either a presidential order or an act of Congress to move the military into action. A series of information warfare attacks could cause hundreds of billions of dollars in damage by the time civilian authorities order a military response.

Civilian law enforcement agencies will have a very significant role as a first line of detection and defenses against information warfare attacks. These civilian law enforcement agencies will need to be better equipped to respond. In addition, civilian law enforcement personnel will need considerable training to bring their skills up to the level necessary for dealing with information warfare attacks. This training involves the improvement of computer skills, computer incident investigation techniques, an understanding of information warfare strategies and tactics, as well as an understanding of the various information warrior mentalities.

Training for all levels of law enforcement is necessary. Federal law enforcement agencies have already placed a high priority on computer-related incident training programs. But local and state agencies remain behind the training curve in investigating and dealing with computer-related criminal or terrorist incidents. This chapter examines the need for this training and the obstacles to successfully building a cyber response capability that are inherent in law enforcement systems of computer-dependent nations. These needs include:

- How to broaden the perspectives of civilian law enforcement personnel and expand their understanding of information warfare strategies and tactics

- Developing a cadre of civilian law enforcement personnel who have technical skills necessary to respond to information warfare attacks

- ▶ The knowledge and skills required for civilian law enforcement personnel to respond to information warfare attacks

- ▶ The establishment of an information highway patrol force

- ▶ The use of profiling techniques to identify and track military, terrorist, and rogue information warriors and their activities

- ▶ The development of investigation and apprehension methods that are appropriate for dealing with information warriors

The Good Guys: Poorly Paid and Under-Trained

According to the U.S. Bureau of Labor Statistics (BLS), police and detectives held about 764,000 jobs in the United States in 1998. Local governments, primarily in cities with more than 25,000 inhabitants, employ about 64 percent of all police detectives and investigators. Large cities, of course, have very large police forces, while most small communities employ fewer than 25 officers each. State police agencies employ about 11 percent of all police, detectives, and investigators, and various federal agencies employ the other 25 percent. Seventy local, special, and state agencies employ 1,000 or more full-time sworn officers, including 41 local police agencies, 15 state police agencies, 12 sheriff's departments, and two special police agencies—the New York City public school system and the Port Authority of New York/New Jersey.

The pay scale for civilian law enforcement personnel (shown in Table 11-1) is lower than the pay scale for computer programmers and analysts (shown in Table 10-2). Given this disparity, it does not make economic sense for an individual with good computer skills to enter a law enforcement career. On the low end and at the median point of the pay scale, computer professionals are earning about $4,000 more per year than the law enforcement workers. On the high end of the pay scale, computer professionals are earning as much as $10,000 more per year than the law enforcement worker earns. In addition, the computer professional has a relatively safe job compared to the law enforcement worker. Working for local law enforcement agencies is economically detrimental to the earning power of a computer professional.

Table 11-1: Annual Salaries for Police and Detective Supervisors and Detectives and Criminal Investigators (from the U.S. Bureau of Labor Statistics)

Salary Levels	Police and Detective Supervisors	Detectives and Criminal Investigators
1998 median	$48,700	$46,180
2001 median at 4% annual growth	$54,840	$51,950
1998 highest 10%	$84,710	$80,120
2001 highest 10% at 4% annual growth	$95,300	$90,140
1998 middle 50%	$37,130 to $69,440	$35,540 to $62,520
2001 middle 50% at 4% annual growth	$41,770 to $78,120	$39,980 to $70,340
1998 lowest 10%	$28,780	$27,950
2001 lowest 10% at 4% annual growth	$32,380	$31,440

If a trained computer professional decides to pursue a law enforcement career, the most economically beneficial alternative is to work as a federal investigator. Federal law enforcement agents can earn a better annual salary than computer professionals. According to the BLS, federal law provides special salary rates to federal employees who serve in law enforcement. Additionally, federal special agents and inspectors receive law enforcement availability pay (LEAP) or administratively uncontrolled overtime (AUO). The LEAP and AUO supplements are equal to 25 percent of the agent's grade and step and the supplements are awarded because of the large amount of overtime that these agents are expected to work. For example, in 1999, FBI agents entered service as GS 10 employees on the government pay scale at a base salary of $34,400, yet earned about $43,000 a year with availability pay. They could advance to the GS 13 grade level in field non-supervisory assignments at a base salary of $53,800, which is worth almost $67,300 with availability pay. Promotions to supervisory, management, and executive positions were available in grades GS 14 and GS 15, which paid a base salary of about $63,600 or $74,800 a year, respectively, and equaled $79,500 or $93,500 per year, including availability pay. Salaries were slightly higher in selected areas where the prevailing local pay level was higher.

In addition to the pay scale, the basic level of education of law enforcement personnel needs to be addressed in order to bring agents' capabilities up to the level necessary to deal with new technologies and new threats. One of the recommendations of the President's Commission on Law Enforcement and the Administration of Justice, established in 1967, was that all police personnel with general enforcement powers have baccalaureate degrees. Jeremy Travis, director of the National Institute of Justice of the U.S. Department of Justice, addressed the issue of education at the Forum on Police and Higher Education at the Center for Research in Law and Justice, University of Illinois in Chicago, on February 10, 1995. He noted that, in general, various national commissions have recommended that some years of college be required for appointment as a law enforcement officer, that higher requirements be set for promotion, and that education programs be based on formal departmental or national policy. Travis also noted that although the education levels of law enforcement personnel had increased during the last twenty years, there was much more work to be done.

Computers and Beyond: New Requirements for Cops and Special Agents

The belief that there is a need for education and training for law enforcement personnel has few opponents. Traditionally, law enforcement training has focused on policing methods and procedures for the physical world. The scope and subject areas for law enforcement training and education must be rethought in the age of the Internet and information warfare. This does not diminish the need for solid police training in the traditional areas of study. Technology training does not replace traditional training for law enforcement personnel; it improves their ability to deal with a new world—that of cyberspace.

Bringing all law enforcement personnel up to the education levels of a highly skilled information warrior is not achievable or practical. Nor is it particularly advisable because it could create a larger population of people capable of implementing information warfare strategies. Law enforcement training for dealing with information warfare needs to be appropriate for the level of involvement the individual officers and investigators will have with criminal or terrorist acts that impact technology or are accomplished by using computers. However, all law enforcement officers need to have at least a basic understanding of information warfare.

Training for the Civilian Information Warfare Expert

To respond to information warfare attacks, civilian law enforcement agencies need a cadre of people who are as equally qualified as any information warrior in the world. One source of such skilled people is former military information warriors. If former military personnel do fill some of these positions, they will need to be trained in appropriate civilian law enforcement procedures and protocols. This is necessary to ensure that they operate in a complementary manner with civilian law enforcement efforts. It is equally important, however, that there are people with civilian law enforcement backgrounds who are trained in information warfare. This is necessary to ensure a balance of perspectives in this elite group of guardians. Regardless of the source of personnel, the individuals working in civilian agencies who are dealing with information warfare attacks with the highest level of expertise need knowledge and skills in the following areas:

▶ Basic law enforcement procedures, including legal processes, investigative techniques, evidence collection and interpretation, forensic analysis, criminal profiling, and inter-agency communications and protocols.

▶ National and global information and communications architectures, including basic electronics, computer system design, operating systems, communications protocols, wireless and broadcast system design, as well as knowledge of multiple computer programming languages.

▶ Business and financial applications, including requirements analysis, development procedures, object-oriented design procedures, testing and debugging, and applications maintenance processes.

▶ Inter-organizational business and financial applications functions, including the structure of the banking system, credit clearance and debit card systems, stock exchange operation, supply chains, and electronic commerce that are being used, and a knowledge of the organizations that are using the applications.

▶ Commercial software, hardware, and networking products, including knowledge of the manufacturers, installation procedures, known bugs and flaws, and the strengths and weaknesses in designs of various classes of commercial products.

- ▶ Security and encryption methods and products for computer and communications systems, including how the products function, what their capabilities are, and their inherent strengths and weaknesses.

- ▶ Intrusion and hacking techniques that are effective with different product classes, systems, and architectures, along with the design and deployment methods of computer viruses and other destructive or offensive computer code.

- ▶ The future of technology, including work that is currently going on at the product engineering level as well as emerging applications and products that will be available during the next decade.

Training for the Criminal Investigator

All criminal investigators will need some level of knowledge about information warfare tactics and computer crime. The general crime investigator is not expected to defend information systems or necessarily track down cyber-attackers through electronic means. But they will need to be able to identify if there is possible use of computers to commit crimes or to support criminal or terrorist activity. There also needs to be a substantial number of specialized criminal investigators who can use electronic means to track and investigate criminal and terrorist activity.

The general criminal investigator needs training to identify if (and to some extent, how) perpetrators are using computers or communications systems. The investigators will also need to be able to identify computer systems and interpret other evidence that indicates computer usage. Evidence includes receipts for computer equipment or computer services as well as documentation of computer passwords, system designs, or application program code printouts. These basic skills are important for criminal investigators who are among the first law enforcement officers to arrive at a crime scene or who are using search warrants to collect evidence relating to other types of crimes where computer usage may be a factor. The basic criminal investigator needs to identify these materials or determine if there is evidence of computer or communications usage and then turn over those aspects of the investigation to specialized investigators.

Criminal investigators who specialize in computer-related crime or terrorist activity cases need a higher skill level. Those investigators who support the investigative process in cases where lawbreakers substantially relied on computers to assist or facilitate their activities will need specialized skills as well. Computer-related criminal investigative work could involve analysis of healthcare fraud, securities and commodities fraud, money laundering, and intellectual property rights violations. Collecting evidence to support the prosecution of people who commit such crimes will require appropriate forensic accounting skills. These investigators, although they may be viewed as traditional white-collar crime investigators, need to have a solid understanding of information warfare. This is important because any one of these criminal activities may be ultimately related to terrorist groups or rogue criminals who are capable of or planning some type of information warfare attack.

An emerging specialization in the criminal investigation profession is the use of computer and communications systems to identify criminal activity and track down lawbreakers. These investigators need a substantially different skill set from the traditional white-collar criminal investigator even though they may be tracking the same culprits. The computer-centric investigators need the following skills and knowledge:

- ▶ Excellent Internet skills, including technology that supports Internet communication and a thorough understanding of Internet culture. They need to be highly skilled Internet users, and they need to know where on the Internet to look for signs of criminal activity.

- ▶ The ability to create false identities in cyberspace just as they would if they were involved in an undercover operation in the physical world.

- ▶ A sociological and psychological understanding of the type of culprit they are investigating or attempting to apprehend and how these people use the Internet.

- ▶ The ability to record or capture data from Internet sites, chat rooms, or other electronic communities that can serve as evidence or help to compile information to facilitate the investigation of illegal activity.

- ▶ The ability to track Internet usage and activities of specific individuals or groups to facilitate the investigative process.

Training for Field Personnel

Law enforcement agencies, especially local and state organizations, have thousands of people who do field work. These includes patrol officers, border patrol agents, customs agents, and special duty officers. All of these personnel need training to help identify activities related to possible terrorist or rogue information warfare or computer-related domestic crimes. The need for this knowledge is increasing because of the growing use of wireless Internet devices. What is most important is that law enforcement field personnel are able to identify the types of devices that are being used or held by suspects or individuals under observation. The devices they need to be familiar with include smart phones, Palm units, and notebook computers with wireless modems. As more wireless Internet consumer products emerge, field personnel will need to be continually updated as to the types of devices to monitor and include in incident reports.

It is also advisable that field personnel be trained to identify computer printouts, password lists, and credit card number lists. They also need to be able to identify computer media such as floppy disks, hard drives, removable hard drives, and magnetic computer tapes. In addition, they should be familiar with computer components, including desktop and notebook computers, memory chips, modems, and electronic test equipment.

Training for the Criminal Prosecutor

The prosecution of terrorists and master criminals has always been a challenge for the criminal justice system. The successful prosecution of terrorists and criminals who have been involved in information warfare activities is absolutely critical. This is not simply a matter of justice. If terrorists or rogue information warriors are apprehended and prosecution is unsuccessful, they will return to the streets—or in this case, probably return to the Internet—and continue their activities. There are two areas of training that are essential for prosecutors. First is the compilation and presentation of credible evidence, much of which is likely to be in electronic form or collected through electronic means. Second, prosecutors must develop an understanding of technology and the information warfare and computer crime processes at a high enough level to make credible arguments in court during the course of prosecution.

Training for the Judiciary

Many technology cases have already proven to be challenges for judges. But the frequency of technology-related cases will increase in the future, as will the complexity of the cases. This means that judges will also need to be better educated about computer and communications technologies and how they are used by the military, government organizations, and private companies. Judges are certainly not expected to have the knowledge level of network engineers or administrators, but they do need to be comfortable with terminology and have a grasp of how systems work. As with prosecutors, it is important for the judiciary to be able to understand technology at a high enough level to adequately hear cases involving information warfare attacks. The goal is to have as many successful convictions as possible and reduce the number of information warriors who are pursuing terrorist or rogue criminal activities in cyberspace.

The Challenge of Developing Cyber Cops

One of the challenges that law enforcement directors and administrators face in combating terrorists and rogue criminals who are wreaking havoc in cyberspace is recruiting talented people to fight the battle. The pay scale of law enforcement officers being generally lower than that of computer professionals, as previously discussed, is one hurdle. Another hurdle, and perhaps a more difficult one, is the difference in mentalities between people who originally choose computer-oriented careers and those who choose a law enforcement career. Simply stated, geeks may not make good cops. Computer professionals, stereotypically, are not really known for being aggressive, rough-and-tumble people. On the other hand, people who enter law enforcement careers expect to face some danger, and chasing down and apprehending criminals is a dangerous job.

This does make recruitment of former military information warriors to work in civilian law enforcement positions an attractive staffing alternative. Certainly people with military experience, especially those who served until they were eligible for retirement, are prepared to face some level of danger. However, there are a limited number of military information warriors available for hire. In addition, to have a well-rounded cyber police squad requires a mix of people from a variety of backgrounds. This means that civilian law enforcement organizations need to develop a means of attracting computer professionals who may be interested in pursuing an information warfare-oriented law enforcement career. This is a difficult challenge and a tough sales job for the law enforcement recruiter. Going to a college campus to offer students in information technology degree programs a lesser-paying job than they can get elsewhere—and as a bonus, telling them they may get shot at while they are doing their job—is probably not going to be an effective approach.

One alternative is to offer computer professionals willing to enter a law enforcement career some sort of incentive pay to make up for the lower salary level. This approach will probably be rejected in cities where there are strong law enforcement labor unions. It could result in lawsuits or strikes and could make contract negotiations with existing officers far more difficult. It may also cause considerable resentment among personnel already on staff and negatively impact morale. None of these are desirable results.

Another approach, and one that will take longer to achieve results from, is the establishment of education programs at the university level that specialize in computer crime or information warfare training. This is a good idea, but it is also an expensive one. There are already undergraduate degrees in law enforcement available from universities in most areas of the United States. In addition, most states have some sort of official law enforcement academy where new recruits go for their initial training and where most law enforcement officers return from time to time for advanced or specialized training. It is possible that one of the existing education programs may take up the mantle. However, to launch a new program will take time and cost money. One of the biggest challenges in launching the program will be to find qualified instructors willing to work for university-level compensation.

Another approach to developing the skills necessary to fight terrorists and rogue information warriors is to train existing law enforcement personnel. This is also a challenging alternative, and it has many obstacles. One obstacle, of course, is labor unions and how they would respond to the structure of eligibility for the training, as well as numerous other possible labor union objections. Other obstacles could include a lack of interest on the part of law enforcement officers who are mid-career, the lack of formal training programs, and funding to support the training effort.

There are already law enforcement organizations that have established computer-related crime units. The officers staffing these units most often get their positions by choice. They have an interest in computers and developed most of their computer skills on their own time. They were not trained by the organizations they work for, with the exception of perhaps attending a few workshops or seminars at department expense. Interviews conducted by the authors over the last five years found that in jurisdictions where there are computer-related crime units, these units are staffed with just a few people and have a long list of cases to work on. All of these things considered, training existing law enforcement officers to patrol cyberspace and fight terrorists and rogue information warriors really does not seem like a viable solution.

Working for Big Brother: The New Information Highway Patrol

The new information highway patrol is starting to emerge. The U.S. military has had information warrior training programs for more than a decade. The FBI is training computer crime and information warfare investigators and building case experience as they go along. Some local jurisdictions have established computer crime units, while others are starting to think about it. The National Infrastructure Protection Center (NIPC), established in February 1998, is now the national focal point for gathering information on threats to critical infrastructures. The NIPC is the principal means of facilitating and coordinating the federal government's response to an incident, mitigating attacks, investigating threats, and monitoring reconstitution efforts. These infrastructures, which include telecommunications, energy, banking and finance, water systems, government operations, and emergency services, are considered critical to the economy of the United States.

However, all of these efforts are far from adequate to protect the entire spectrum of information technology activities that computer-dependent countries rely on. In a defensive role, the military now focuses on military systems and installations. The definition of infrastructure used by the NIPC is restrictive and rooted in an aging view of what is critical and what is infrastructure. There is a big gap in protection, and ecommerce companies are now easy pickings for terrorists and rogue criminal information warriors. The FBI can investigate, but they can do little to prevent attacks. By the time they get to the scene, virtual or physical, the attacks could be over and the damage done. The local police, as previously mentioned, are just starting to develop their capabilities.

It is also important to realize that many attacks on corporate systems go unreported for economic, political, and public relations reasons. Reported attacks seldom result in the apprehension of an offender and usually just end up causing the reporting company bad press and discomfort. Large corporations have their own computer security staff, and they work diligently to keep intruders out of systems. Many smaller ecommerce companies, as well as many companies that have their Web sites hosted by an Internet service provider (ISP), are greatly exposed and highly vulnerable to attack. Meanwhile, the number of attacks continues to increase as it has over the last two or three years. The FBI has been expending considerable resources dealing with attacks and closing more cases, but each year they end up with more pending cases than at the end of the previous year.

To be effective in tracking attackers, the information highway patrol needs to be on the scene when an attack is in progress. This means that a new model of cyberpolicing is necessary. The traditional response in law enforcement has been to investigate crimes after they happen. The exception to this is sting operations that sometimes prompt crimes to happen, and then undercover agents arrest the culprits. This model is not going to work with cybercrimes, and it is not going to be at all effective in responding to major terrorist or rogue criminal information warfare attacks. The new information highway patrol has to be in cyberspace, working all the time.

The implications for this proposition are staggering, and privacy advocates are going to kick and scream. When industrial countries decided they wanted to reduce terrorist attacks in civil aviation, security systems were established that were designed to check passenger identification and keep weapons and bombs off civilian aircraft. The argument for such security was simple: if civil aviation was going to be safer, appropriate security measures were required. The analogy must be applied to cyberspace—if those organizations that have an Internet presence and if the economies that are computer-dependent are going to be made safer, appropriate security measures will need to be implemented. This means that cyberspace must be policed, and that will require a combination of technology and human resources. It will also mean that some privacy rights of individuals using the public communications infrastructures will be compromised.

Terrorist and Criminal Profiling in Cyberspace

It is certainly possible to track everything that happens in cyberspace. However, it would be incredibly expensive and would not yield a very reasonable return on investment. It is a common and often controversial approach to create profiles of criminals and criminal behavior when policing the physical world. In the judgment of a police officer, if circumstances dictate, he or she will stop, detain, and question individuals who fit the characteristics of a profile. Federal agents, acting within a similar framework, investigate groups of individuals who have a set of characteristics that make them suspect under certain circumstances. These law enforcement procedures have been highly criticized over the last fifty years. These procedures, however, are critical to the contemporary approach of crime prevention.

Tracking all activity in cyberspace and keeping logs on what each of the more than 250 million Internet users do worldwide is prohibitively expensive. Creating a profiling system for cyber-terrorists and rogue criminals will be a more cost-effective means for the information highway patrol to work with in preventing information warfare attacks. From the perspective of the privacy advocate, such a profiling system will definitely result in the privacy of some individuals being compromised. It will also likely raise potential constitutional questions in the United States and other computer-dependent nations.

Profiling is not a complicated process, but it will require considerable effort on the part of military and civilian law enforcement agencies in all of the computer-dependent nations. Profiling parameters and methods need to be created, and technologies that can track culprits need to be developed and tested. In addition to profiling, computer-dependent nations will need to cooperate in sharing information on suspected or known hackers, cyber-terrorists, and people who commit computer crimes. This is a large undertaking, but there has been successful international cooperation in the past and more will be required in the future.

Conclusions and Agenda for Action

Civilian law enforcement officers and the entire criminal justice system are facing new challenges in dealing with information warfare. They will be fighting a war with a military force that is not automatically engaged to help them fight it. New and advanced training is necessary, and there is a need to recruit and retain a new breed of law enforcement officer, prosecutor, and judge. This is going to be a long and complicated process, and it will also be an expensive one. It is an absolute necessity if computer-dependent nations are going to successfully protect their information infrastructures and their increasingly computer-based economies. Basic conclusions as a result of analyzing law enforcement training requirements are as follows.

Conclusions on the Need for Law Enforcement Training

▶ Recruiting, training, and retaining law enforcement personnel qualified to deal with cyber-terrorists and rogue criminals will be difficult because of an overall shortage of computer professionals and because law enforcement agencies do not offer competitive salaries compared to what computer professionals can make in other positions.

▶ Fighting cybercrime requires new skill sets that do not presently exist in the law enforcement workforce. Training officers will be an expensive and time-consuming process.

▶ In addition to training law enforcement officers, prosecutors and judges also need to be trained to deal with the new levels of complexity involved in computer terrorism and computer crime cases.

▶ Policing cyberspace will require the deployment of a highly qualified information highway patrol force, combining new technology with traditional policing methods to effectively track and apprehend terrorists and criminals.

▶ A profiling system for identifying potential terrorist or criminal behaviors and actions will aid the information highway patrol in preventing information warfare attacks.

An Agenda for Action for Law Enforcement Training

The governments of the United States and other computer-dependent nations need to set an agenda for action to develop cyberpolicing methods and deploy an information highway patrol force. Action steps should include, but not be limited to, the following areas:

▸ Compensation plans need to be reconsidered for law enforcement personnel who require high-level computer skills. A process needs to be developed to create compensation approaches that make it easier to hire these skilled people for civilian law enforcement agencies.

▸ National training programs need to be established and funded to help develop a cadre of law enforcement personnel capable of fighting against extremely intelligent and skilled information warriors.

▸ A profiling system should be developed for identifying potential terrorists and rogue criminals who are capable of or prone to involvement in information warfare activities. This system needs to be implemented on a global basis with input from law enforcement and military organizations in all of the computer-dependent nations.

Chapter 12

Final Words for Policy Makers, Military Planners, and Corporate Executives

The goal of this book was to establish a framework for analysis of information warfare strategies and to formulate agendas for action for policy makers, military planners, and corporate executives. Information warfare is a new type of warfare strategy, but it has much in common with previous warfare strategies. To counter information warfare attacks or to use information warfare strategies as an offensive mechanism will require the same coordinated response of legislative bodies, military organizations, and private industries as all other forms of warfare have required in the past.

The information age, very much symbolized by the Internet, presents new challenges in policymaking, military preparedness, and industrial mobilization. However, many other past challenges have been successfully faced and overcome. The abilities of modern societies to deal with past threats are what will enable the economic and military powers of the twenty-first century to successfully deal with the threat of information warfare. It is vital that the triad of civilian government, military organizations, and industry capitalize on its strengths in addressing this adversity.

The future of information warfare is uncertain. There is much debate as to how information warfare will occur, when it will occur, and who will be the first to launch major information warfare attacks. But uncertainty is a fact of life. Wars have come and gone in the past, some of which were massive efforts while others were slow, long, and draining to societies, military organizations, and the lands in which the wars were fought. Modern government, militaries, and industries have found that they must be prepared for a variety of types of war. The ten information warfare strategies, like other types of warfare strategies, must also be met with high levels of preparedness. This chapter presents my final words for policy makers, military planners, and corporate executives.

Cutting Through the Rhetoric

The level of uncertainty there is about any situation is an excellent predictor of the breadth and depth of rhetoric that surrounds a situation. There has been no shortage of rhetoric about information warfare, what it means, how it will happen, and which country will be the best prepared to attack and the best prepared to defend. The analysis of the ten information strategies, which is presented from several perspectives in this book, illustrates that one of the greatest threats in information warfare is that so many different types of organizations and individuals can employ so many different types of information warfare strategies. This is what makes information warfare one of the greatest threats to the future of peace and the stability of economies.

Policy makers, military planners, and corporate executives need to take a broad look at information warfare. In evaluating the ten strategies, they need to develop defenses against attacks as well as the ability to use offensive information warfare strategies when and where they may be called for.

There must be military preparedness to deal with all ten strategies. Offensive ruinous information warfare and defensive ruinous information warfare attacks can result in extensive damage to nations, industrial infrastructures, and economies. Offensive containment and defensive responsive containment information warfare attacks can also be very devastating. Random and sustained terrorist information warfare attacks can be launched by small groups of people and do extensive damage. Random and sustained rogue information warfare attacks can be executed by totally unknown groups of people and have severe repercussions for the targets at which they are directed. Amateur rogue information warfare attacks have been commonplace and will grow more severe in the future. It is necessary for all nations to participate in developing and supporting defensive preventive information warfare strategies.

Preparation will not be thorough and will not be timely if the process to establish and fund adequate responsive structures and training for military organizations and civilian law enforcement agencies is not accelerated. Those who doubt that information warfare is a threat are fools.

Funding National Defense

Defense funding has always been controversial. There have always been lobbying forces that have so often turned the funding of national defense into political battlegrounds. In funding information warfare efforts there are several things to bear in mind. First, the occurrence of traditional warfare incidents is not over. Wars of many shapes and forms will continue to be fought. Second, information warfare strategies will most likely be used in conjunction with other warfare strategies, which means that a fighting force that is capable of dealing with several types of warfare strategies simultaneously will be the most effective fighting force. Third, the possibility of information warfare will likely increase the costs of defense programs and military operations.

Many people would like to believe that the world is at peace and therefore nations need to spend less on defense. It is true that many old enemies have been shattered and no longer pose as drastic a threat as they did in days gone by. But information warfare does not require the existence of massive polarized superpowers. Many nations, both large and small, can wage information warfare. Terrorists, rogue criminals, and even amateur information warriors can cause considerable damage and economic disruption. Complacency in defense funding courts nothing but disaster.

Risk Management in the Corporate Environment

Private corporations have always felt the impact of both large and small wars. Information warfare does not decrease the potential impact of war on corporations. In fact, information warfare strategies put corporations at greater risk than they have ever been in conventional warfare situations. Corporations can become direct targets of information warfare attacks or suffer many negative consequences because of the indirect impact of information warfare attacks. Again, to be unprepared is to court nothing else than disaster.

In many ways, information warfare puts an end to the possibility of corporations economically benefiting from war without suffering the consequences of war. The cooperation of private industry does not have to be purchased in information warfare. The companies that would prefer to wait for the military to pay for their assistance are ignoring the realities of information warfare. If private companies that are the potential target of information warfare attacks do not cooperate with the military in formulating defenses and supporting military efforts, they are part of the problem, not part of the solution.

It is simply a matter of due diligence that private companies cooperate with NIPC and similar organizations in the countries in which they operate. Anything short of extensive and full cooperation is a dangerous path. However, it must be recognized that cooperation in planning defenses and reporting information warfare incidents is only the first step. Information warfare is not like the Y2K problem, which came and went. The threat of information warfare is permanent. If private companies want to be protected they must fully participate in the process of protecting themselves, their nations, and their future.

Ecommerce and Information Warfare

The most vulnerable companies in a war are those who live in the battlefield. Ecommerce companies live in cyberspace, and cyberspace is one of the battlefields in information warfare. This puts ecommerce companies at much higher risk when information warfare attacks are launched.

The conclusion is simple: ecommerce companies are among the most vulnerable and therefore must be among those that are the most cooperative in assisting military organizations and civilian law enforcement agencies in formulating defenses against information warfare.

Ecommerce companies need to rapidly mature in their understanding of cyber threats and view their business efforts from a more holistic viewpoint. They also must participate in cyber defense, and they must support the efforts of their governments in establishing systems for reporting and responding to information warfare attacks. This is an essential to assure that ecommerce can thrive in a potentially hostile cyber landscape.

Closing Comments

The future is at once unpredictable and predictable. Information warfare will happen. It will happen many times. When it will happen, how severe the attacks will be, and who will launch the first major attacks are not predictable. The threat of information warfare is like the threat of nuclear war. There will always be hope that it does not occur, but the only logical defense is to be prepared. In information warfare, the world will not be destroyed, as it would be in nuclear warfare. But economies can be laid waste in information warfare just as the planet could be turned into a wasteland after a nuclear attack. Once again the United States and allied nations of Europe and Asia have no choice at all. They must once again become the defenders of peace and freedom.

Glossary

Information Warfare Tactics

This glossary covers information warfare tactics. Each of the tactics defined can be used in many of the ten information warfare strategies discussed in the book. There are numerous tactics that can be utilized in information warfare that can be combined in endless combinations.

ALTERED SOFTWARE DISTRIBUTION

Unauthorized distribution of software that has been intentionally altered to malfunction under certain conditions or that has malicious code embedded in parts of the software that will execute under preset conditions or on a preset date and time.

APPLICATION SOFTWARE ALTERATION

Modification of installed application software to render it inoperable or cause it to malfunction.

APPLICATION SOFTWARE REMOVAL

Removing, erasing, or uninstalling application software from a system resulting in system users not having access to an application.

ATTACK SOURCE TRACING

Locating sources of information warfare attacks.

ATTACKER MASQUERADING

Information warriors disguising their identity to make it appear that a different group of people launched an attack.

ATTACKER TRAPS

Drone systems used to lure information warriors into an attack in order to trace the source of the attack.

AVIATION CONTROL SYSTEM ATTACKS

Attacking a civilian or military aviation control system to cause disruption of air traffic.

BANKING SYSTEM ATTACKS

Attacking national banking computers and communications systems to cause economic disruption to a specific bank or a nation.

CELLULAR COMMUNICATIONS SYSTEM ATTACKS

Attacking cellular systems to disrupt communications.

CIVILIAN GOVERNMENT INFORMATION SYSTEM ATTACKS

Attacking civilian government computers and telecommunications systems to disrupt government operations.

DATA ALTERATION

Modification of datasets or databases to render them unusable or to cause results of analysis to be incorrect.

DATA TRAPPING

Intercepting, mirroring, or capturing data or email traffic between systems.

DEFENSE COMMUNICATIONS SYSTEMS ATTACKS

Attacking defense communications systems to hinder military operations.

DESTRUCTIVE CODE ATTACKS

Malicious code, viruses, worms, or other types of destructive code designed to disable computer or telecommunications systems.

DIPLOMAT-ASSISTED ATTACKS

Attacking a computer or telecommunications system with the assistance of diplomats and government representatives.

DRONE ATTACKS

Reprogramming computers located at numerous locations to act as drone information warriors to launch attacks at target systems.

ECOMMERCE ATTACKS

Attacking electronic commerce websites to cause economic disruption to a company or a nation.

ELECTRICAL GRID MANAGEMENT ATTACKS

Attacking computer systems that manage the distribution of electricity to disrupt military operations, manufacturing, and commerce.

ELECTRONIC EAVESDROPPING

Monitoring communications of military organizations to ascertain activities and movements of military units.

ELECTRONIC WEAPONS ATTACKS

Attacking electronic and computer-dependent weapons systems to make them malfunction or to disable them.

EMAIL FLOODING

Replicating worms or viruses designed to flood email servers or client systems with email messages that hinder the operation of the systems.

EMERGENCY SERVICES SYSTEM ATTACKS

Attacking civilian emergency services systems, including police, fire, and private security systems, to disrupt the ability of government agencies to respond to emergency situations.

ENCRYPTION CRACKING

Breaking encryption that is used to protect the contents of data and voice transmissions, electronic messages, software, or commercial electronic content packaging.

ENERGY SOURCE OBSTRUCTION

Rendering computer or telecommunications equipment inoperable by obstructing the flow of electricity or other forms of energy necessary for the systems to run.

FACILITIES CONTROL SYSTEM ATTACKS

Attacking civilian or military facilities, management systems, and control systems, including security, electrical services, and water distribution, to disrupt building or campus operations.

FACILITIES OCCUPATION

Taking physical control of computer and telecommunications facilities to control systems and keep other parties from utilizing or controlling the systems.

FREQUENCY JAMMING

Overloading a specific transmission frequency with signals that are designed to flood receivers.

GAS ATTACKS

Injecting poisonous or noxious gas into a computer or telecommunications systems facility to rendering the personnel or the facility inoperative so the facility can be physically entered and controlled by information warriors.

HARBOR CONTROL SYSTEM ATTACKS

Attacking civilian or military seaport control systems to disrupt port operations.

HEALTH SYSTEM ATTACKS

Attacking civilian or military health systems, including life support, laboratory equipment, diagnostics systems, and information systems to disrupt healthcare operations.

INSIDER-ASSISTED ATTACKS

Attacking a computer or telecommunications system with the assistance of an inside person who has legitimate access to the systems.

INSIDER RECRUITMENT

Recruiting personnel who work on computer or telecommunications systems to aid in an information warfare attack by providing information, access, or other forms of assistance.

INSTANT MESSENGER SYSTEM ATTACKS

Attacking instant messenger systems to disrupt communications.

INTERNET SERVICE PROVIDER ATTACKS

Attacking Internet service providers to disrupt communications.

LOGISTICS MANAGEMENT SYSTEMS ATTACKS

Attacking logistics management systems to disrupt the movement of material, supplies, and personnel.

MAGNETIC WEAPONS ATTACKS

The use of weapons that disrupt the magnet and electronic fields that are part of system operations.

MASS CYBER ATTACKS

Dozens or even hundreds of cyberwarriors launching remote system attacks on a specific system.

MASS TRANSPORTATION SYSTEMS ATTACKS

Attacking mass transit control systems to disrupt commuting activities.

MILITARY COMMAND SYSTEM ATTACKS

Attacking military command systems to disrupt military communications and activities.

MUNICIPAL MANAGEMENT SYSTEM ATTACKS

Attacking municipal control and management systems to disrupt city operations.

ONLINE SERVICE PROVIDER ATTACKS

Attacking online services to disrupt communications.

ONSITE SYSTEM ATTACKS

Disabling or otherwise altering the operability of computer or telecommunications systems at the physical location of the system.

OPERATING SYSTEM SABOTAGE

Disabling computer or telecommunications systems by rendering the operating system of equipment inoperable.

PASSWORD TAMPERING

Entering a system and altering or destroying user passwords to deny legitimate users access to system resources.

PASSWORD THEFT

Stealing user passwords to gain access to a system.

PHYSICAL SYSTEM DESTRUCTION

Annihilation of computer or telecommunications equipment and systems through any means possible, including explosion, implosion, precision bombing, incendiary devices, or dismantling.

PRECISION BOMBING

Destroying selected computer or telecommunications facilities and equipment through the use of aerial-launched bombs or missiles.

PROCESS CONTROL ATTACKS

Launching an information warfare attack on the systems that control processes in industrial plants and manufacturing facilities.

PRODUCT-SPECIFIC ATTACKS

Targeting information technology products manufactured by specific companies such as Microsoft or Lucent Technologies.

RAILROAD CONTROL SYSTEM ATTACKS

Attacking railroad control systems to disrupt the movement of freight and passenger trains.

REMOTE SYSTEM ATTACKS

The use of telecommunications or Internet connections to enter and disable or otherwise alter the operability of computer or telecommunications systems from a geographically distant location.

SATELLITE TAMPERING

Unauthorized modification of a satellite or satellite transmissions.

SPACE CONTROL SYSTEM ATTACKS

Attacking civilian or military space control systems to disrupt the operations of space vehicles and satellite systems.

SPOOF ATTACKING

Simulating system attacks or launching system attacks to attract the attention of system security personnel and consume human resources as a cover for other operations.

STAFF INFILTRATION

Planting a mole or saboteur in a computer or telecommunications facility.

SYSTEM INTRUSION

Entering a computer system without the proper authority for the purpose of data collection, alteration, disablement, or destruction.

SYSTEM ISOLATION

Severing communications to the system through virtual or physical means.

SYSTEM OVERLOADING

Sending excessive commands to a system from multiple sources to consume the resources of the system.

TELECOMMUNICATIONS GRIDLOCKING

Exceeding the capacity of a telecommunications system by flooding the system with artificially generated traffic.

TELECOMMUNICATIONS SYSTEM ATTACKS

Attacking a civilian or military telecommunications system to cause disruption of voice and data communications.

TELECOMMUNICATIONS SYSTEM REPROGRAMMING

Altering the function of a telecommunications system by reprogramming settings or parameters of system operation.

TIME-BOMBING

Placing malicious code on a system that launches on a preset date and time.

UPGRADE TAMPERING

Modifying system upgrades being distributed to users to malfunction under certain conditions or embedding malicious code in parts of the software that will execute under preset conditions or at a preset date and time.

VENDOR-ASSISTED ATTACKS

Attacking a computer or telecommunications system with the assistance of a manufacturer or maintenance company that has legitimate access to the systems.

VIRTUAL PRIVATE NETWORK ATTACKS

Attacking virtual private network (VPN) communications systems to disrupt the use of the networks or isolate systems attached to the networks.

WAN ATTACKS

Attacking wide area network (WAN) communications systems to disrupt the use of the networks or isolate systems attached to the networks.

WATER ATTACKS

Flooding computer or telecommunications equipment facilities with water.

WATER DISTRIBUTION SYSTEM ATTACKS

Attacking water distribution control systems to disrupt civilian, government, and military operations.

WEBSITE MODIFICATION

Unauthorized alteration of website contents or functionality.

WEB TRAPS

Using websites to attract visitors to obtain information about the visitor or infect visiting systems with destructive code.

WIRELESS SYSTEM AND DEVICE ATTACKS

Attacking wireless systems or devices that use cellular communications or wireless LAN systems to disrupt communications and operations of organizations that depend on the systems.

Index

INTERNATIONAL CONTACT INFORMATION

AUSTRALIA
McGraw-Hill Book Company Australia Pty. Ltd.
TEL +61-2-9417-9899
FAX +61-2-9417-5687
http://www.mcgraw-hill.com.au
books-it_sydney@mcgraw-hill.com

CANADA
McGraw-Hill Ryerson Ltd.
TEL +905-430-5000
FAX +905-430-5020
http://www.mcgrawhill.ca

GREECE, MIDDLE EAST,
NORTHERN AFRICA
McGraw-Hill Hellas
TEL +30-1-656-0990-3-4
FAX +30-1-654-5525

MEXICO (Also serving Latin America)
McGraw-Hill Interamericana Editores S.A. de C.V.
TEL +525-117-1583
FAX +525-117-1589
http://www.mcgraw-hill.com.mx
fernando_castellanos@mcgraw-hill.com

SINGAPORE (Serving Asia)
McGraw-Hill Book Company
TEL +65-863-1580
FAX +65-862-3354
http://www.mcgraw-hill.com.sg
mghasia@mcgraw-hill.com

SOUTH AFRICA
McGraw-Hill South Africa
TEL +27-11-622-7512
FAX +27-11-622-9045
robyn_swanepoel@mcgraw-hill.com

UNITED KINGDOM & EUROPE
(Excluding Southern Europe)
McGraw-Hill Publishing Company
TEL +44-1-628-502500
FAX +44-1-628-770224
http://www.mcgraw-hill.co.uk
computing_neurope@mcgraw-hill.com

ALL OTHER INQUIRIES Contact:
Osborne/McGraw-Hill
TEL +1-510-549-6600
FAX +1-510-883-7600
http://www.osborne.com
omg_international@mcgraw-hill.com